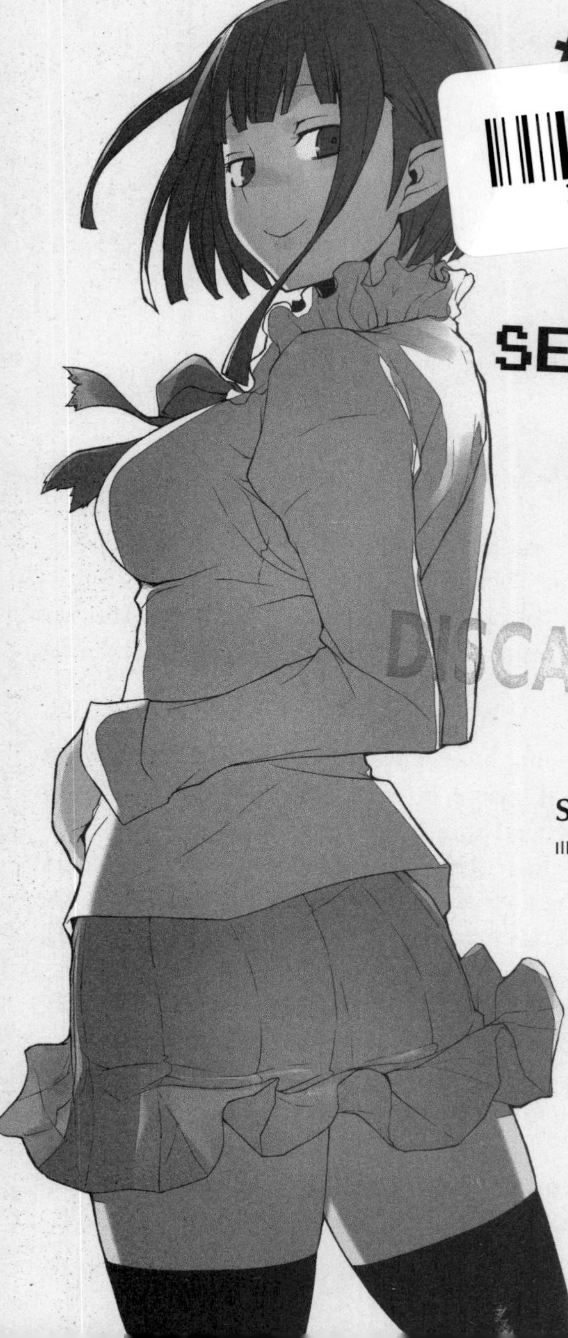

SPECIAL CHAPTER

BROTHER SEPARATED FROM SISTER?

Story: Fujino Omori

Illustration: Suzuhito Yasuda

"Hey, Eina, that little brother of yours is really tearing it up!"

It was just past noon. Their lunch break was almost over.

Misha Frot walked over to her coworker Eina Tulle, who was behind the reception counter inside the Guild Headquarters' main lobby.

"Brother......?"

"You know, your subordinate adventurer! White hair, red eyes, looks like a rabbit? Of course, other adventurers don't know who he is, but we've all noticed him!"

The two of them had been friends since their school days. Misha's light pink hair gently swished from side to side as she talked to her former classmate about the adventurer Bell Cranell.

Bell had been advancing at breakneck speed over the past month. His abilities had allowed him to progress to deeper and deeper floors much more quickly than normal.

Just as Misha said, the boy ought to still be a newbie, and yet his exploits were starting to get noticed.

"That boy, he's solo, right? There's no one else there to support him, but he just keeps going deeper...and now he's on the tenth floor! Everyone's really impressed, you know!"

The Guild kept information on every adventurer down to the lowliest newbie. Since every new detail was quickly recorded and organized, Guild employees tended to be the first to hear about individual adventurers' activities. Eina, however, was nowhere near as excited about Bell's progress as Misha was. In fact, her expression turned sour.

Bell's growth was much too fast, and she didn't know why. Eina had wanted the boy to venture into the Dungeon and gain experience, but his pace was making her more worried than happy for him.

She knew that sometimes it was easiest to fall into a trap in the Dungeon when everything was going smoothly.

"At this rate, he'll level up and pass the twelfth floor, moving into the middle levels in no time, don't you think?"

"—He's not going to the middle levels. I won't let him." Eina closed her eyes and quipped at her coworker's excitement. Misha was stunned into silence. Eina continued, her voice almost pathetically protective as she spoke.

"No matter how much stronger he gets, leveling up is a different story…Anyway, leveling up, middle levels, it's much too soon to talk about any of that. Bell takes too many risks as it is……"

Eina cast her eyes to the floor and recounted the events when he'd put himself in a lot of danger to save his supporter. Then she said, "In any case, I don't care if he does level up. I'm not letting him anywhere near the middle levels without a battle party."

Misha cracked a smile and said, "I feel like we've had this conversation before. But you know he'll join a party eventually. What would you do if he suddenly jumped from the thirteenth floor to the eighteenth? You'd get one heck of a bonus if he made it all the way down to the safe point, right?"

"Ah-ha-ha, no, no," Eina laughed to herself, saying that of course that wouldn't happen.

That's when *she* arrived.

The lobby suddenly got noisy. There were only a few adventurers and Guild employees present, but Eina couldn't help following their eyes to a figure standing at the lobby entrance.

Eina was just as surprised as the others to see flowing locks of golden hair that could rival goddesses' in their beauty.

The girl seemed to be looking for someone in particular. She caught Eina's eyes and quickly made her way to the reception desk.

"...Miss Wallenstein?"

The top-class adventurer Aiz Wallenstein planted her feet in front of the reception window and gave a brief greeting. "...Good morning."

Thanks to Reveria, Eina had met *Loki Familia*'s star adventurer only a few days ago. However, she didn't know how she should respond and looked at the blond girl in confusion. Aiz, on the other hand, cut straight to the point.

"I, um, have something I'd like to...return to one of your subordinates..."

Eina tilted her head, but all became clear when Aiz held out a piece of armor toward her. It was an emerald-green vambrace wrapped in a white cloth. Eina had bought it for Bell after becoming concerned with his cheap armor less than a week earlier.

Aiz, a girl of few words, did her best to explain the situation. Eina had asked her to help Bell after he got mixed up in one of Lilly's problems; she found the vambrace on the tenth floor where Bell was being attacked by a group of orcs.

The blond girl had first met the boy during the Minotaur incident. She finished explaining their most recent encounter, placed her hand on her chest, and exhaled with a long "whew." A smile grew on Eina's lips as she looked at Aiz's expression. "Understood," she responded with a nod. "I'll give it to Bell...I will give the vambrace to Bell Cranell and inform him of the situation."

Misha picked up on the sudden change in tone and went back to her desk. Meanwhile, Aiz's face suddenly became firm—like she was working up courage but also nervous—as she opened her mouth to speak.

"Um……"

"?"

"…I'd like to…give it to him directly."

Aiz looked down as she revealed her true intention.

The Minotaur incident had caused him so much trouble, so she wanted to use this opportunity to return his vambrace as well as apologize—the boy always ran away like a scared rabbit whenever he saw her. She couldn't let this chance go to waste.

Aiz suddenly met Eina's gaze, the blond girl's eyes timid and uneasy. Eina adjusted her glasses before taking on a serious air and nodding once again.

"I understand. I would like to offer my cooperation as well."

"?"

"I will create a situation that he won't escape from, can't escape from, such that the two of you will be able to talk face-to-face."

She sounded almost like a parent, or perhaps like a protective older sister, as she made her suggestion.

"He has some nerve. I would like to extend an apology to you, Miss Wallenstein, on behalf of my very rude subordinate." A fretful Eina quickly apologized for all the times that Bell had disrespected her by running away. Aiz couldn't help but smile. The two young women smiled at each other before starting to discuss their plan.

"First, I will lure him into one of our consultation rooms. Then, you'll enter the room. You'll be able to talk when he doesn't have an escape route."

"Is this…okay? We'd be…tricking him."

"It's fine. Anything less won't work."

Loki Familia would soon embark on an expedition. So they decided to execute their plan to trap Bell in a consultation room before Aiz left. They were just about to choose the day when suddenly—

Eina happened to notice a figure coming toward the reception desk, behind Aiz.

Her shoulders shook. Aiz quickly turned around and saw who had arrived in the Guild lobby.

It was the white-haired boy, Bell Cranell.

"......"

"......"

"......"

*What timing...*Eina thought to herself as the three of them froze in place.

Bell turned his back on them almost instantly and made a break for the door.

"B-Bell! Stop right there!" Eina yelled at the boy who was flying through the lobby at full speed. However, he didn't look back.

—*Oh! What a pain!*

Eina's mind screamed out, but all she could do was watch him go. She quickly turned to Aiz and said, "Chase after him, Miss Wallenstein!"

A switch seemed to flip inside Aiz when she heard Eina's voice.

A moment later, the sword princess took off with enough vigor to leave Eina standing, stunned behind the counter, as she watched the girl pursue the rabbit with the ferocity of a hurricane.

🔥

"—Bell, the two of you need to talk, alone," Eina said to Bell after Aiz had captured him on the Guild's front lawn.

The boy's face went bright red. "Please stay here!" he squeaked in desperation.

"There are a lot of things that need to be said, so make sure you say them." On that strict note, Eina left Aiz and Bell by themselves.

She returned to the Guild lobby—but kept an eye on them through a window the entire time.

Her cheeks pulled back into a smile when she saw the boy thrust his head down into an unmistakable bow.

"Eina, do you happen to have any brothers or sisters?"

Misha left her desk and joined Eina in front of the window. "…I do. A little sister." *What about it?* she asked with her eyes, and tilted her head.

Misha grinned. "You standing here watching him like that, it's like he's your little brother. That look in your eyes, it's like you can't just let him be. It's like that when you talk to him, too. Sometimes angry and worried, and sometimes gentle with a smile.

"Just like a big sister," she added.

Eina's eyes popped open a little wider. Misha giggled to herself before continuing.

"Are you sure it's okay to leave him alone out there?"

"……"

Eina looked back out the window in time to see a very nervous Bell turn an even deeper shade of red as Aiz smiled back at him.

Something about seeing them smiling together made her feel warm inside. Her next words seemed to drip out of her mouth.

"I'm sure…He can't be my little brother forever."

It was impossible for her to help him indefinitely.

No, that wasn't it. There would come a time when he would no longer depend on her, spreading his wings and taking off on his own.

After all, he was an adventurer.

Eina thought about that day in the future, the pride and joy she would feel, as well as the loneliness.

She was the one who, inevitably, would have to be separated from her "little brother" at some point.

Eina looked on with a hint of loneliness in her eyes as the boy, red-faced, mustered his courage and asked some favor of the girl.

"He can't just go on as your little brother, eh?...So you're saying that once he's properly grown, you'll have a go at him yourself?"

"Wha...? Misha!"

"My, my, how devious!"

Misha's teasing had hit home. Eina snapped back at her.

When the time for them to part did arrive, how would their relationship change?

Even as she scolded her coworker, the tips of Eina's ears turned red as the thought crossed her mind.

IS it WRONG to TRY to PiCK UP GIRLS iN A DUNGEON?

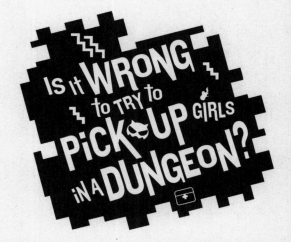

HEY! FLIP THE BOOK TO
READ A SPECIAL, PREVIOUSLY
UNPUBLISHED STORY STRAIGHT
FROM FUJINO OMORI!

IS IT WRONG TO TRY TO PICK UP GIRLS IN A DUNGEON? ⑤

FUJINO OMORI
KUNIEDA
SUZUHITO YASUDA

Translation: Andrew Gaippe • Lettering: Brndn Blakeslee

DUNGEON NI DEAI WO MOTOMERU NO WA MACHIGATTEIRUDAROUKA vol. 5
© 2015 Fujino Omori / SB Creative Corp.
© 2015 Kunieda / SQUARE ENIX CO., LTD.
First published in Japan in 2015 by SQUARE ENIX CO., LTD.
English Translation rights arranged with SQUARE ENIX CO., LTD.
and Hachette Book Group through Tuttle Mori Agency, Inc.

Translation © 2016 SQUARE ENIX CO., LTD.

Yen Press
Hachette Book Group
1290 Avenue of the Americas
New York, NY 10104

www.HachetteBookGroup.com
www.YenPress.com

Yen Press is an imprint of Hachette Book Group, Inc. The Yen Press name and logo are trademarks of Hachette Book Group, Inc.

The publisher is not responsible for websites (or their content) that are not owned by the publisher.

Library of Congress Control Number: 2016931002

First Yen Press Edition: May 2016

ISBN: 978-0-316-27225-4

10 9 8 7 6 5 4 3 2 1

BVG

Printed in the United States of America

HAVE YOU BEEN TURNED ON TO LIGHT NOVELS YET?

IN STORES NOW!

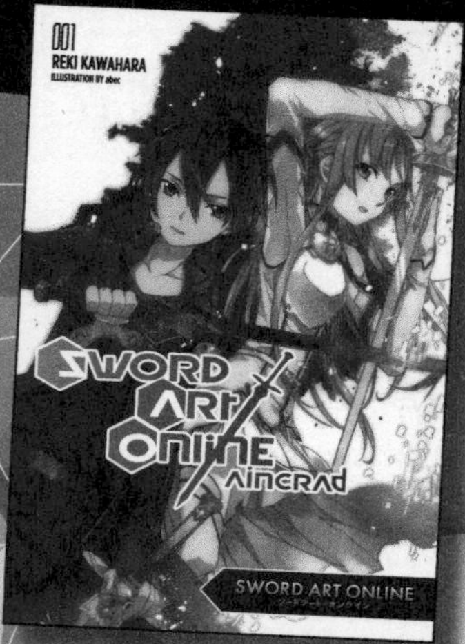
001
REKI KAWAHARA
ILLUSTRATION BY abec
SWORD ART ONLINE
AINCRAD
SWORD ART ONLINE

SWORD ART ONLINE, VOL. 1–7
SWORD ART ONLINE, PROGRESSIVE 1–3

The chart-topping light novel series that spawned the explosively popular anime and manga adaptations!

MANGA ADAPTATION AVAILABLE NOW!

ACCEL WORLD, VOL. 1–6

Prepare to accelerate with an action-packed cyber-thriller from the bestselling author of *Sword Art Online*.

MANGA ADAPTATION AVAILABLE NOW!

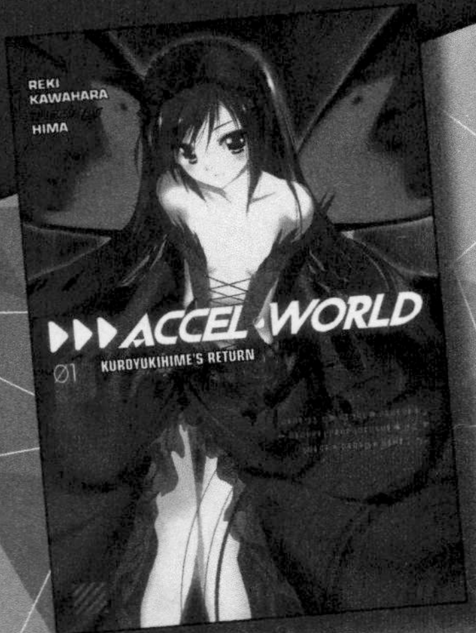
REKI
KAWAHARA
HIMA
ACCEL WORLD
01
KUROYUKIHIME'S RETURN

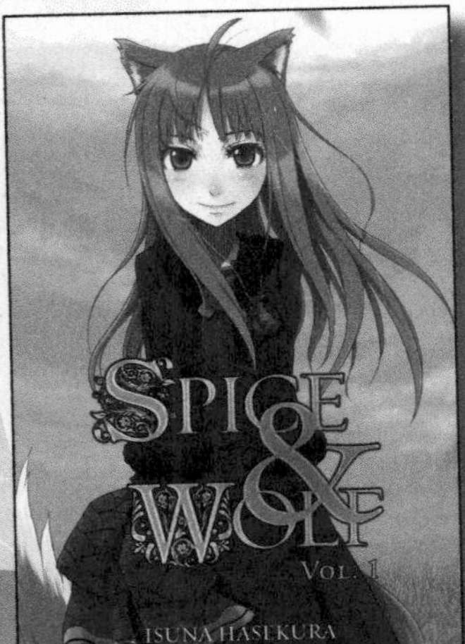
SPICE & WOLF
VOL. 1
ISUNA HASEKURA

SPICE AND WOLF, VOL. 1–17

A disgruntled goddess joins a traveling merchant in this light novel series that inspired the *New York Times* bestselling manga.

MANGA ADAPTATION AVAILABLE NOW!

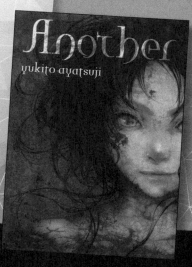

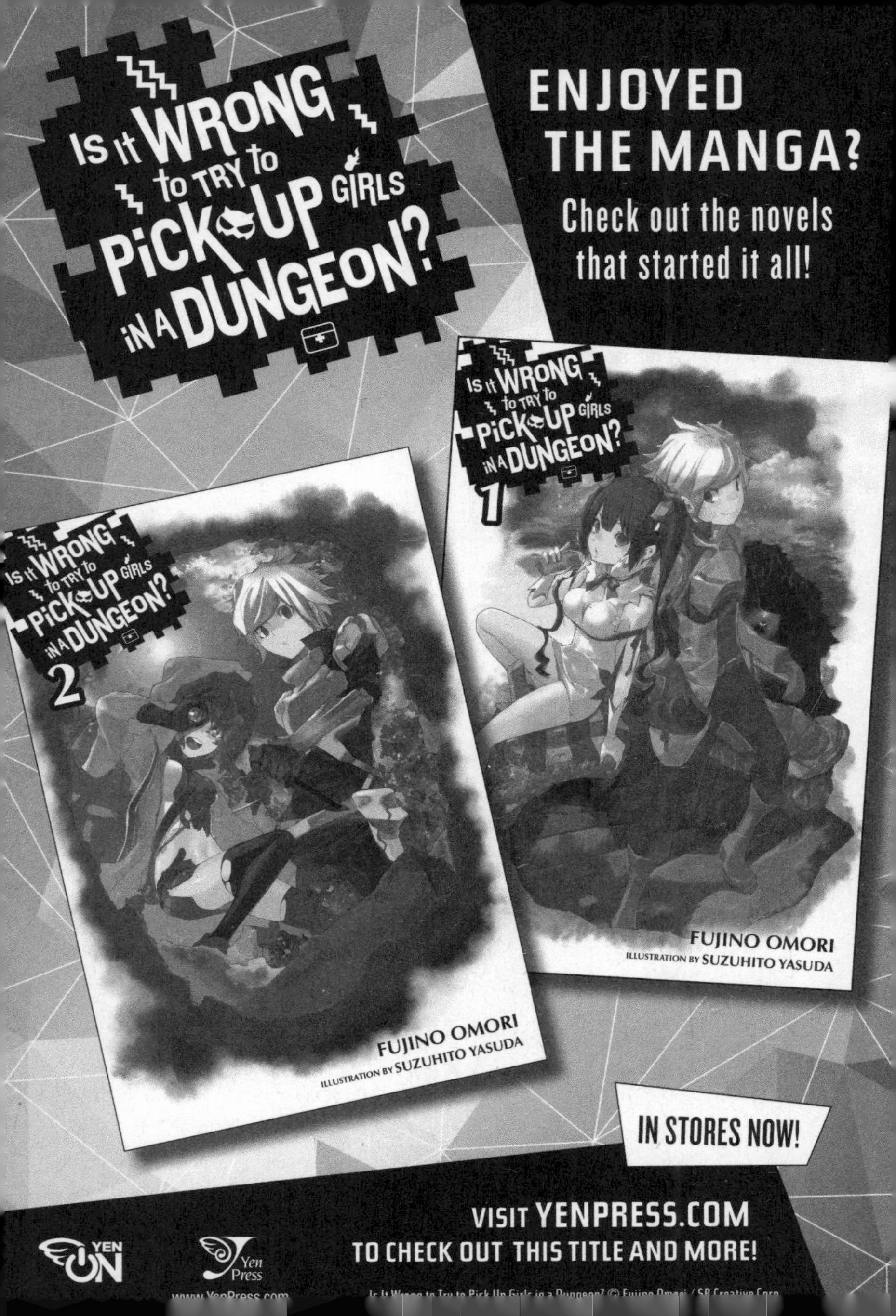

Is it WRONG to TRY to PiCK UP GIRLS iN A DUNGEON?
ENJOYED THE MANGA?
Check out the novels that started it all!
Is it WRONG to TRY to PiCK UP GIRLS iN A DUNGEON? 1
FUJINO OMORI
ILLUSTRATION BY SUZUHITO YASUDA
Is it WRONG to TRY to PiCK UP GIRLS iN A DUNGEON? 2
FUJINO OMORI
ILLUSTRATION BY SUZUHITO YASUDA
IN STORES NOW!
VISIT YENPRESS.COM
TO CHECK OUT THIS TITLE AND MORE!
YEN ON
Yen Press

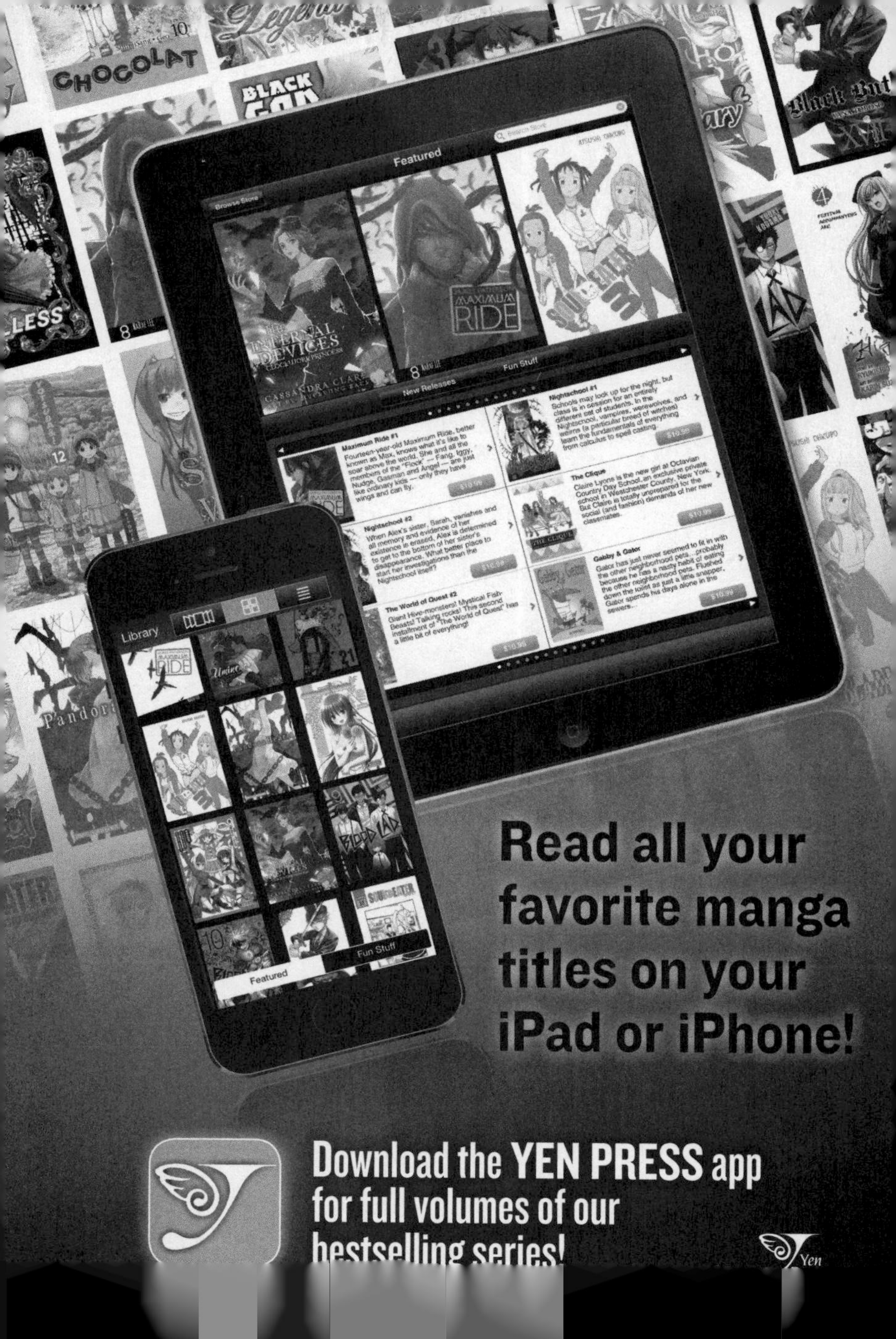
Read all your favorite manga titles on your iPad or iPhone!
Download the YEN PRESS app for full volumes of our bestselling series!
Yen

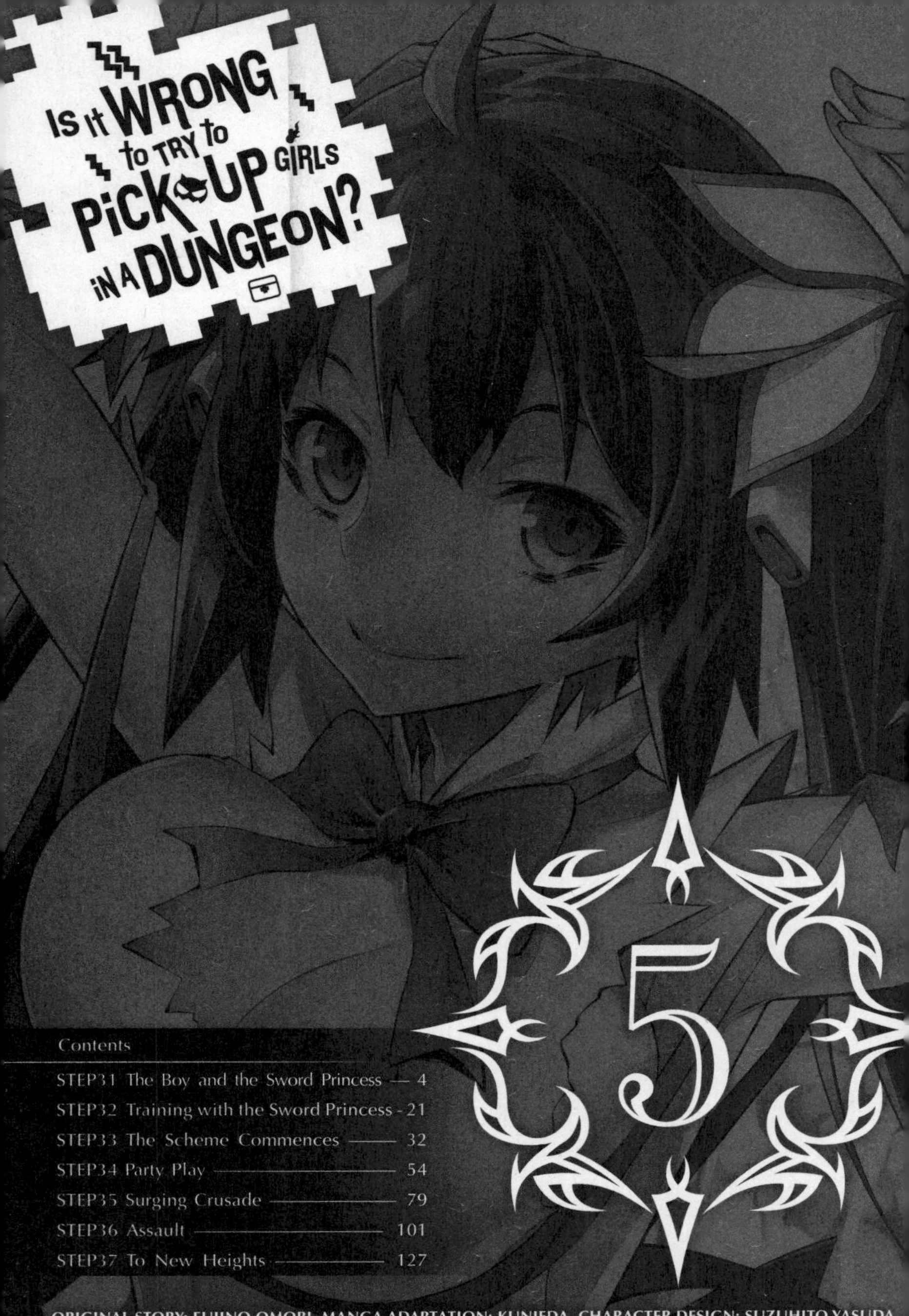

Is it Wrong to Try to Pick Up Girls in a Dungeon?

5

Contents

ORIGINAL STORY: FUJINO OMORI MANGA ADAPTATION: KUNIEDA CHARACTER DESIGN: SUZUHITO YASUDA

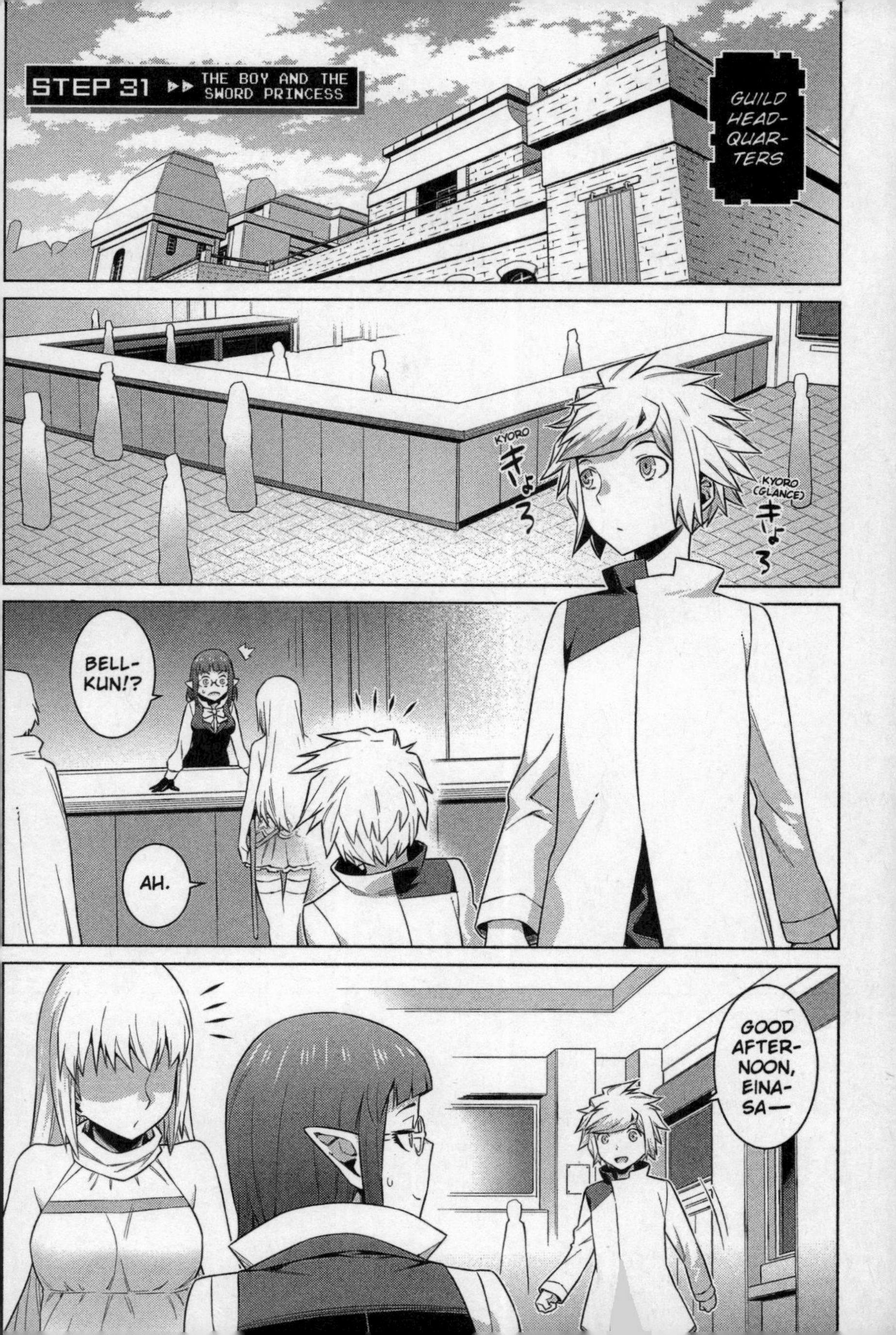
GUILD HEADQUARTERS
STEP 31 ▶▶ THE BOY AND THE SWORD PRINCESS
KYORO (GLANCE) キょろ
KYORO キょろ
BELL-KUN!?
AH.
GOOD AFTERNOON, EINA-SA—

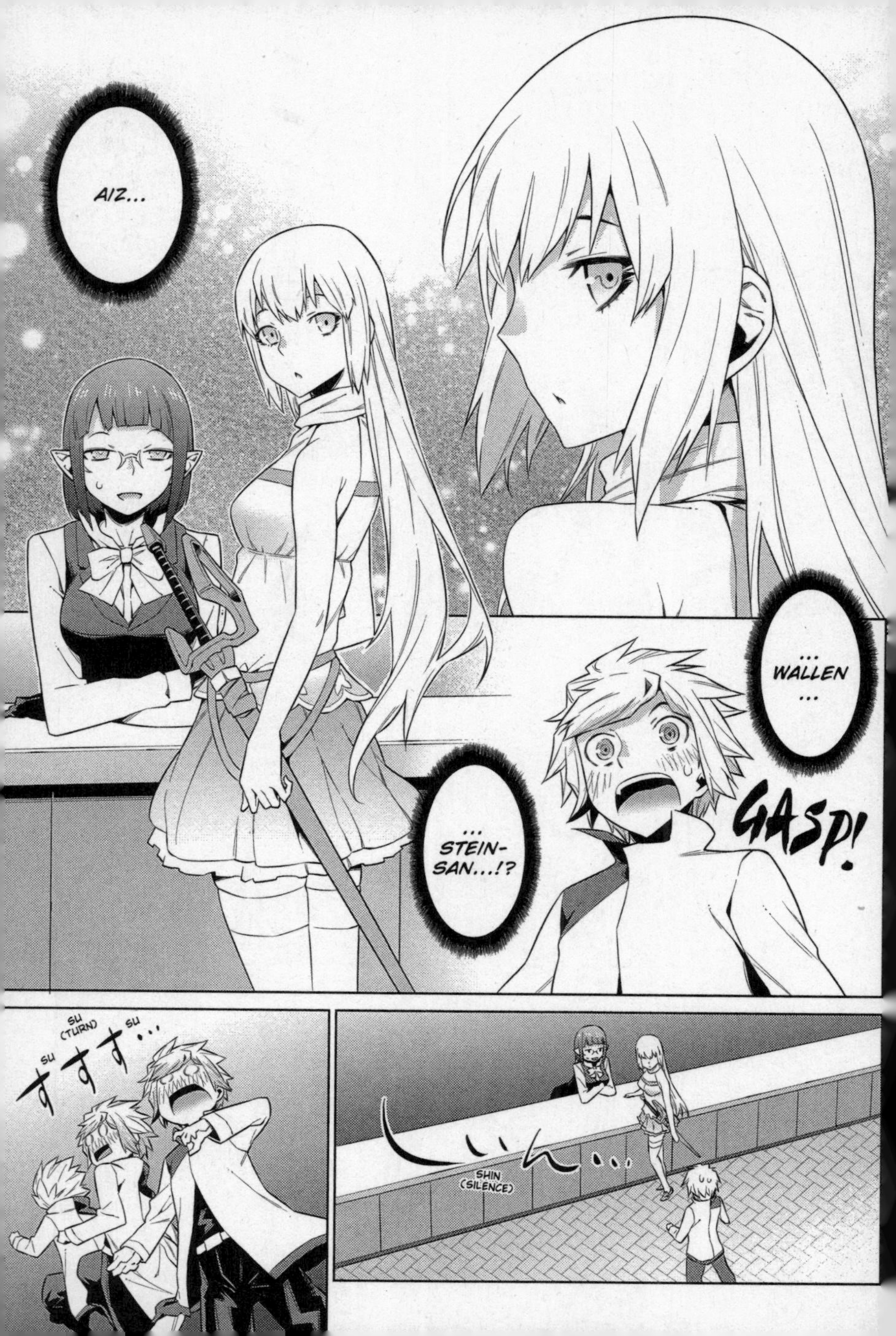
...WALLEN...
...STEIN-SAN...!?
GASP!
AIZ...
しいん...
SHIN (SILENCE)
すすす...
SU SU SU (TURN)

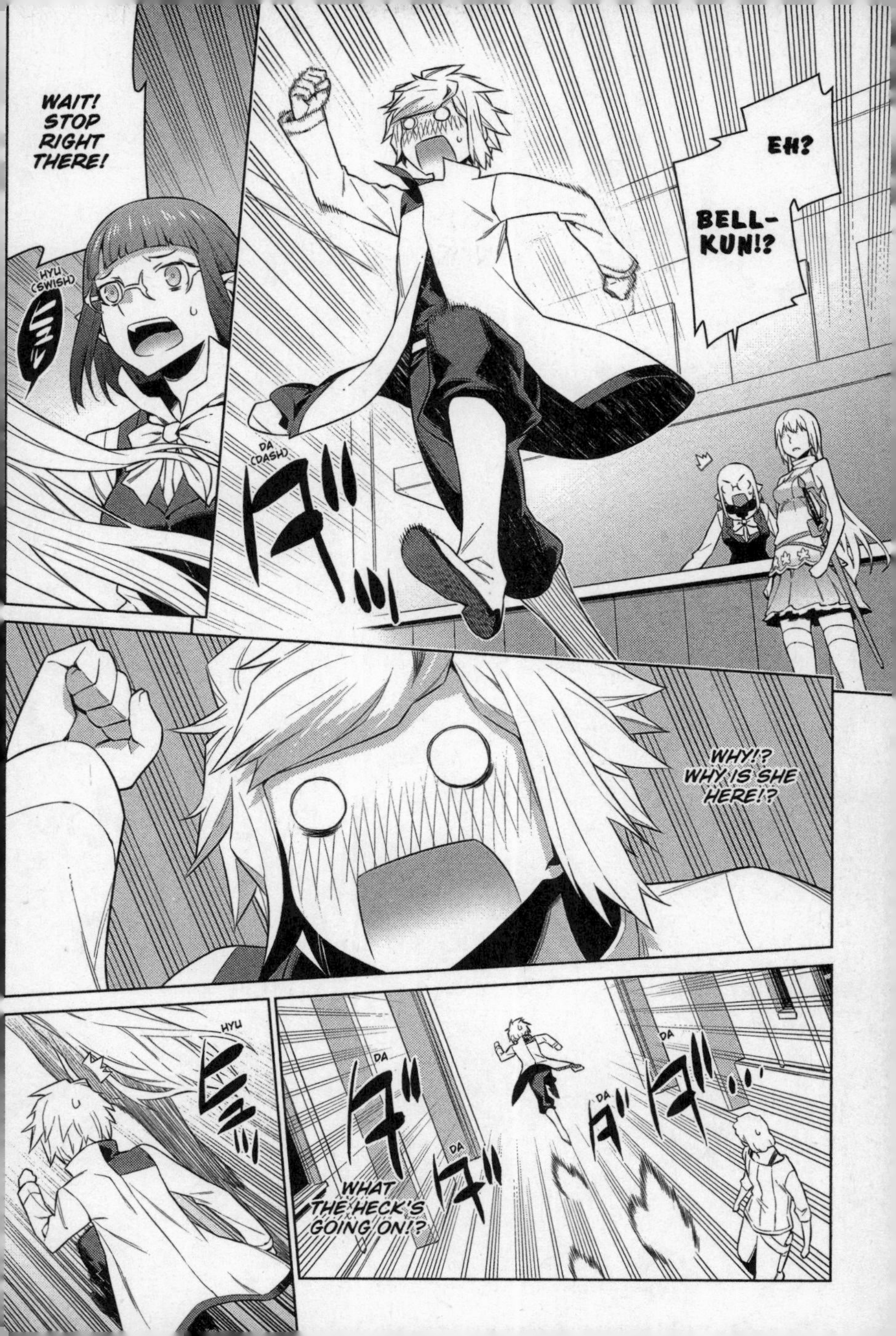
EH?
BELL-KUN!?
DA (DASH)
WAIT! STOP RIGHT THERE!
HYU (SWISH)
WHY!? WHY IS SHE HERE!?
DA
DA
DA
DA
WHAT THE HECK'S GOING ON!?
HYU

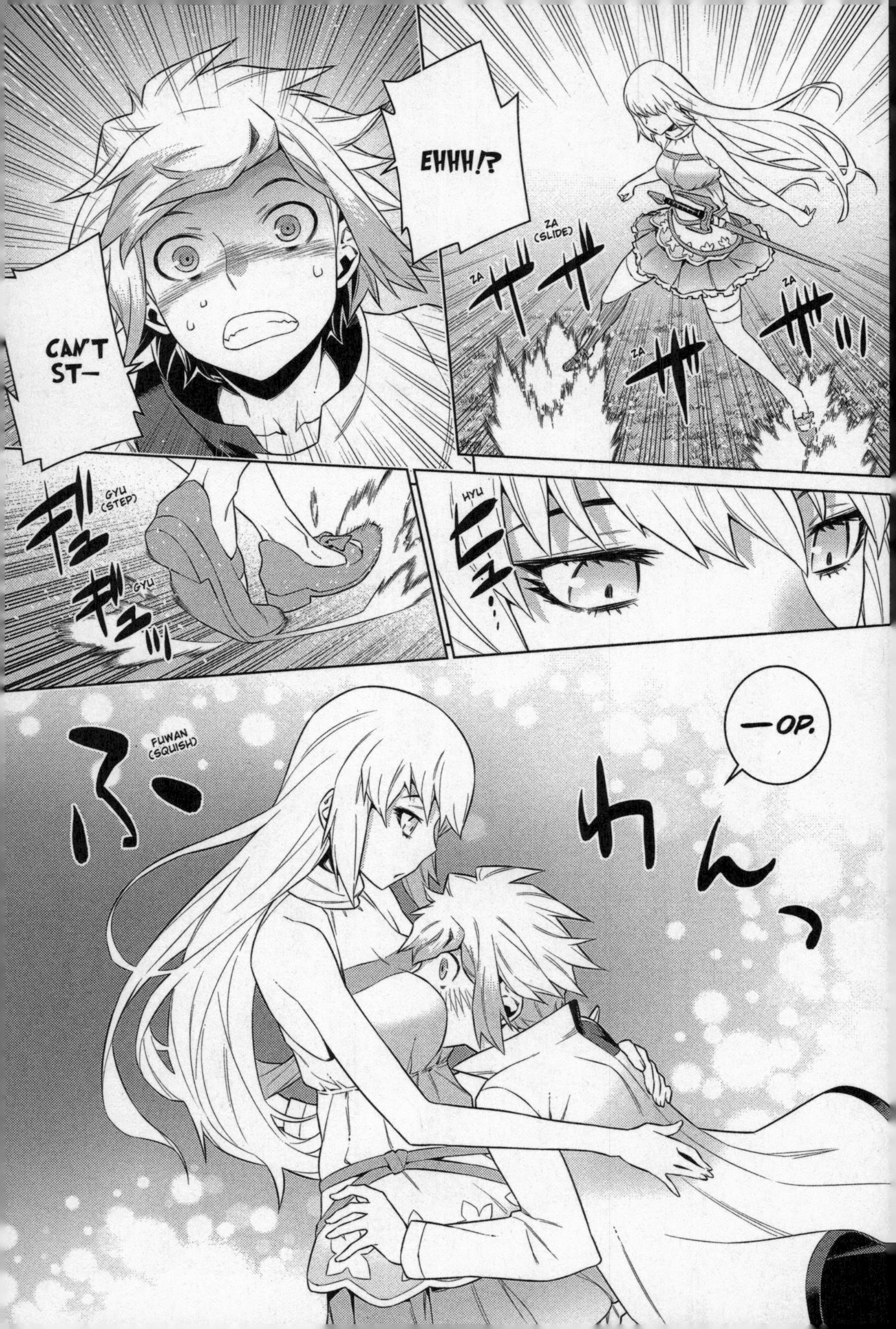
ZA (SLIDE)
ZA
ZA
ZA
EHHH!?
CAN'T ST—
HYU
GYU (STEP)
GYU
FUWAN (SQUISH)
—OP.

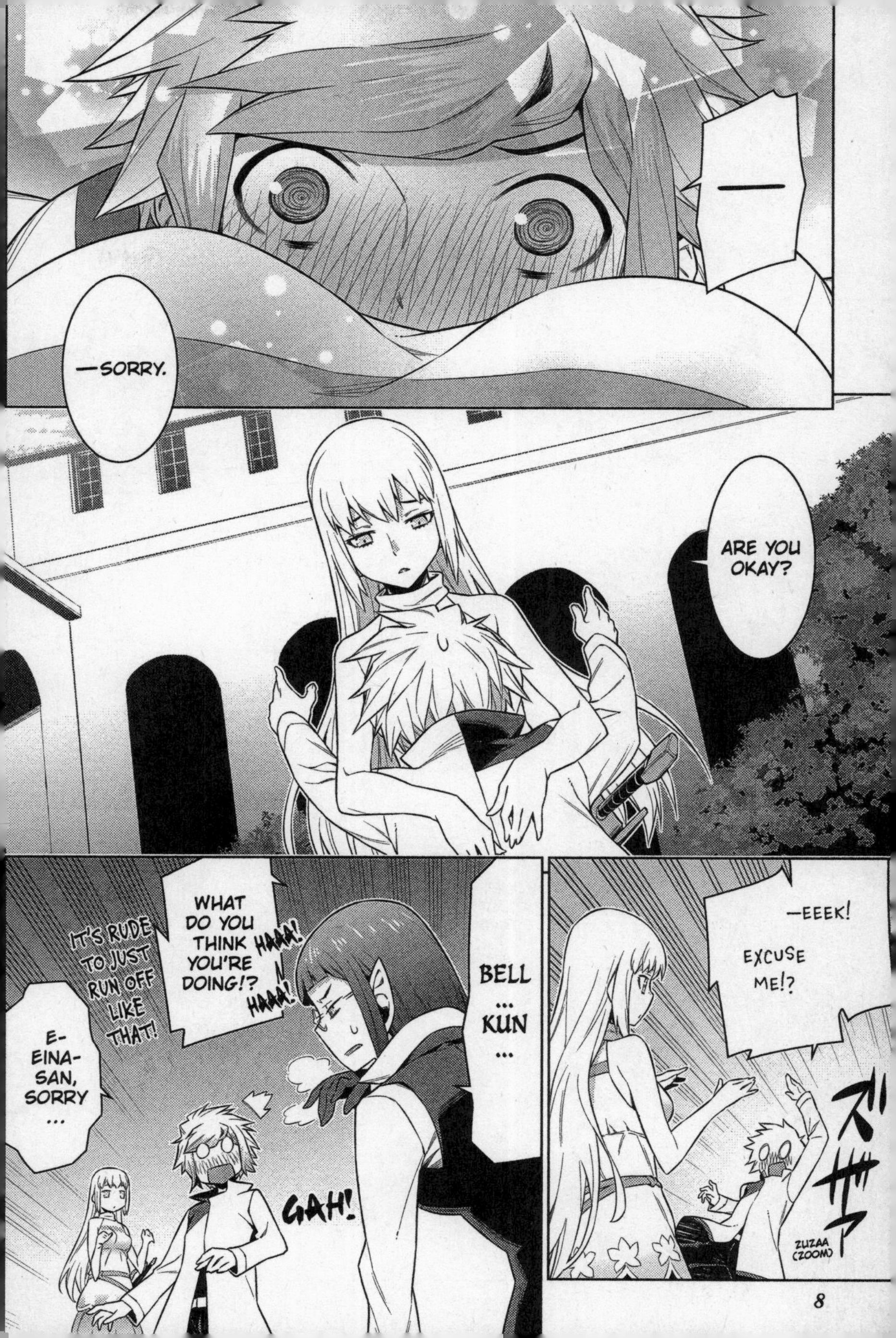
—
—SORRY.
ARE YOU OKAY?
—EEEK!
EXCUSE ME!?
ズザァ
ZUZAA (ZOOM)
BELL ... KUN ...
WHAT DO YOU THINK YOU'RE DOING!?
HAAA! HAAA!
IT'S RUDE TO JUST RUN OFF LIKE THAT!
E-EINA-SAN, SORRY ...
GAH!

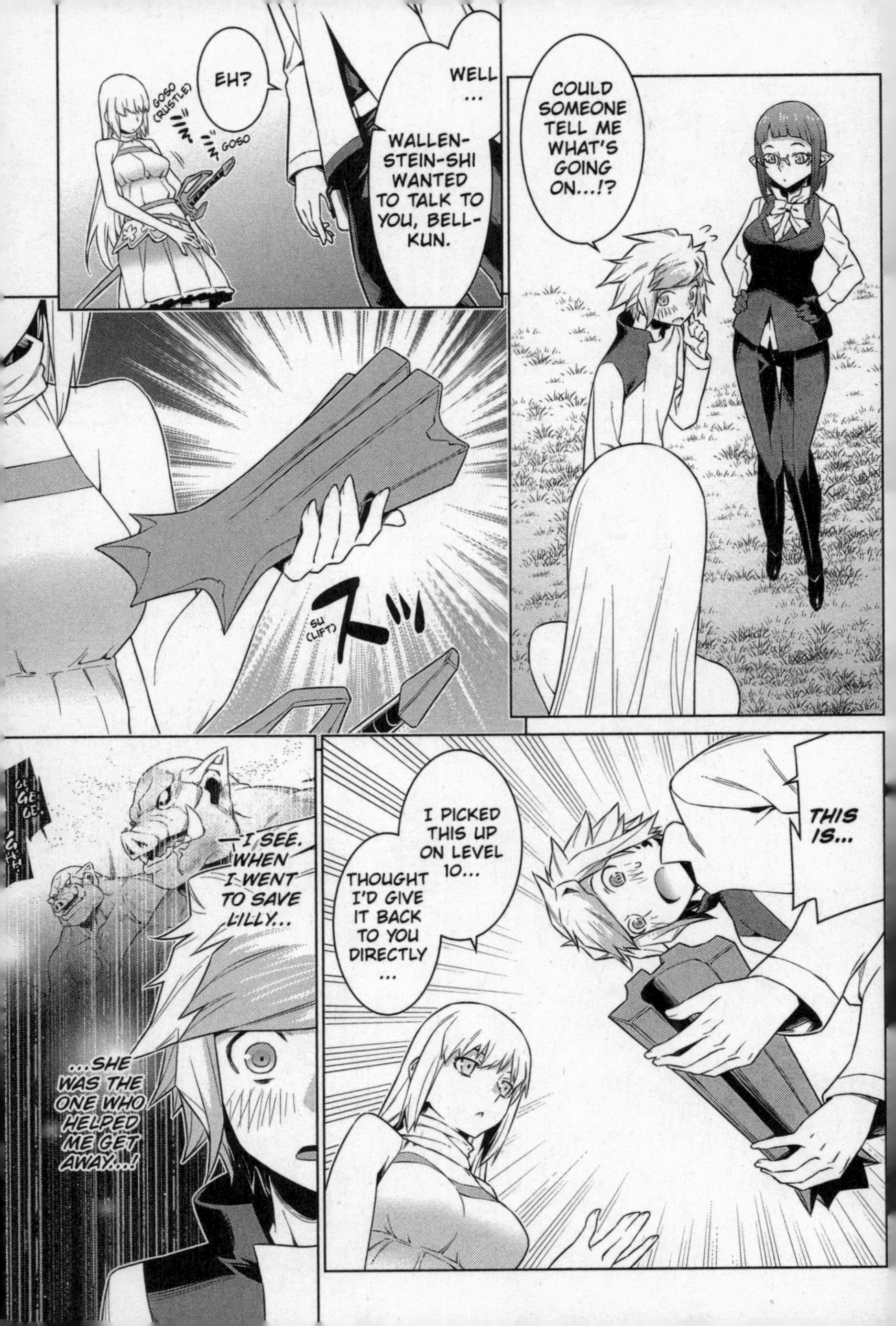
COULD SOMEONE TELL ME WHAT'S GOING ON...!?
EH?
GOSO (RUSTLE)
GOSO
WELL ...
WALLEN-STEIN-SHI WANTED TO TALK TO YOU, BELL-KUN.
SU (LIFT)
THIS IS...
I PICKED THIS UP ON LEVEL 10...
THOUGHT I'D GIVE IT BACK TO YOU DIRECTLY ...
—I SEE. WHEN I WENT TO SAVE LILLY...
GE GE GE.
...SHE WAS THE ONE WHO HELPED ME GET AWAY...!

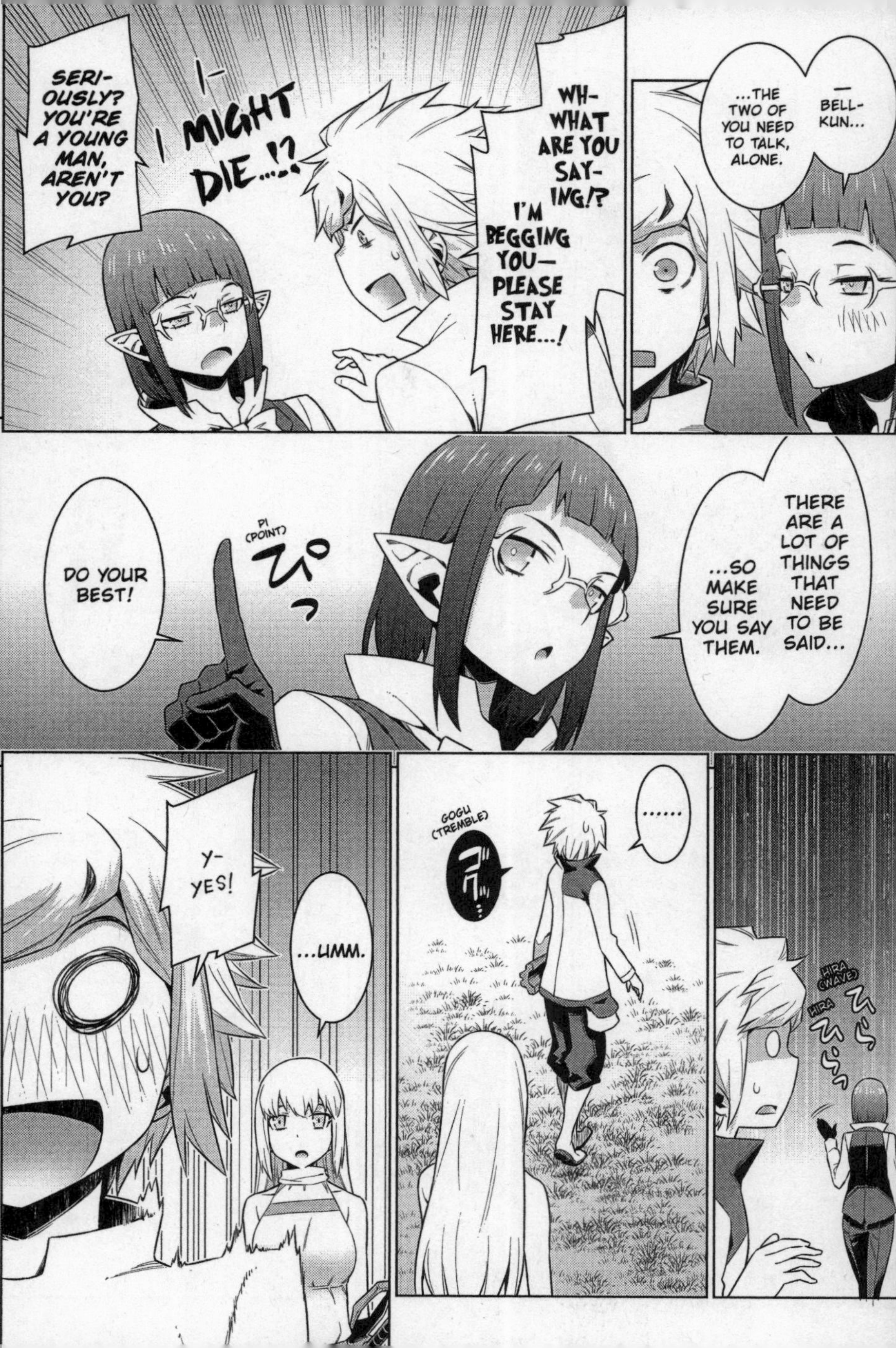
—BELL-KUN...
...THE TWO OF YOU NEED TO TALK, ALONE.
WH-WHAT ARE YOU SAYING!?
I'M BEGGING YOU—PLEASE STAY HERE...!
I-I MIGHT DIE...!?
SERIOUSLY? YOU'RE A YOUNG MAN, AREN'T YOU?
THERE ARE A LOT OF THINGS THAT NEED TO BE SAID...
...SO MAKE SURE YOU SAY THEM.
PI (POINT)
ぴっ
DO YOUR BEST!
HIRA (WAVE)
HIRA
ひら
ひら
......
GOGU (TREMBLE)
Y-YES!
...UMM.

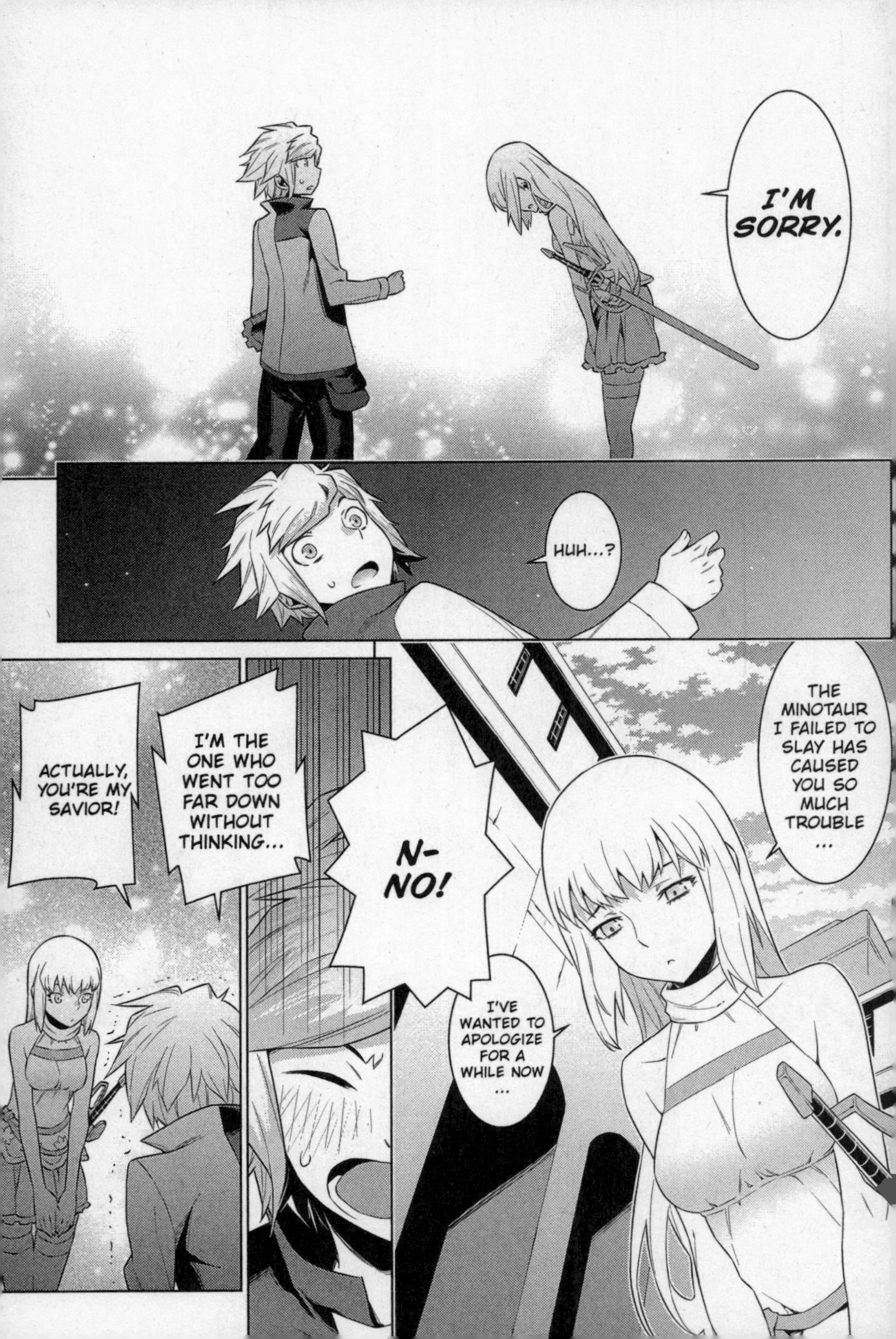
I'M SORRY.
HUH...?
THE MINOTAUR I FAILED TO SLAY HAS CAUSED YOU SO MUCH TROUBLE ...
I'VE WANTED TO APOLOGIZE FOR A WHILE NOW ...
N-NO!
I'M THE ONE WHO WENT TOO FAR DOWN WITHOUT THINKING...
ACTUALLY, YOU'RE MY SAVIOR!

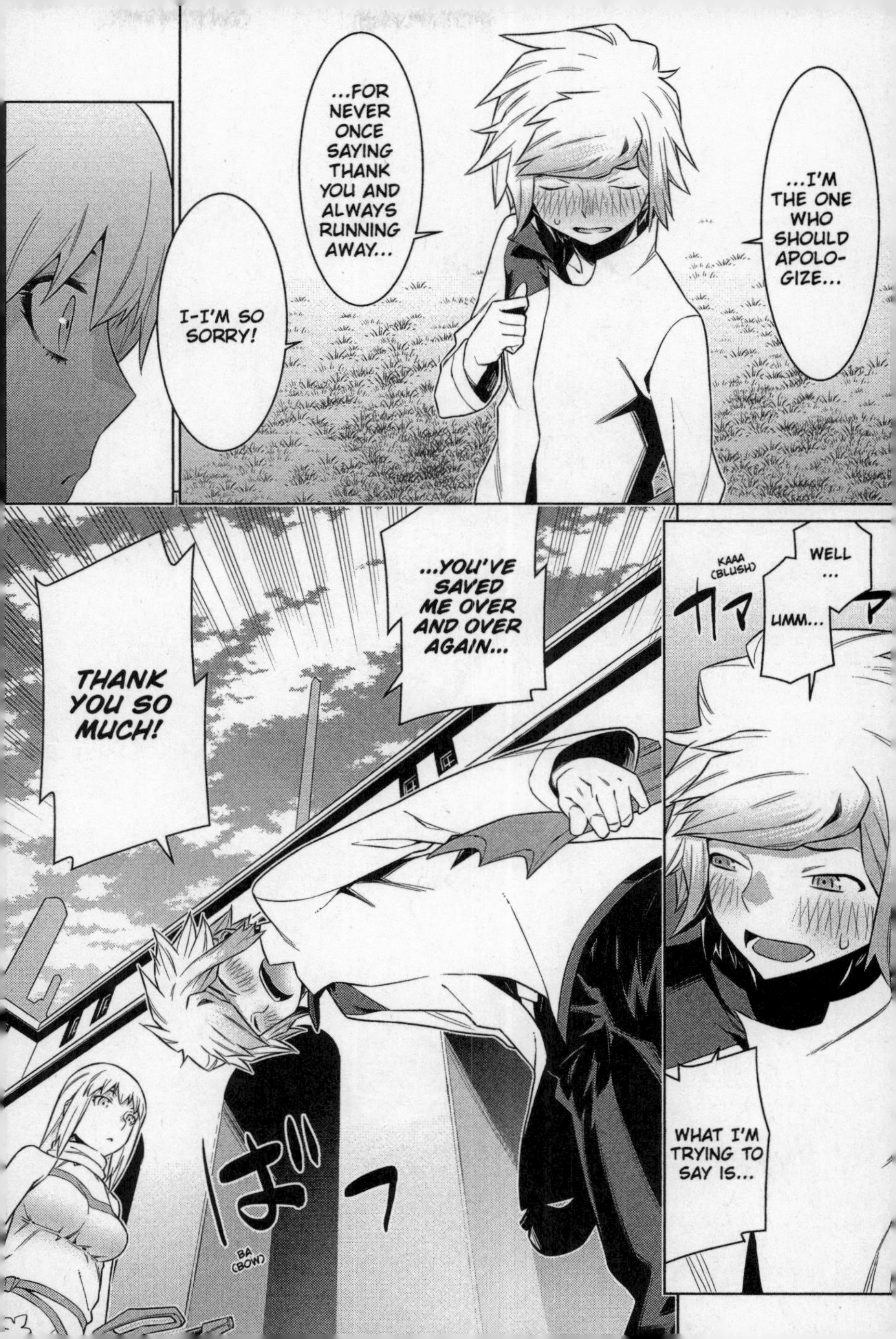
...I'M THE ONE WHO SHOULD APOLOGIZE...
...FOR NEVER ONCE SAYING THANK YOU AND ALWAYS RUNNING AWAY...
I-I'M SO SORRY!
KAAA (BLUSH)
WELL...
UMM...
WHAT I'M TRYING TO SAY IS...
...YOU'VE SAVED ME OVER AND OVER AGAIN...
THANK YOU SO MUCH!
BA (BOW)

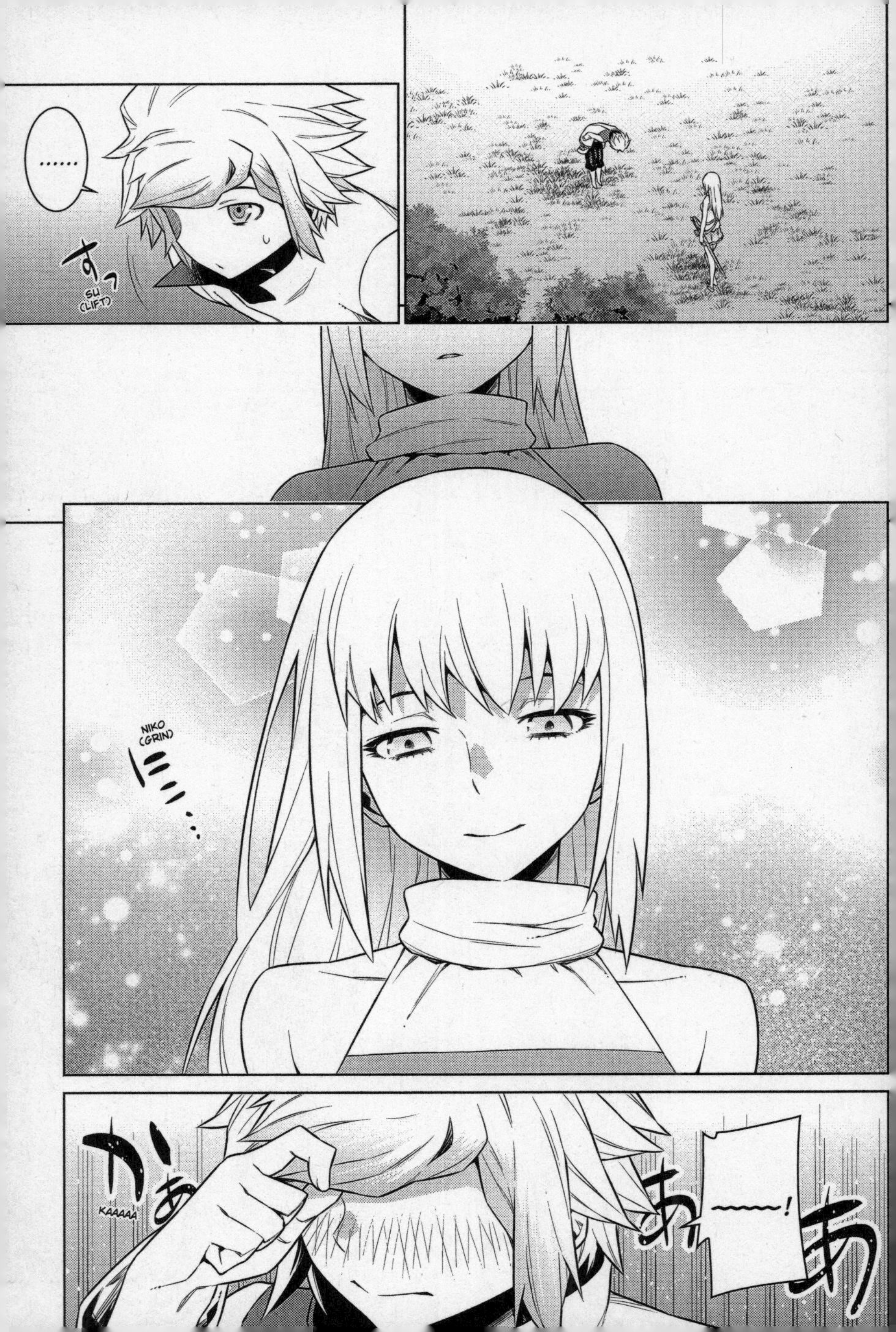

......
すっ
SU (LIFT)
NIKO (GRIN)
にこ…
かぁ
KAAAAA
あ
~~~~~!
あ
~~~~~

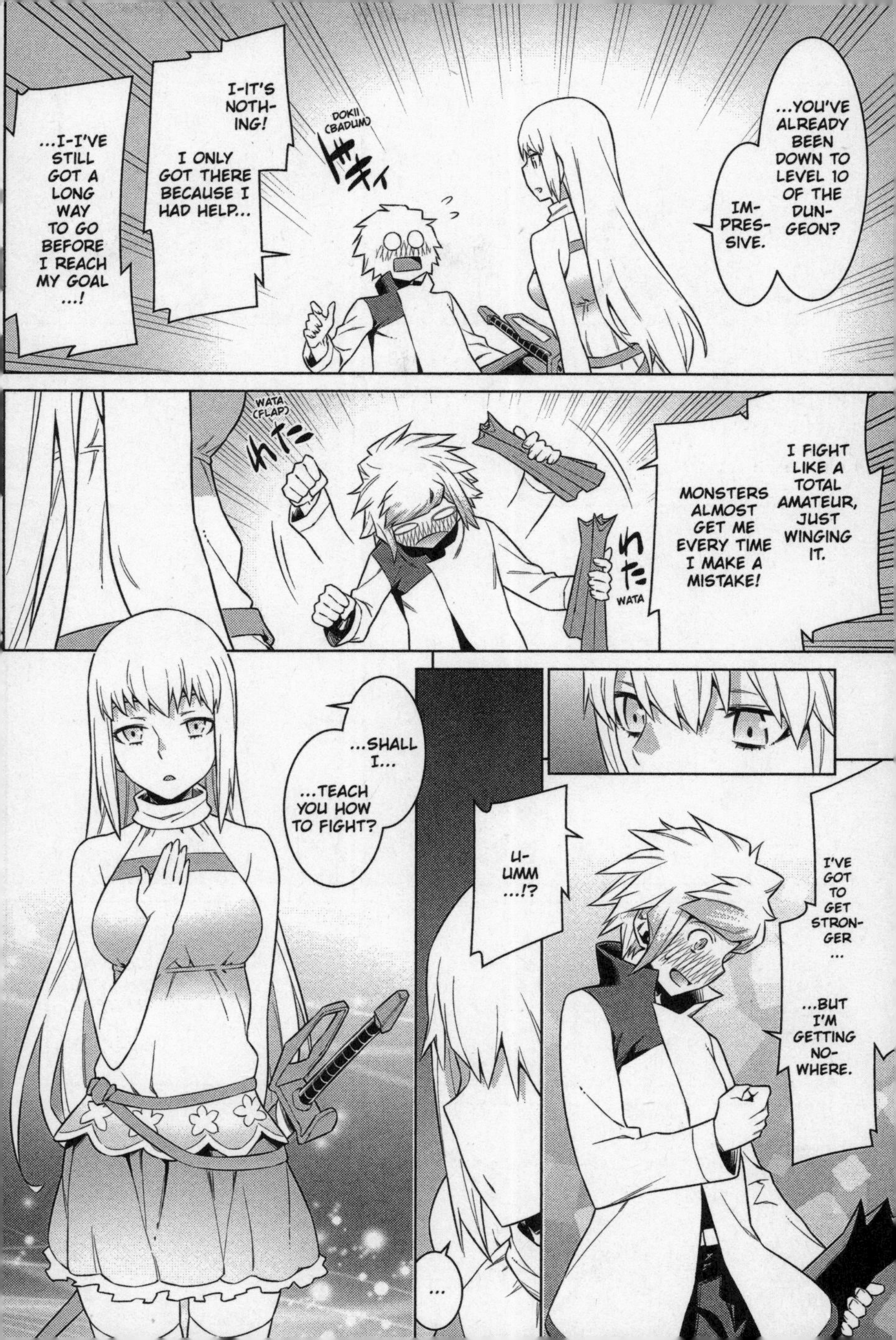
...YOU'VE ALREADY BEEN DOWN TO LEVEL 10 OF THE DUN-GEON?
IM-PRES-SIVE.
DOKII (BADUM)
ドキィ
I-IT'S NOTH-ING!
I ONLY GOT THERE BECAUSE I HAD HELP...
...I-I'VE STILL GOT A LONG WAY TO GO BEFORE I REACH MY GOAL...!
I FIGHT LIKE A TOTAL AMATEUR, JUST WINGING IT.
MONSTERS ALMOST GET ME EVERY TIME I MAKE A MISTAKE!
わた
WATA
WATA (FLAP)
わた
I'VE GOT TO GET STRON-GER...
...BUT I'M GETTING NO-WHERE.
U-UMM...!?
...
...SHALL I...
...TEACH YOU HOW TO FIGHT?

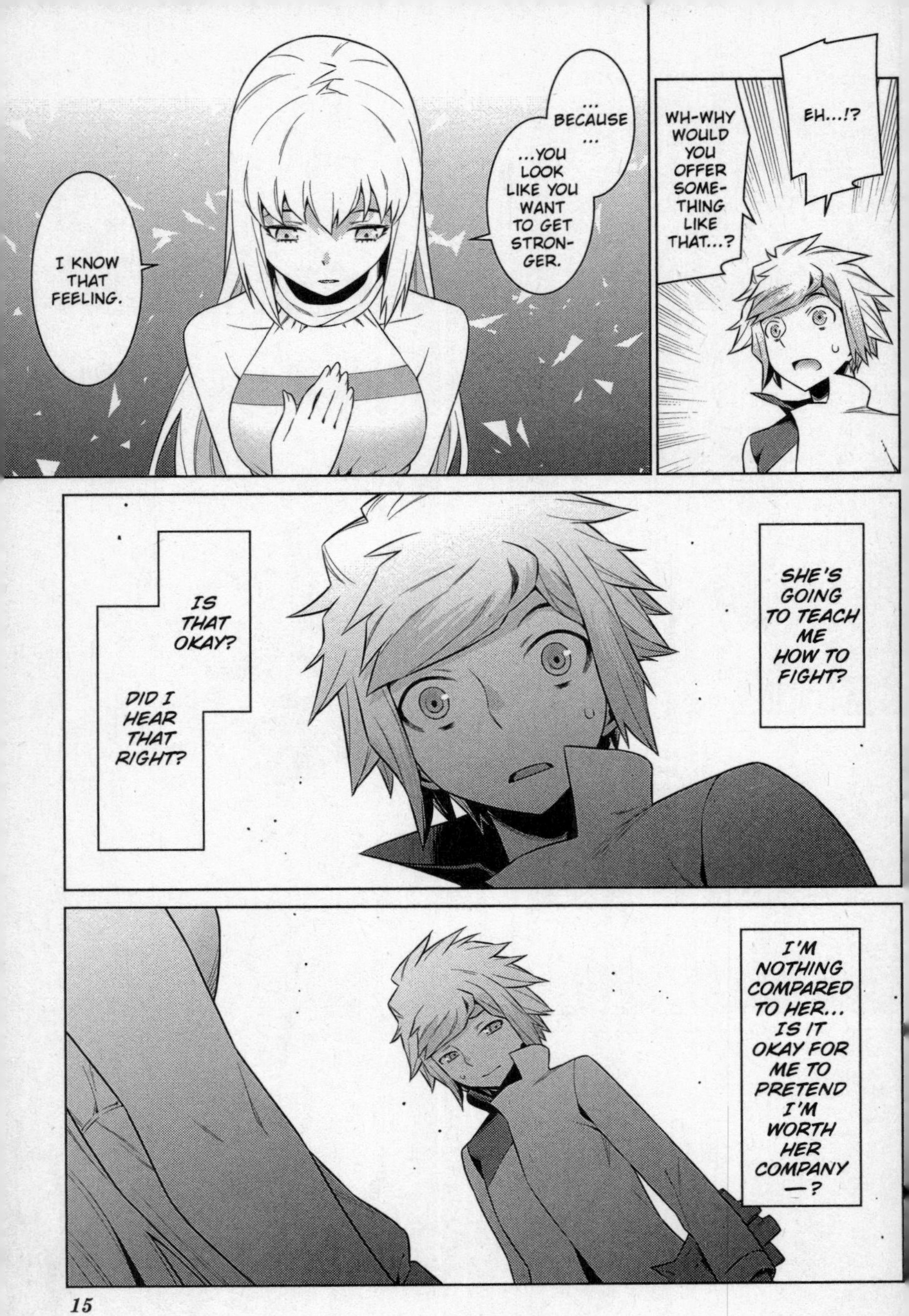
EH...!?
WH-WHY WOULD YOU OFFER SOME-THING LIKE THAT...?
... BECAUSE ...
...YOU LOOK LIKE YOU WANT TO GET STRON-GER.
I KNOW THAT FEELING.
SHE'S GOING TO TEACH ME HOW TO FIGHT?
IS THAT OKAY?
DID I HEAR THAT RIGHT?
I'M NOTHING COMPARED TO HER... IS IT OKAY FOR ME TO PRETEND I'M WORTH HER COMPANY —?

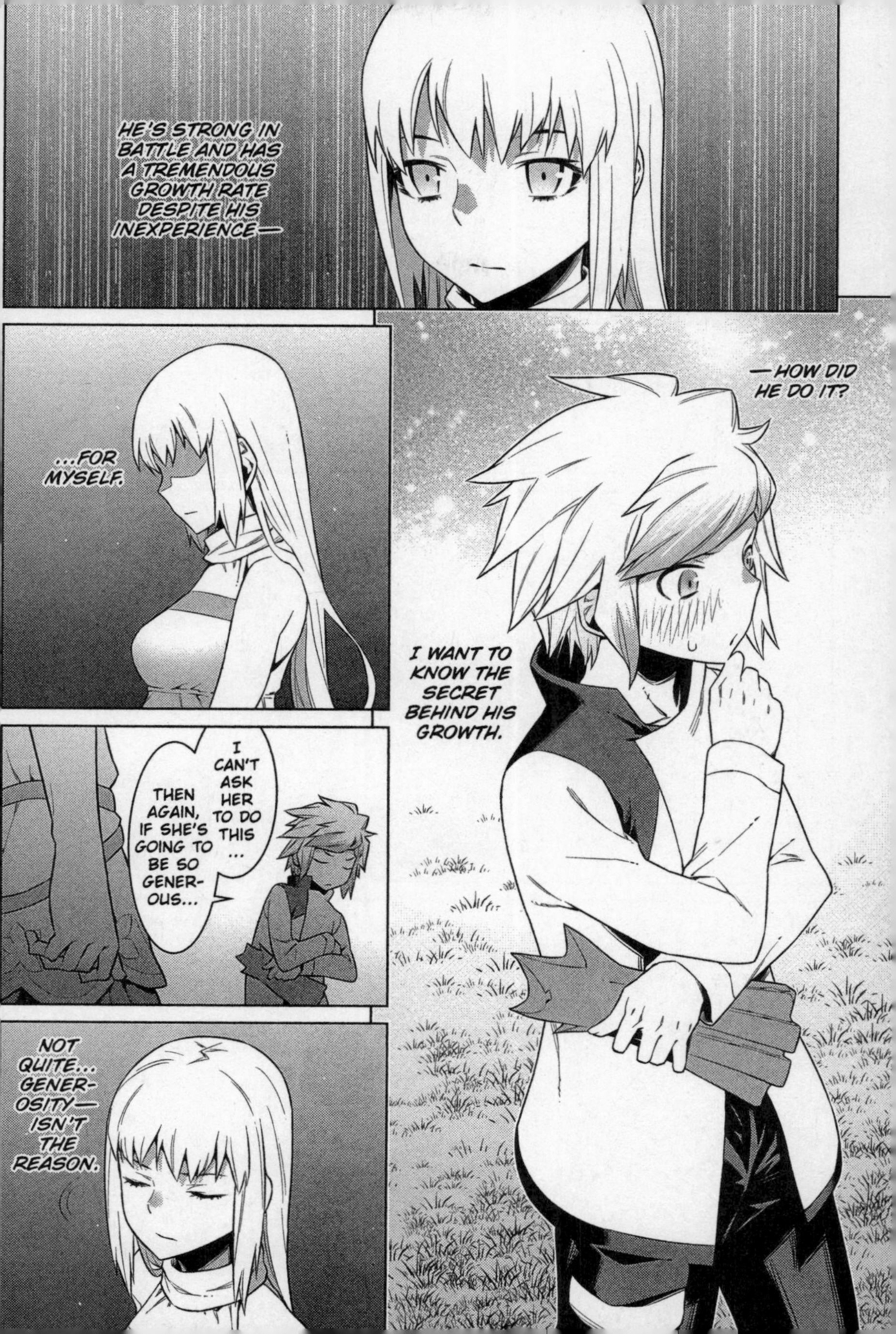
HE'S STRONG IN BATTLE AND HAS A TREMENDOUS GROWTH RATE DESPITE HIS INEXPERIENCE—
—HOW DID HE DO IT?
I WANT TO KNOW THE SECRET BEHIND HIS GROWTH.
...FOR MYSELF.
I CAN'T ASK HER TO DO THIS...
THEN AGAIN, IF SHE'S GOING TO BE SO GENEROUS...
NOT QUITE... GENEROSITY—ISN'T THE REASON.

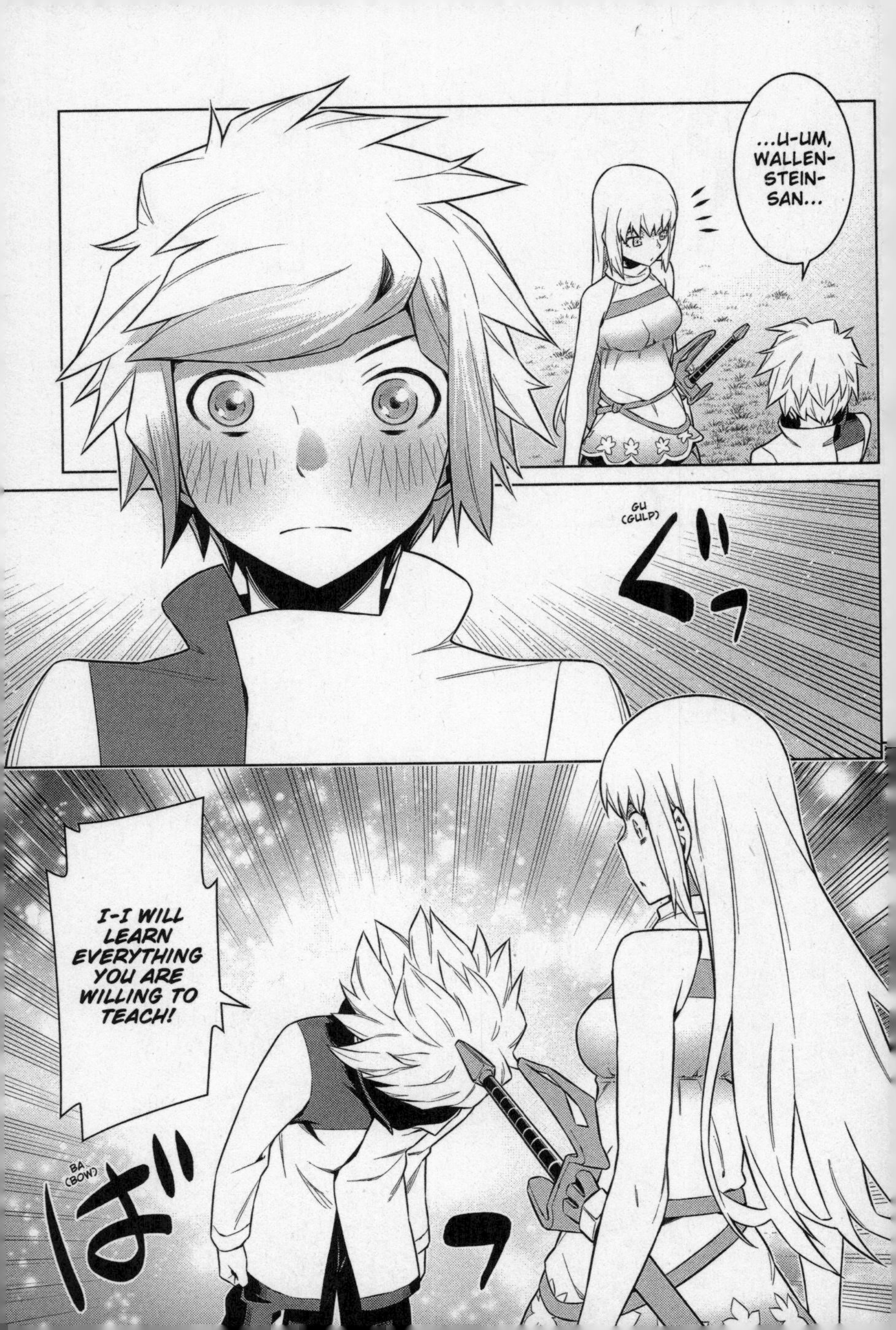
...U-UM, WALLEN-STEIN-SAN...
GU (GULP)
ぐっ
I-I WILL LEARN EVERYTHING YOU ARE WILLING TO TEACH!
BA (BOW)
ばっ

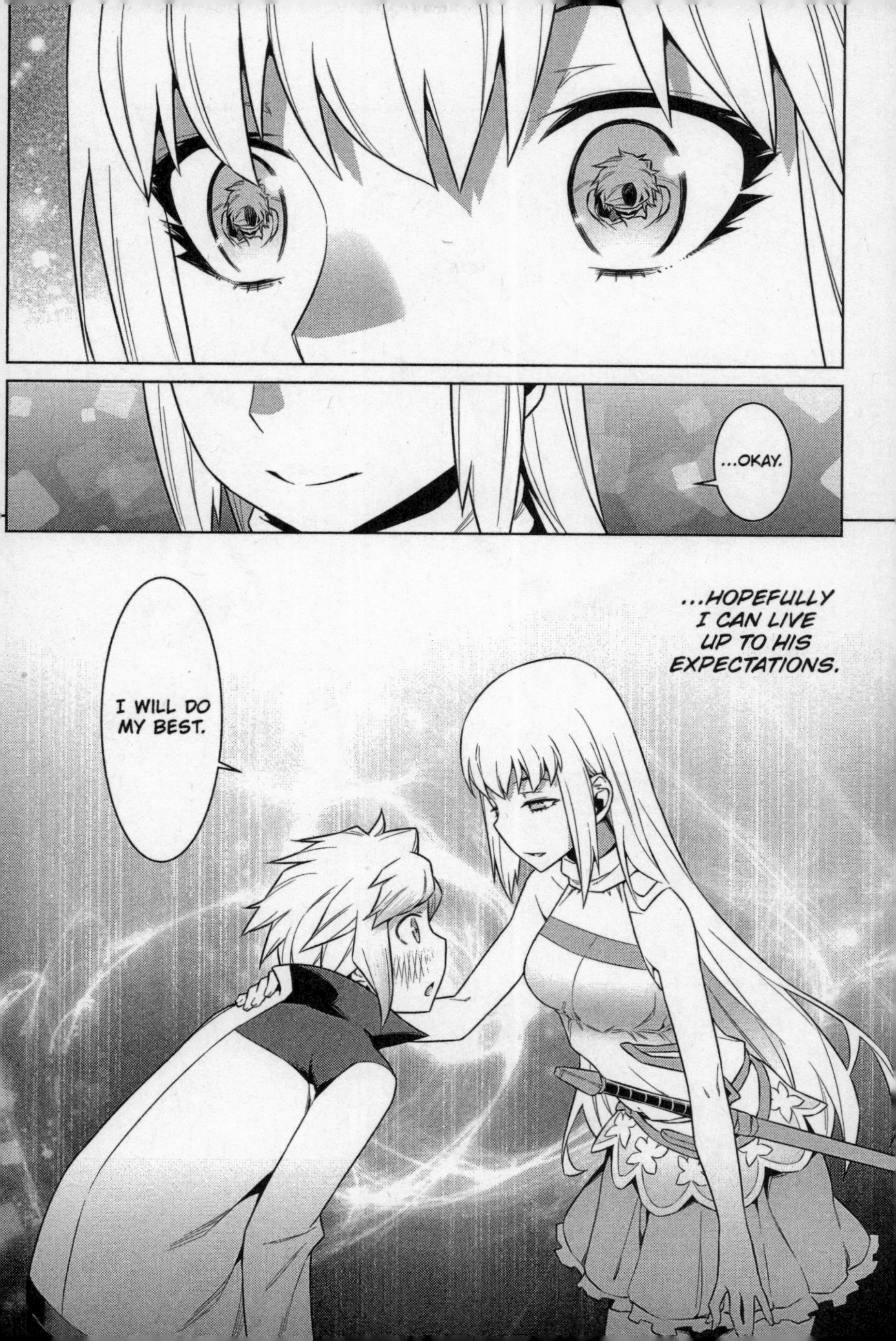
...OKAY.
...HOPEFULLY I CAN LIVE UP TO HIS EXPECTATIONS.
I WILL DO MY BEST.

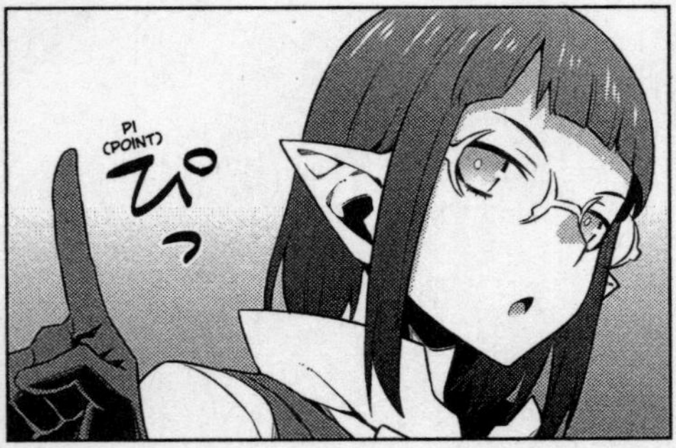
PI
(POINT)
ぴっ

IS it WRONG to TRY to PICK UP GIRLS IN A DUNGEON?

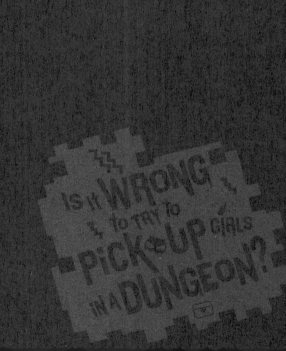

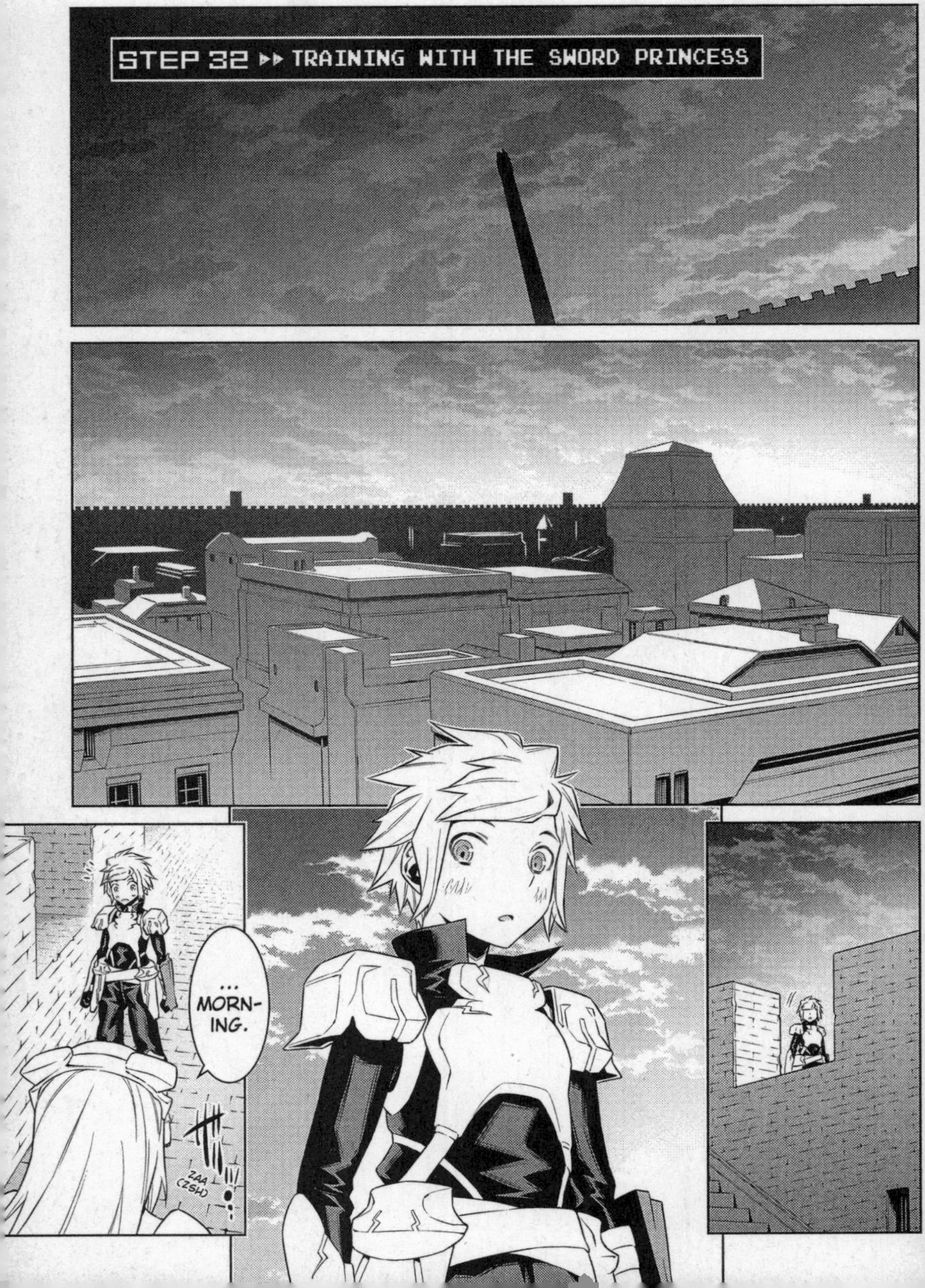
STEP 32 ▸▸ TRAINING WITH THE SWORD PRINCESS
... MORNING.
ZAA (ZSH)

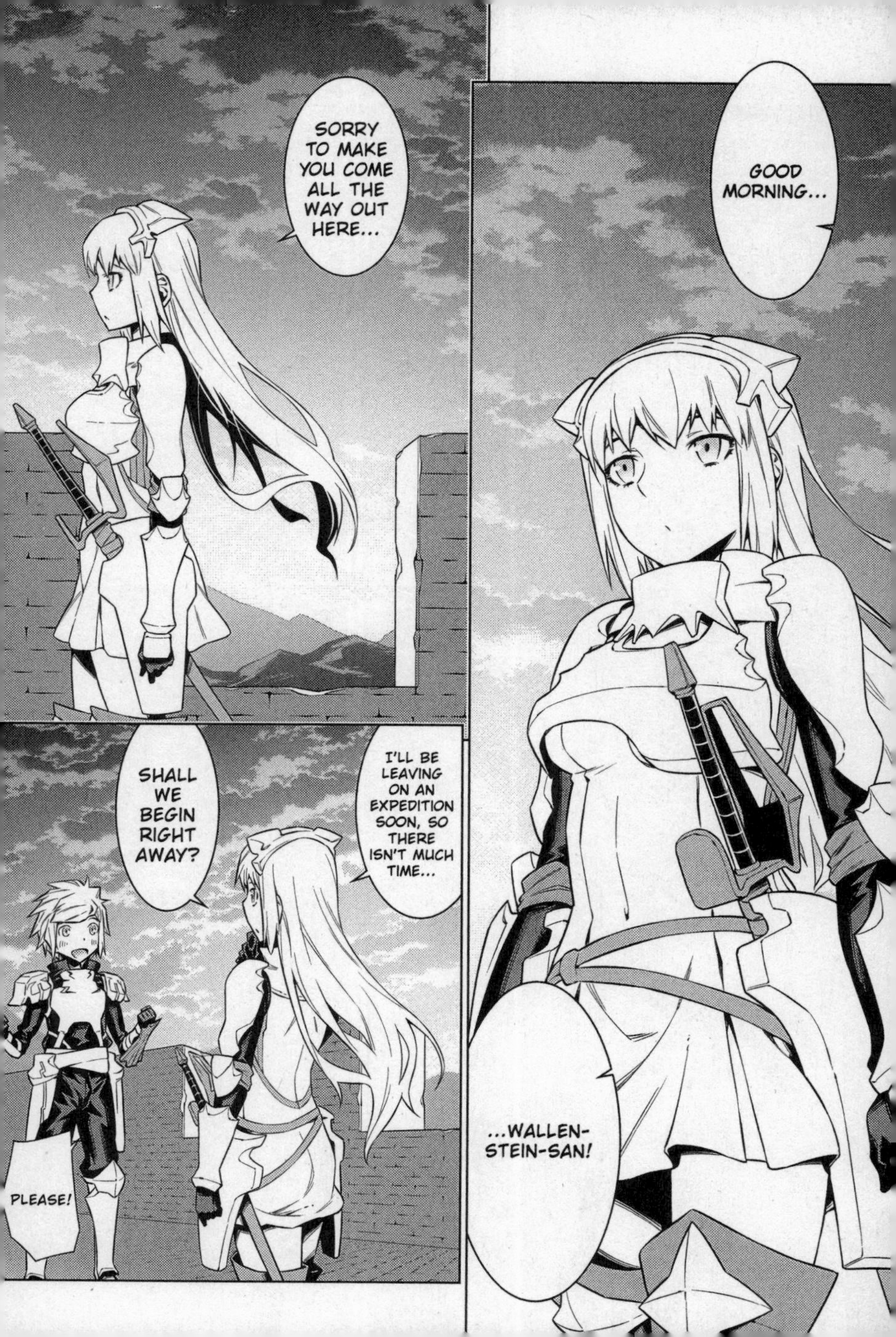
GOOD MORNING...
...WALLEN-STEIN-SAN!
SORRY TO MAKE YOU COME ALL THE WAY OUT HERE...
I'LL BE LEAVING ON AN EXPEDITION SOON, SO THERE ISN'T MUCH TIME...
SHALL WE BEGIN RIGHT AWAY?
PLEASE!

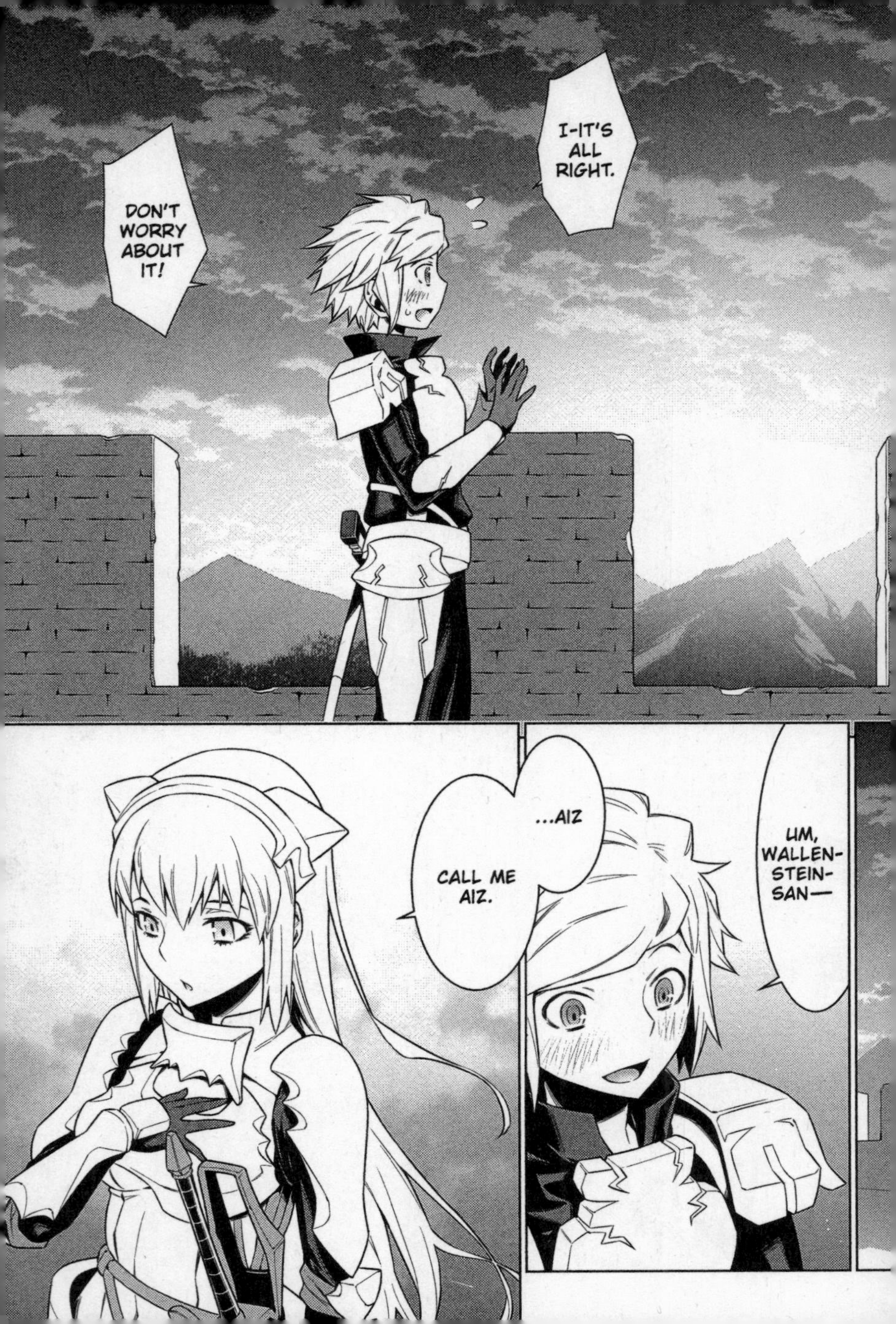
I-IT'S ALL RIGHT.
DON'T WORRY ABOUT IT!
UM, WALLEN-STEIN-SAN—
...AIZ
CALL ME AIZ.

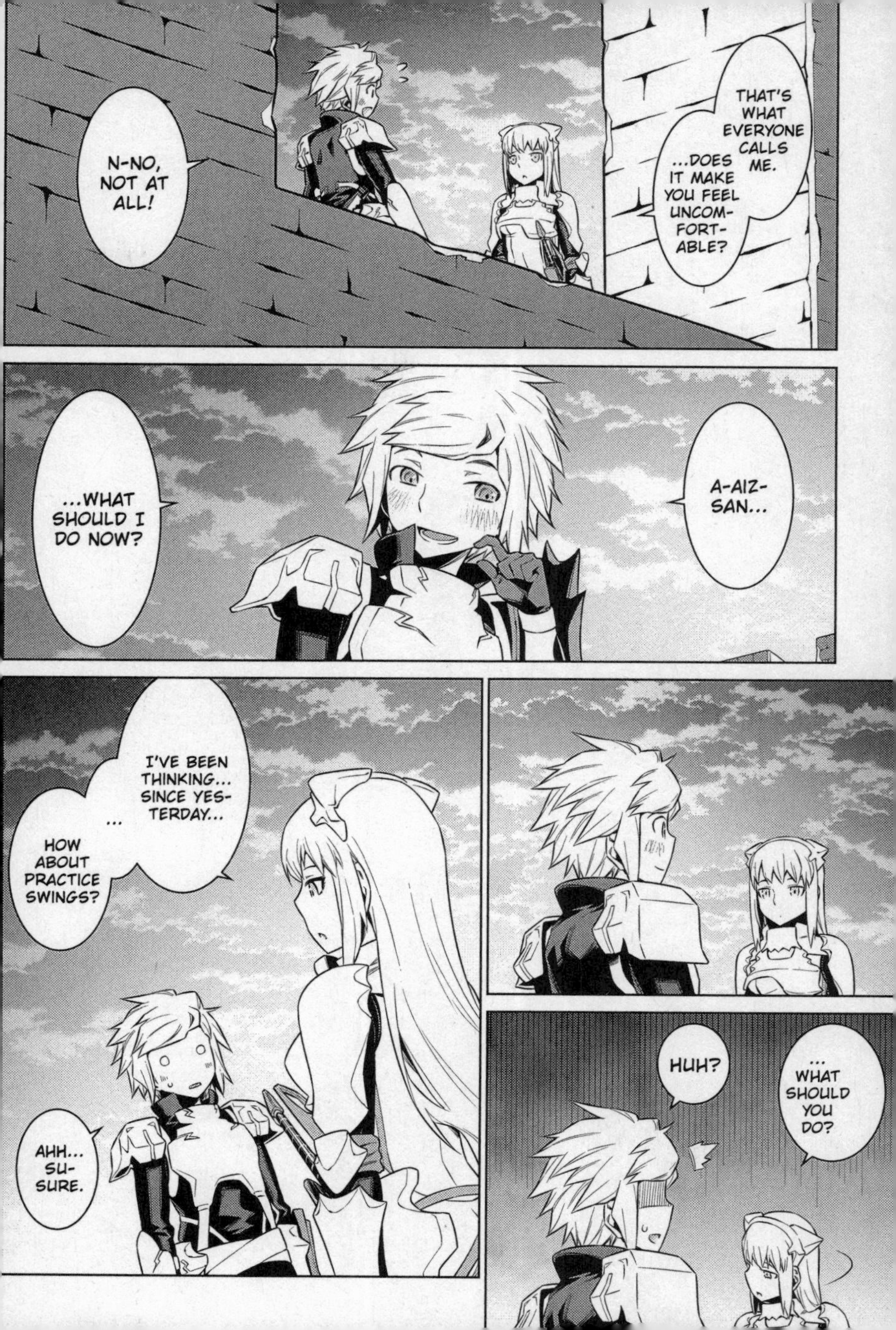
THAT'S WHAT EVERYONE CALLS ME.
...DOES IT MAKE YOU FEEL UNCOM-FORT-ABLE?
N-NO, NOT AT ALL!
A-AIZ-SAN...
...WHAT SHOULD I DO NOW?
... WHAT SHOULD YOU DO?
HUH?
I'VE BEEN THINKING... SINCE YES-TERDAY...
... HOW ABOUT PRACTICE SWINGS?
AHH... SU-SURE.

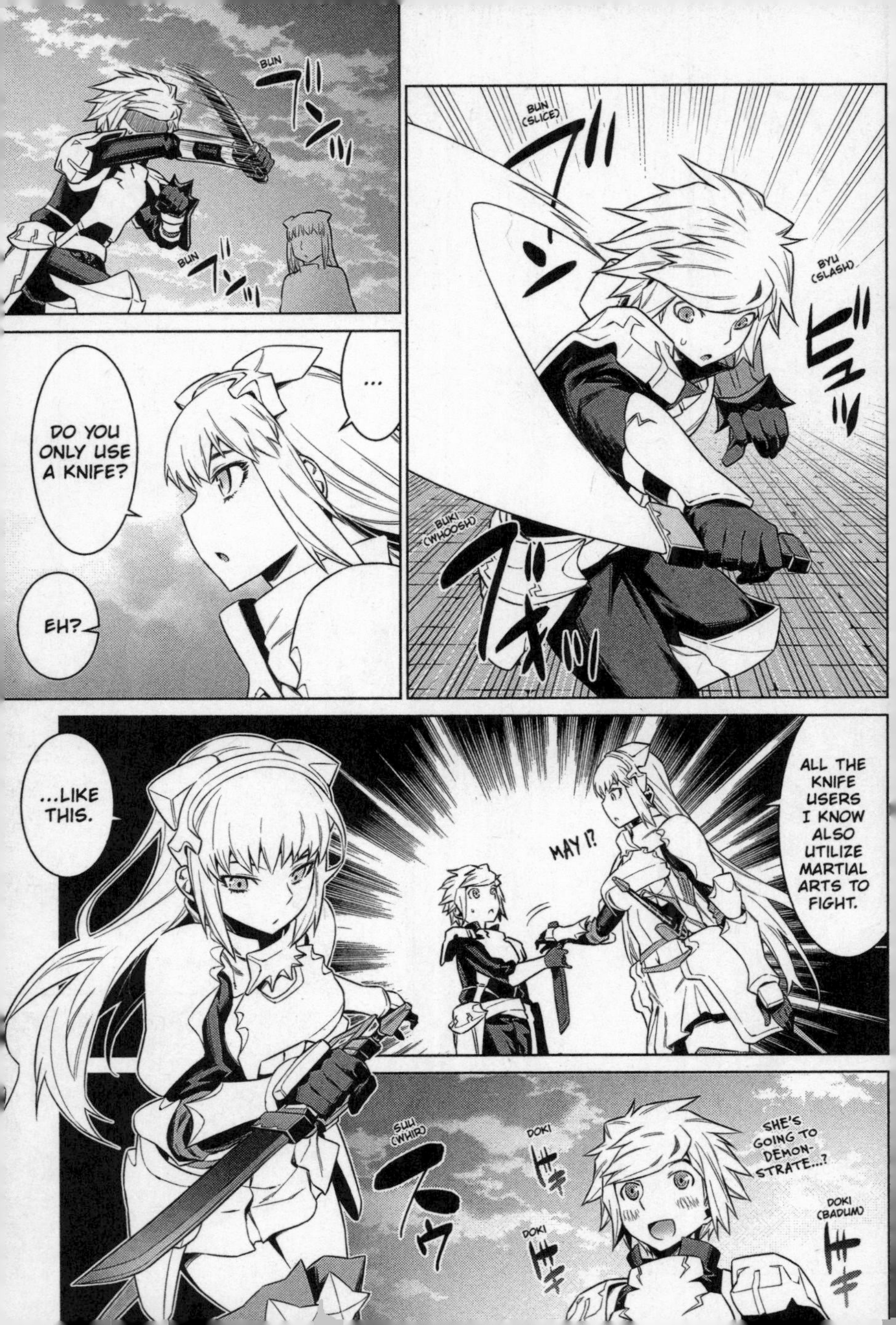
BUN (SLICE)
BYU (SLASH)
BUKI (WHOOSH)
BUN
BUN
...
DO YOU ONLY USE A KNIFE?
EH?
ALL THE KNIFE USERS I KNOW ALSO UTILIZE MARTIAL ARTS TO FIGHT.
MAY I!?
...LIKE THIS.
SHE'S GOING TO DEMON-STRATE...?
DOKI
DOKI
DOKI (BADUM)
SUU (WHIR)

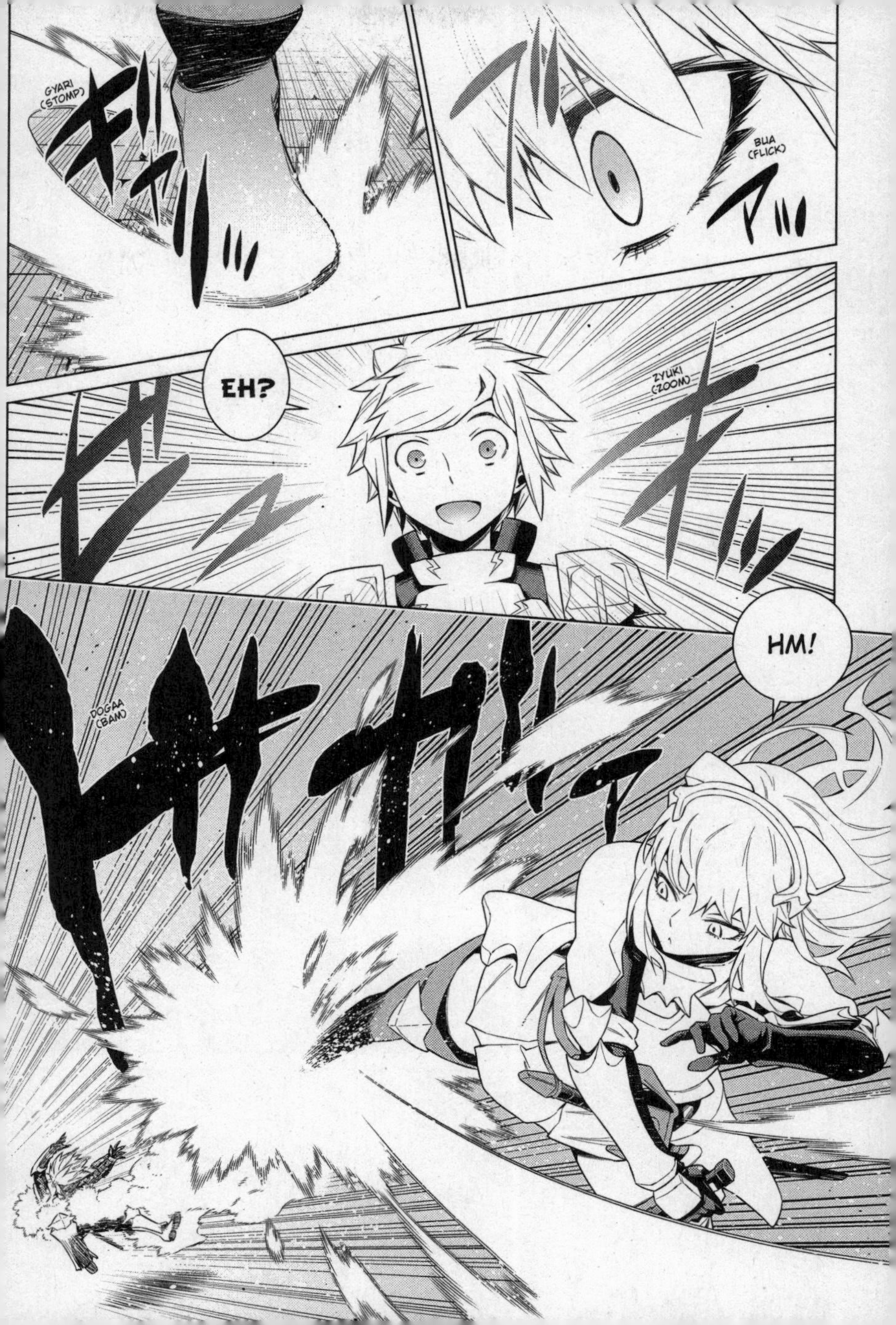
BUA
(FLICK)
GYARI
(STOMP)
ZYUKI
(ZOOM)
EH?
HM!
DOGAA
(BAM)

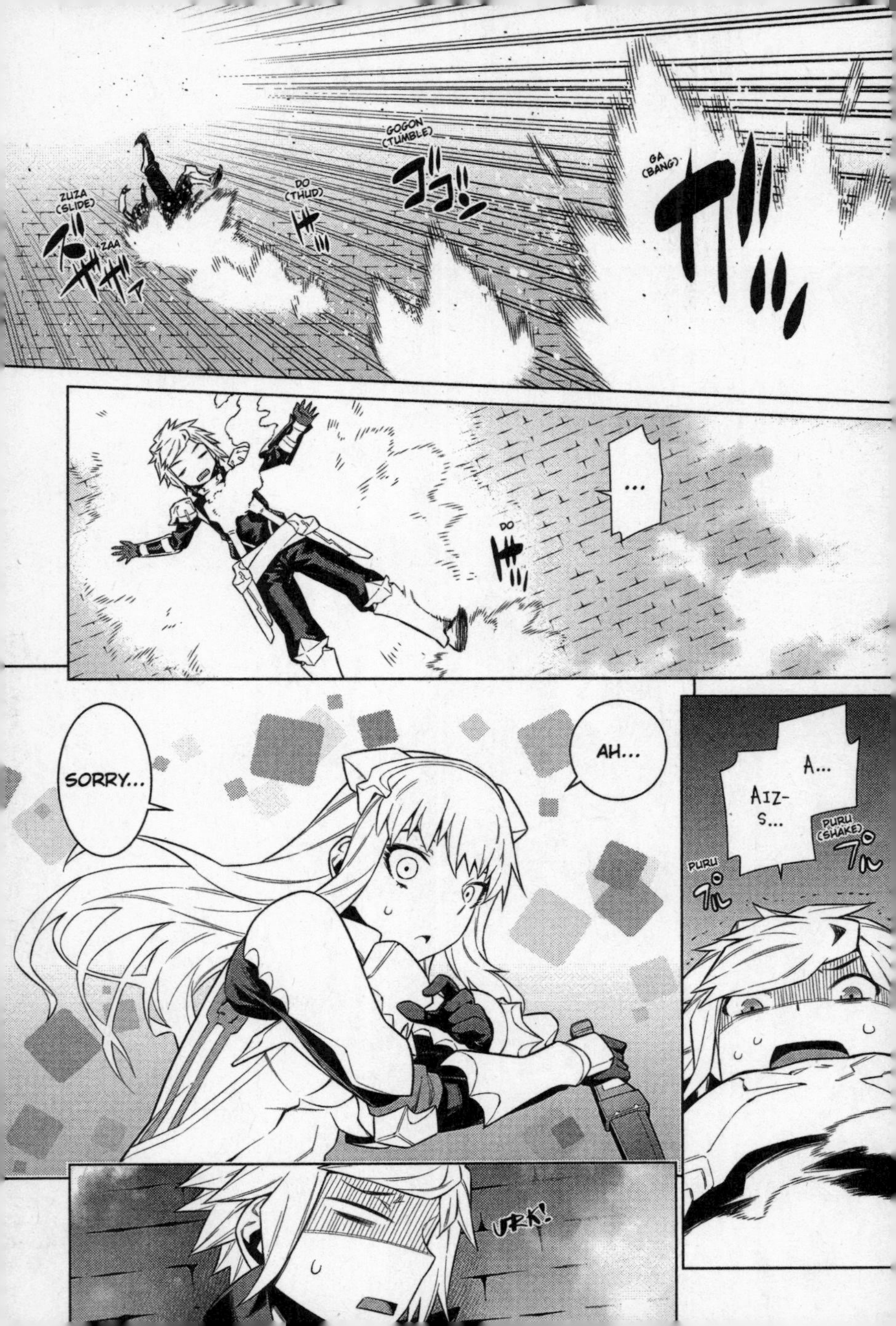
GA (BANG)
GOGON (TUMBLE)
DO (THUD)
ZUZA (SLIDE)
ZAA
...
DO
A... AIZ-S...
PURU (SHAKE)
PURU
AH...
SORRY...
URK!

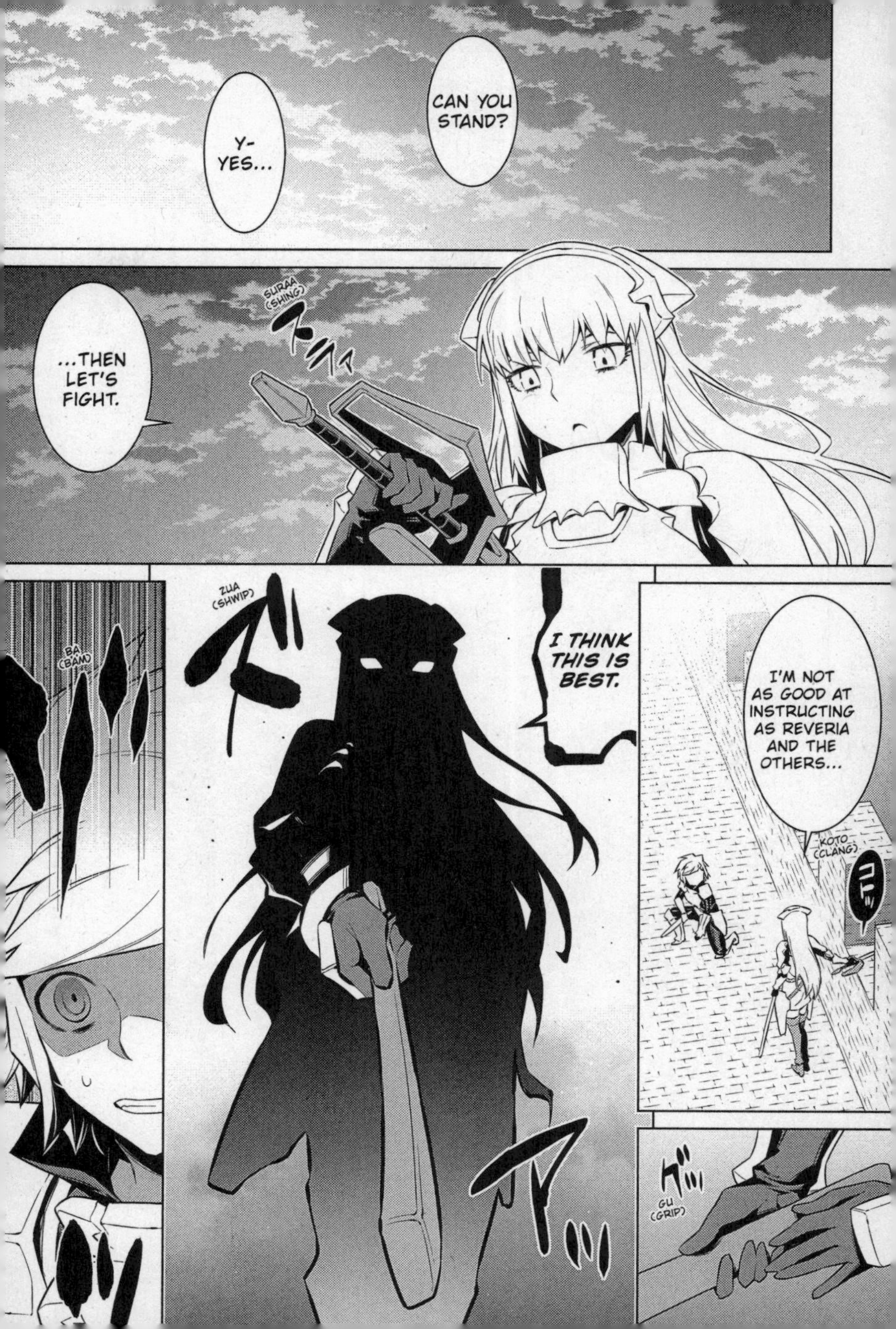
CAN YOU STAND?
Y- YES...
SURAA (SHING)
...THEN LET'S FIGHT.
I'M NOT AS GOOD AT INSTRUCTING AS REVERIA AND THE OTHERS...
KOTO (CLANG)
GU (GRIP)
ZUA (SHWIP)
I THINK THIS IS BEST.
BA (BAM)

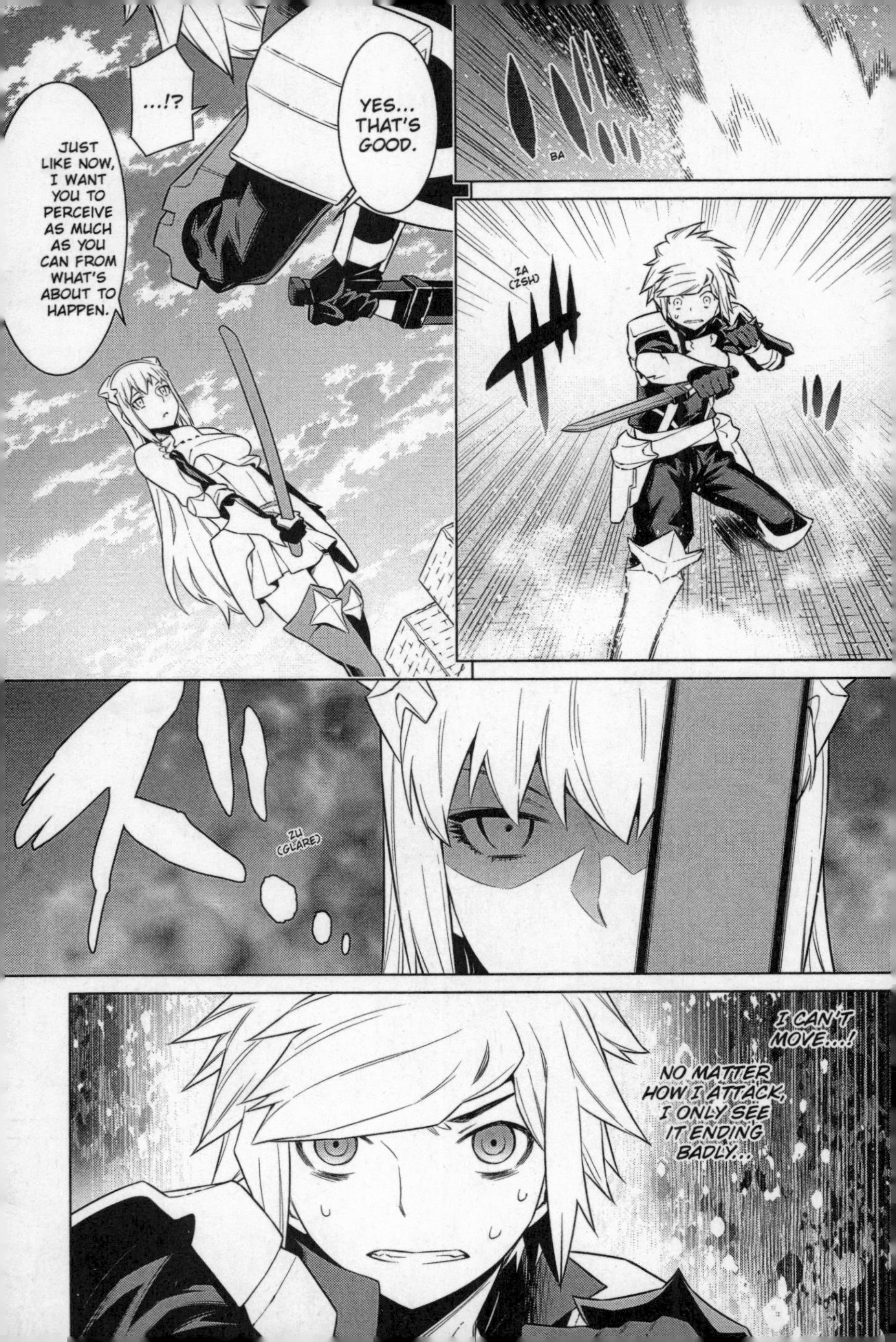
BA
ZA (ZSH)
YES... THAT'S GOOD.
...!?
JUST LIKE NOW, I WANT YOU TO PERCEIVE AS MUCH AS YOU CAN FROM WHAT'S ABOUT TO HAPPEN.
ZU (GLARE)
I CAN'T MOVE...!
NO MATTER HOW I ATTACK, I ONLY SEE IT ENDING BADLY...

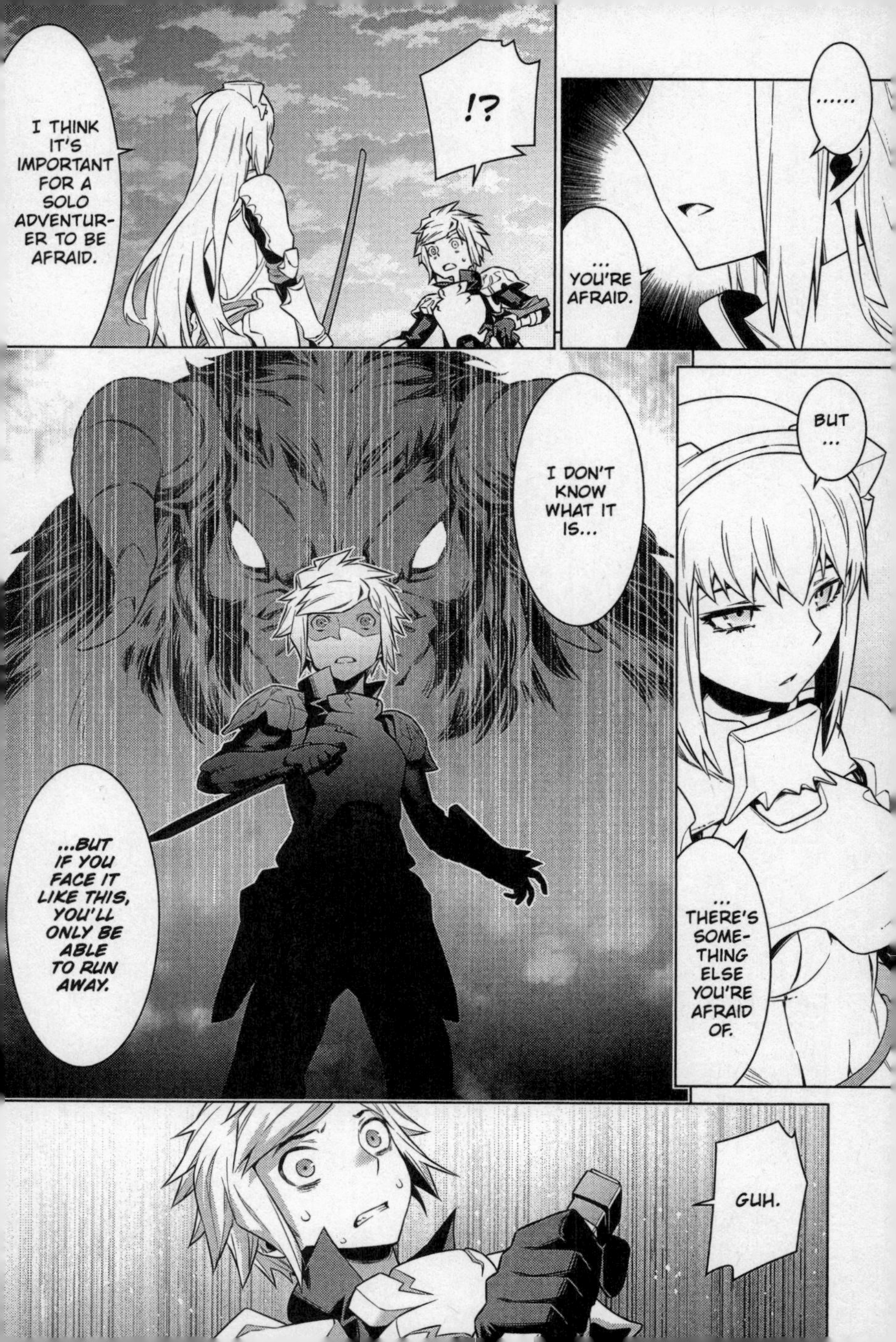
......
... YOU'RE AFRAID.
!?
I THINK IT'S IMPORTANT FOR A SOLO ADVENTURER TO BE AFRAID.
BUT ...
... THERE'S SOMETHING ELSE YOU'RE AFRAID OF.
I DON'T KNOW WHAT IT IS...
...BUT IF YOU FACE IT LIKE THIS, YOU'LL ONLY BE ABLE TO RUN AWAY.
GUH.

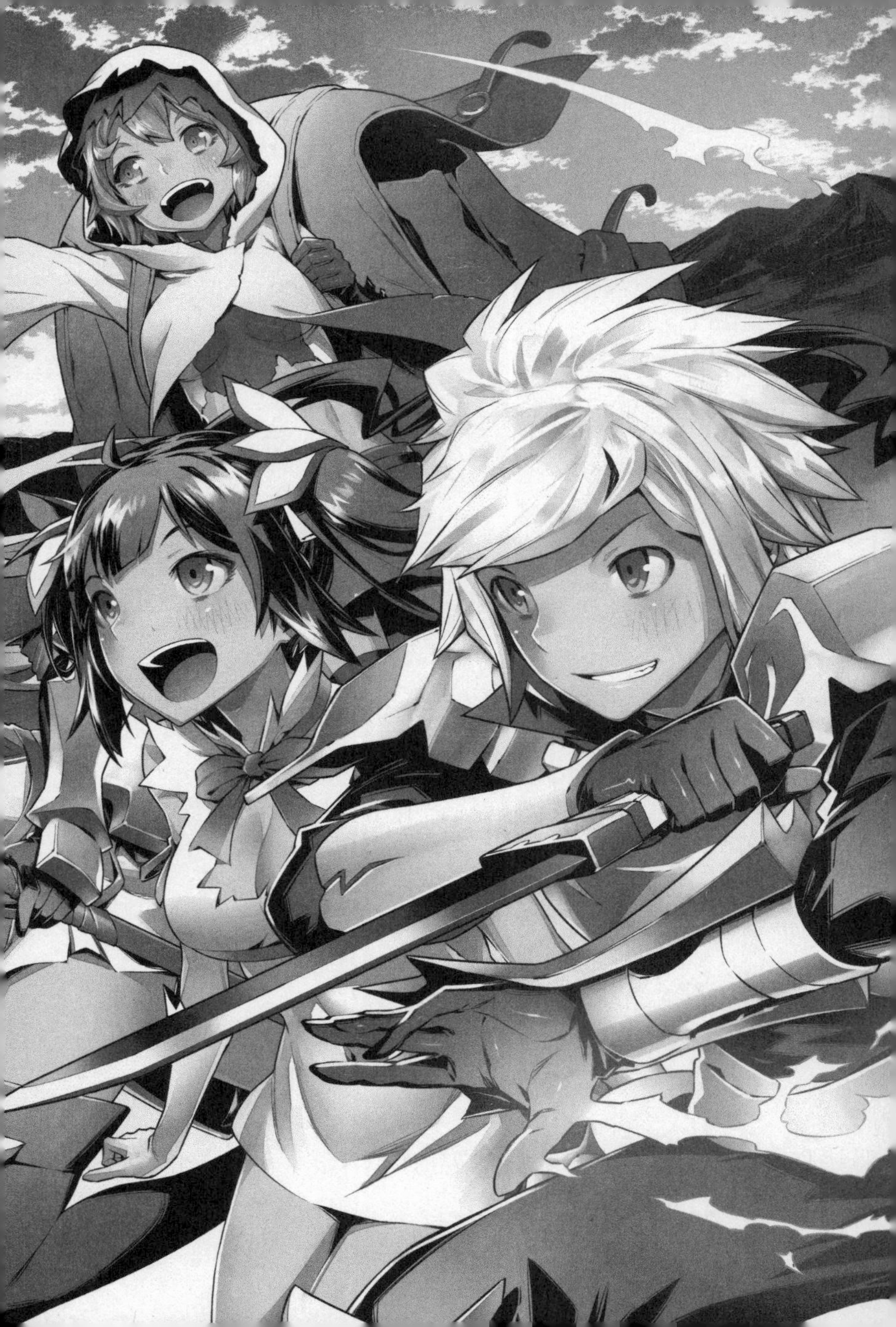

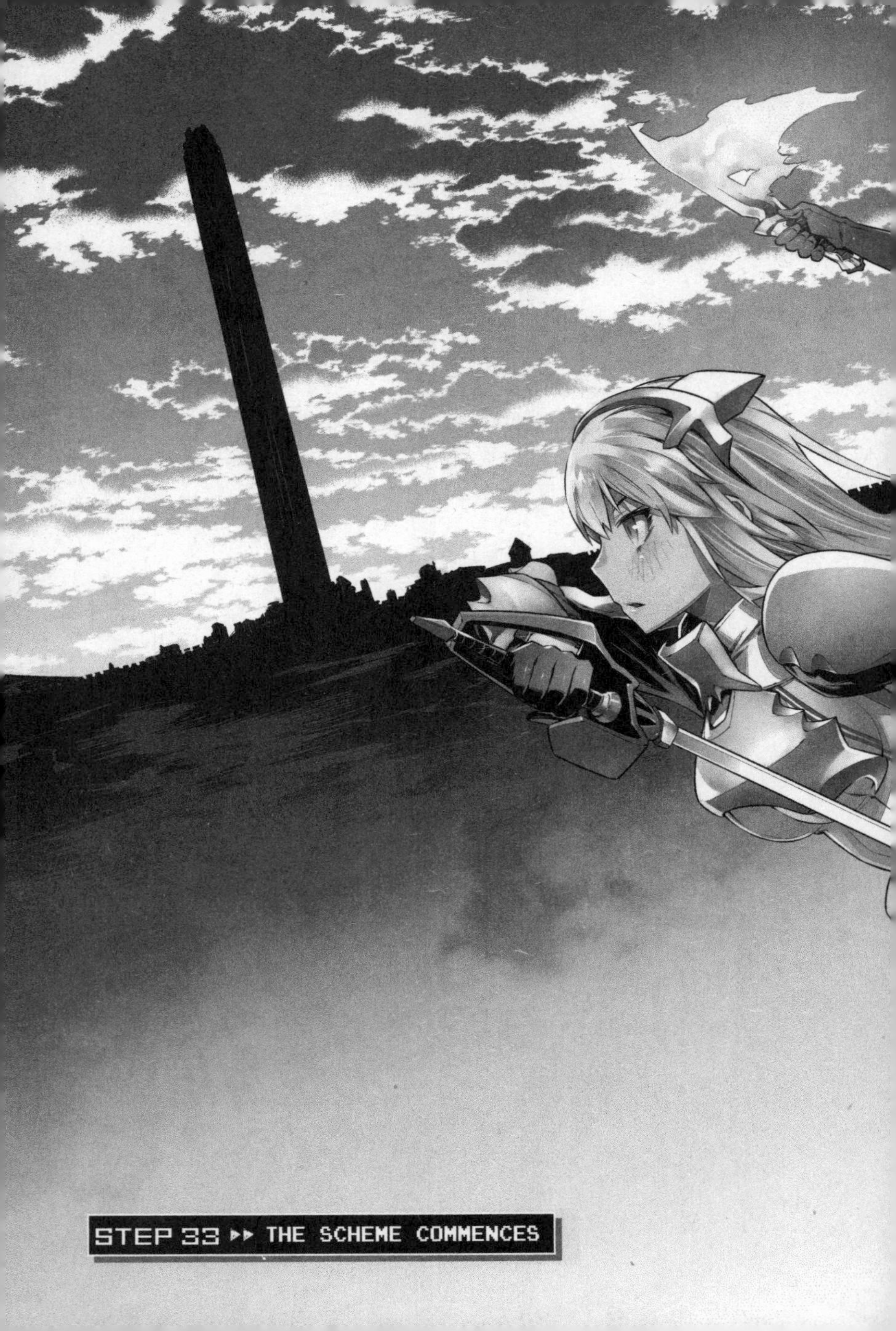

STEP 33 ▸▸ THE SCHEME COMMENCES

Is It Wrong to Try to Pick Up Girls in a Dungeon?

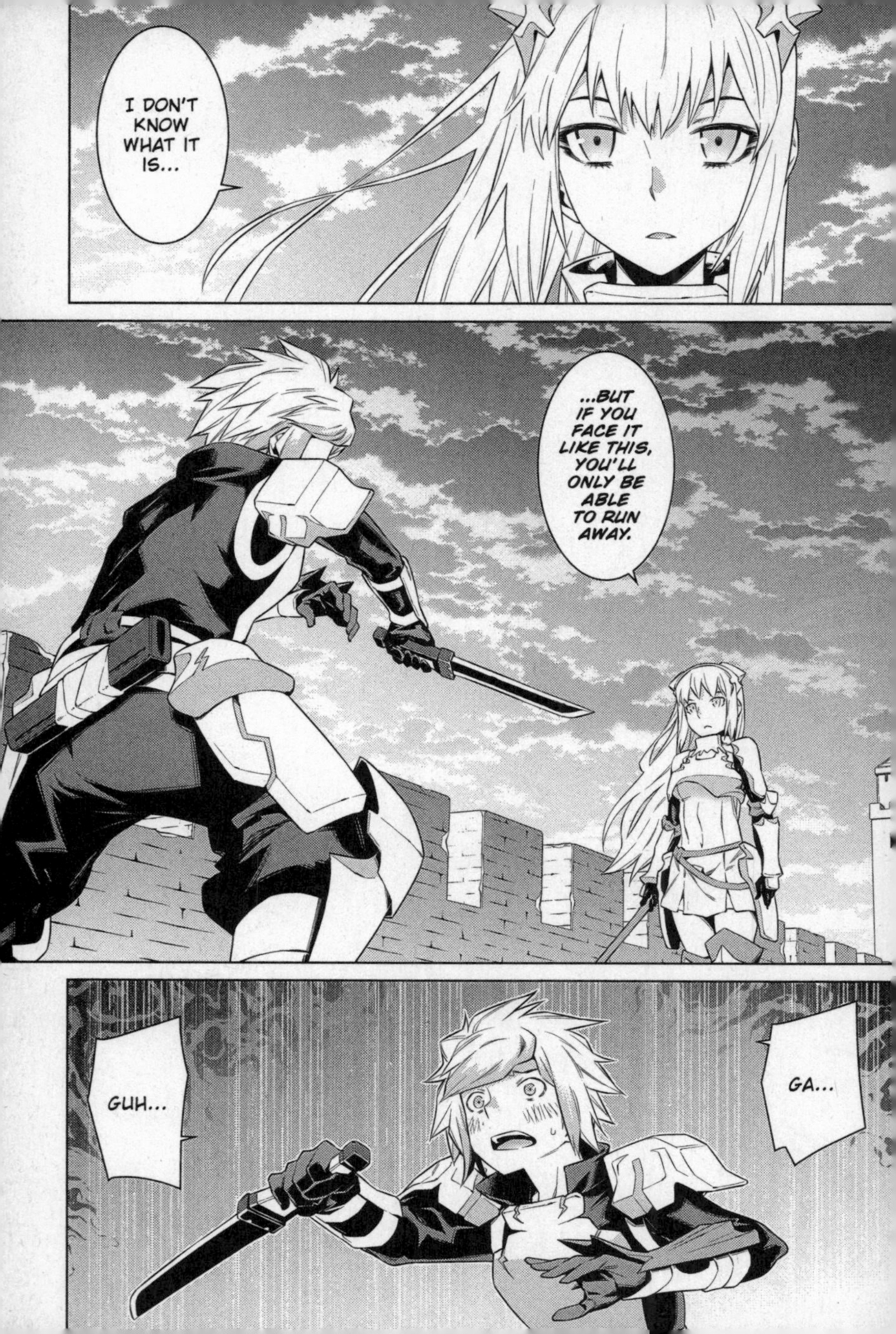
I DON'T KNOW WHAT IT IS...
...BUT IF YOU FACE IT LIKE THIS, YOU'LL ONLY BE ABLE TO RUN AWAY.
GA...
GUH...

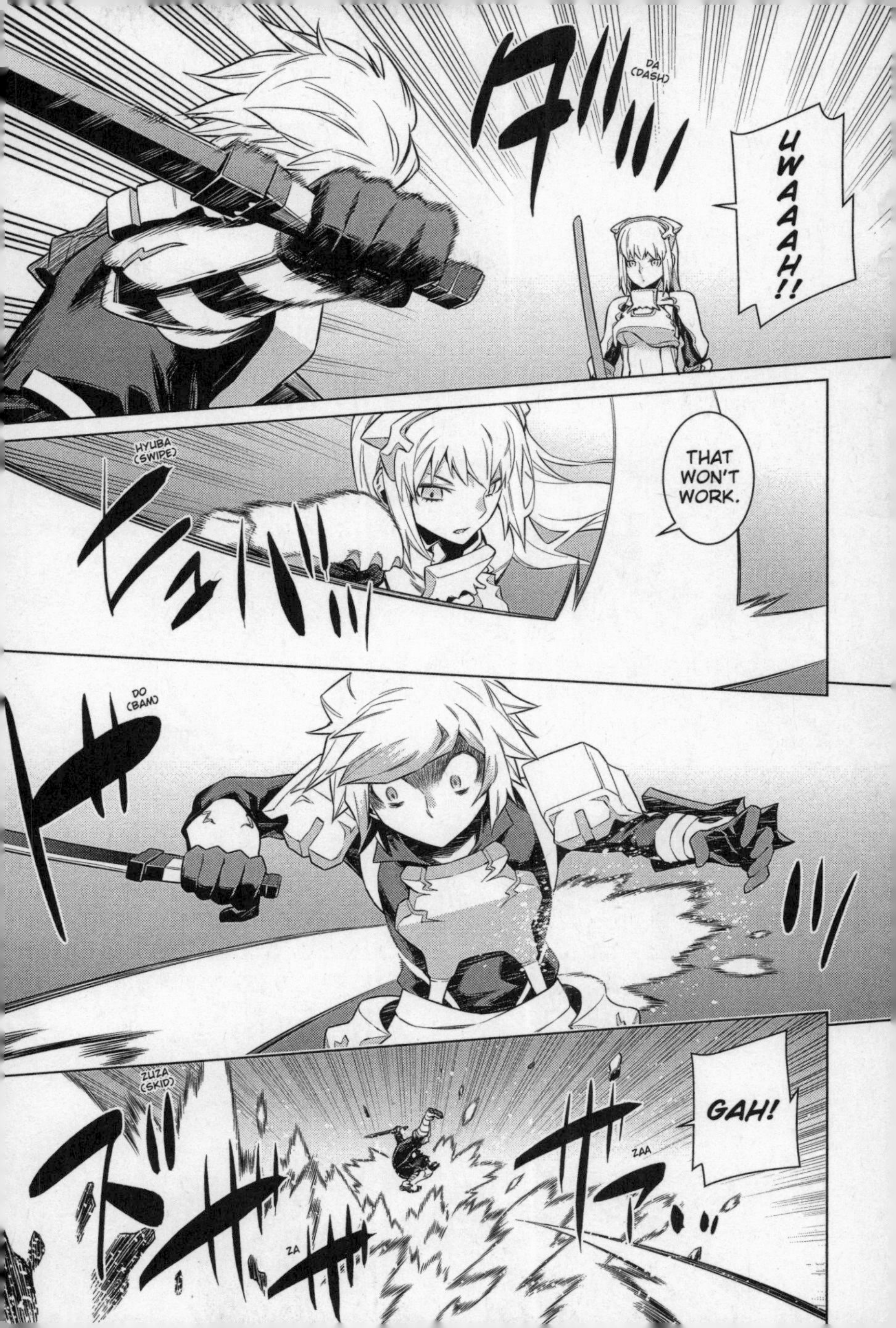
UWAAAAH!!
DA (DASH)
THAT WON'T WORK.
HYUBA (SWIPE)
DO (BAM)
GAH!
ZAA
ZUZA (SKID)
ZA

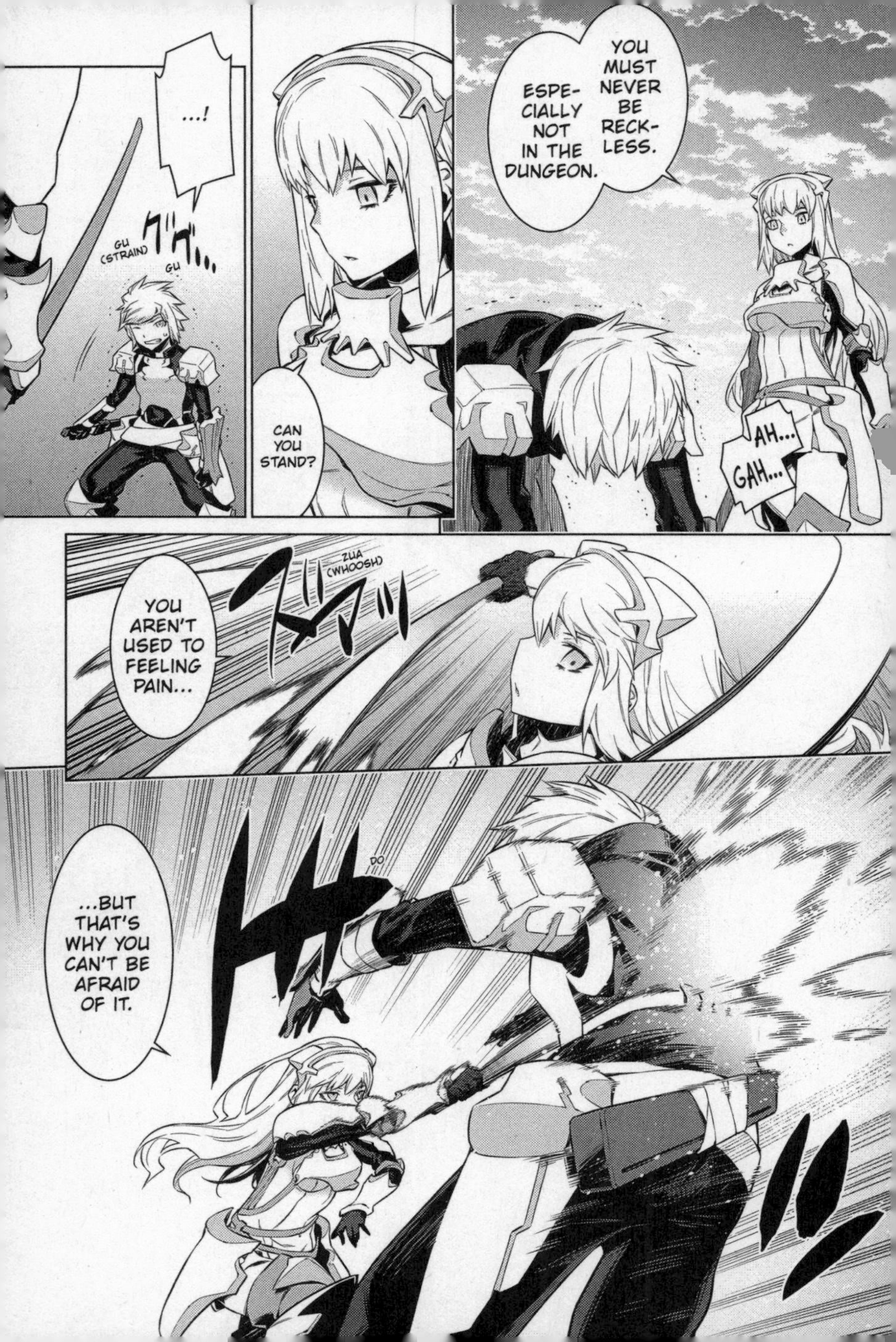
YOU MUST NEVER BE RECK-LESS.
ESPE-CIALLY NOT IN THE DUNGEON.
AH... GAH...
CAN YOU STAND?
...!
GU (STRAIN) GU
ZUA (WHOOSH)
YOU AREN'T USED TO FEELING PAIN...
DO
...BUT THAT'S WHY YOU CAN'T BE AFRAID OF IT.

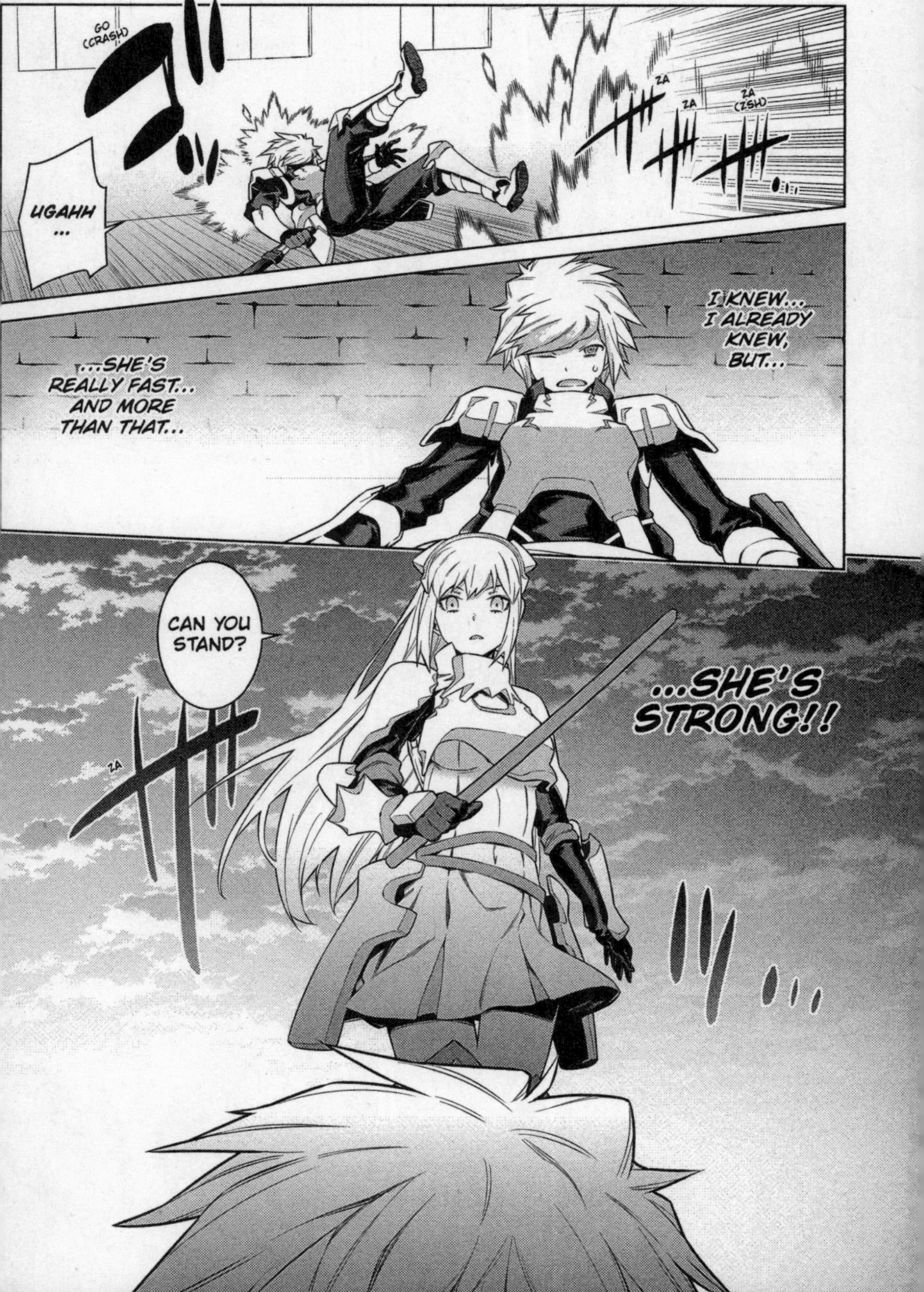
ZA
ZA
ZA (ZSH)
GO (CRASH)
UGAHH ...
I KNEW... I ALREADY KNEW, BUT...
...SHE'S REALLY FAST... AND MORE THAN THAT...
CAN YOU STAND?
...SHE'S STRONG!!
ZA

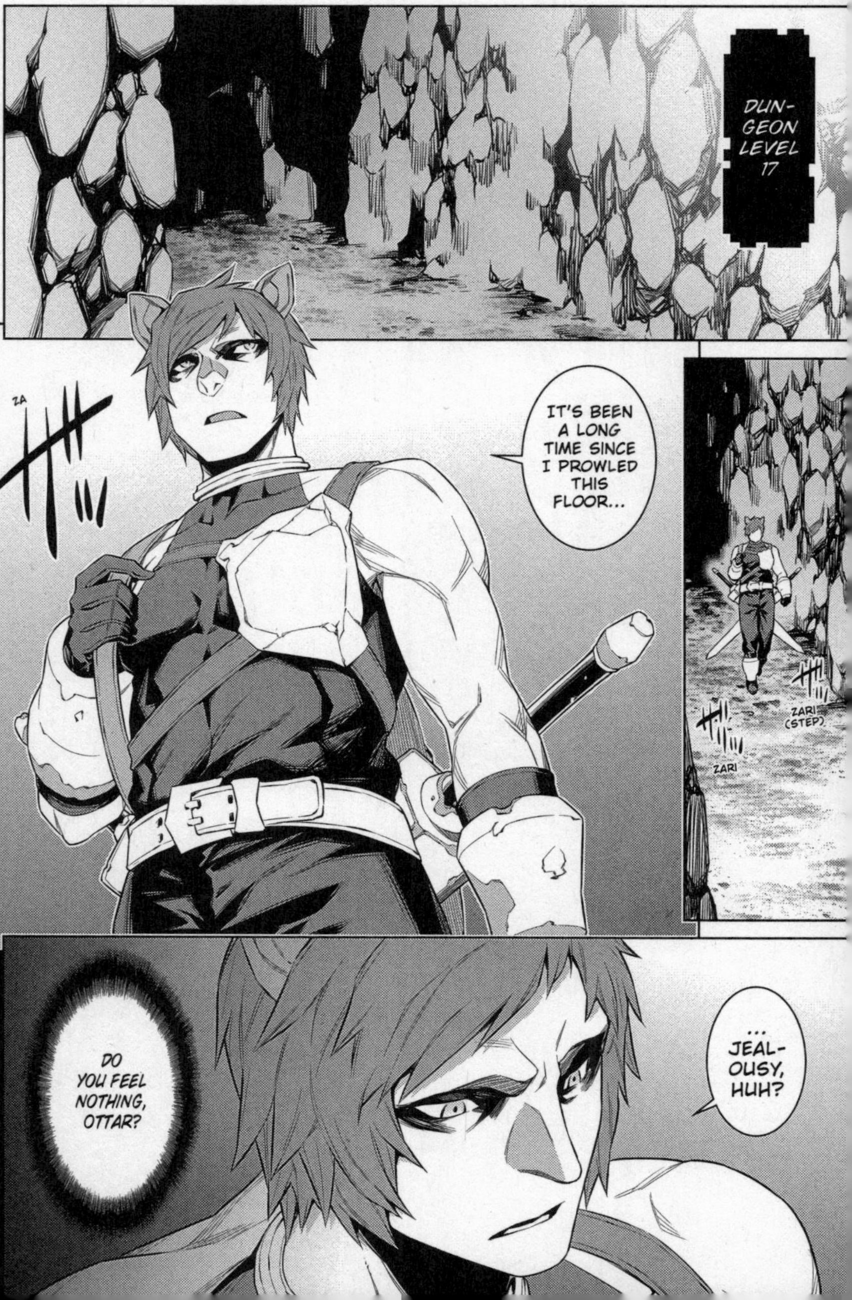
DUN-GEON LEVEL 17
ZARI (STEP)
ZARI
IT'S BEEN A LONG TIME SINCE I PROWLED THIS FLOOR...
ZA
... JEAL-OUSY, HUH?
DO YOU FEEL NOTHING, OTTAR?

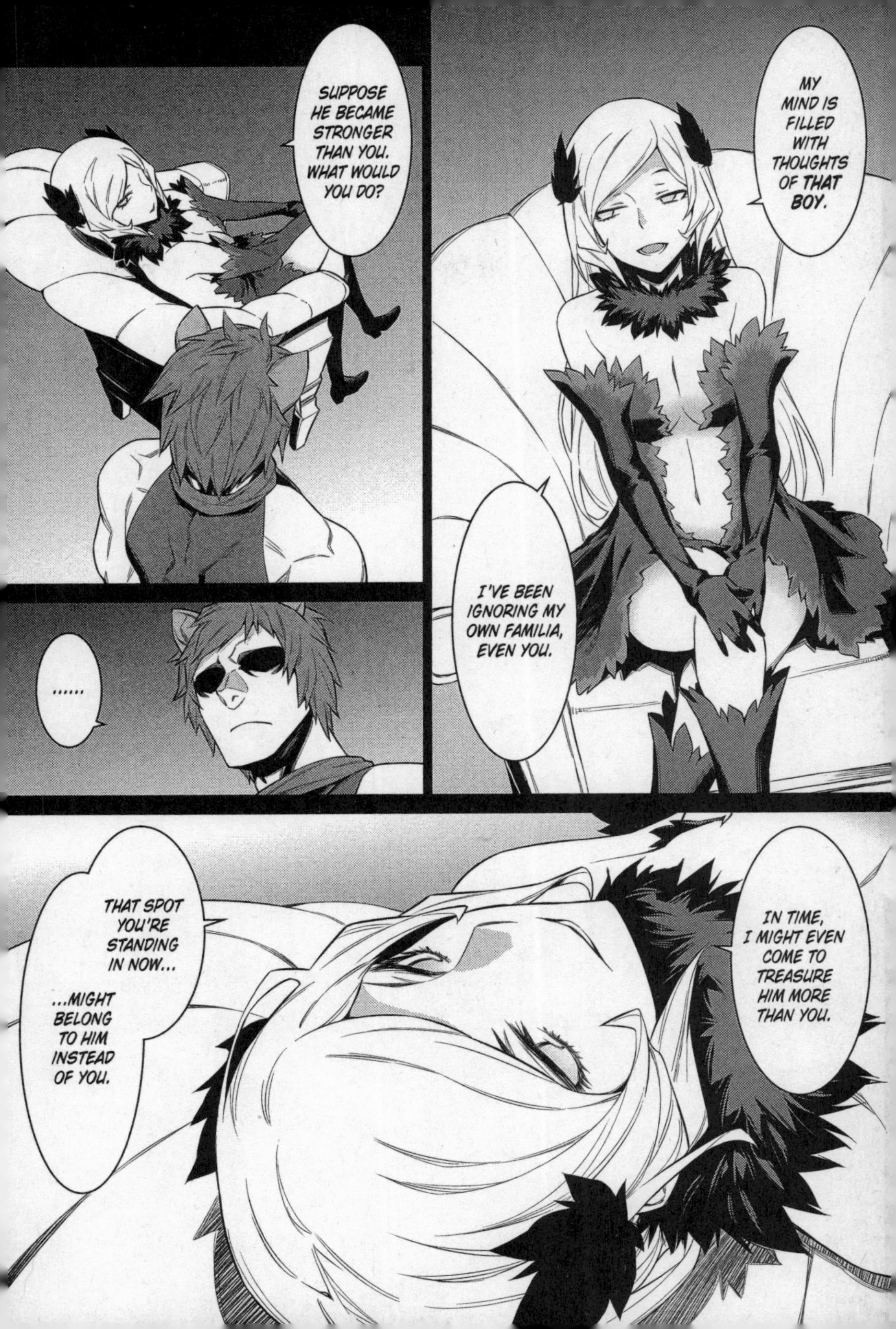
MY MIND IS FILLED WITH THOUGHTS OF THAT BOY.
I'VE BEEN IGNORING MY OWN FAMILIA, EVEN YOU.
SUPPOSE HE BECAME STRONGER THAN YOU. WHAT WOULD YOU DO?
......
IN TIME, I MIGHT EVEN COME TO TREASURE HIM MORE THAN YOU.
THAT SPOT YOU'RE STANDING IN NOW...
...MIGHT BELONG TO HIM INSTEAD OF YOU.

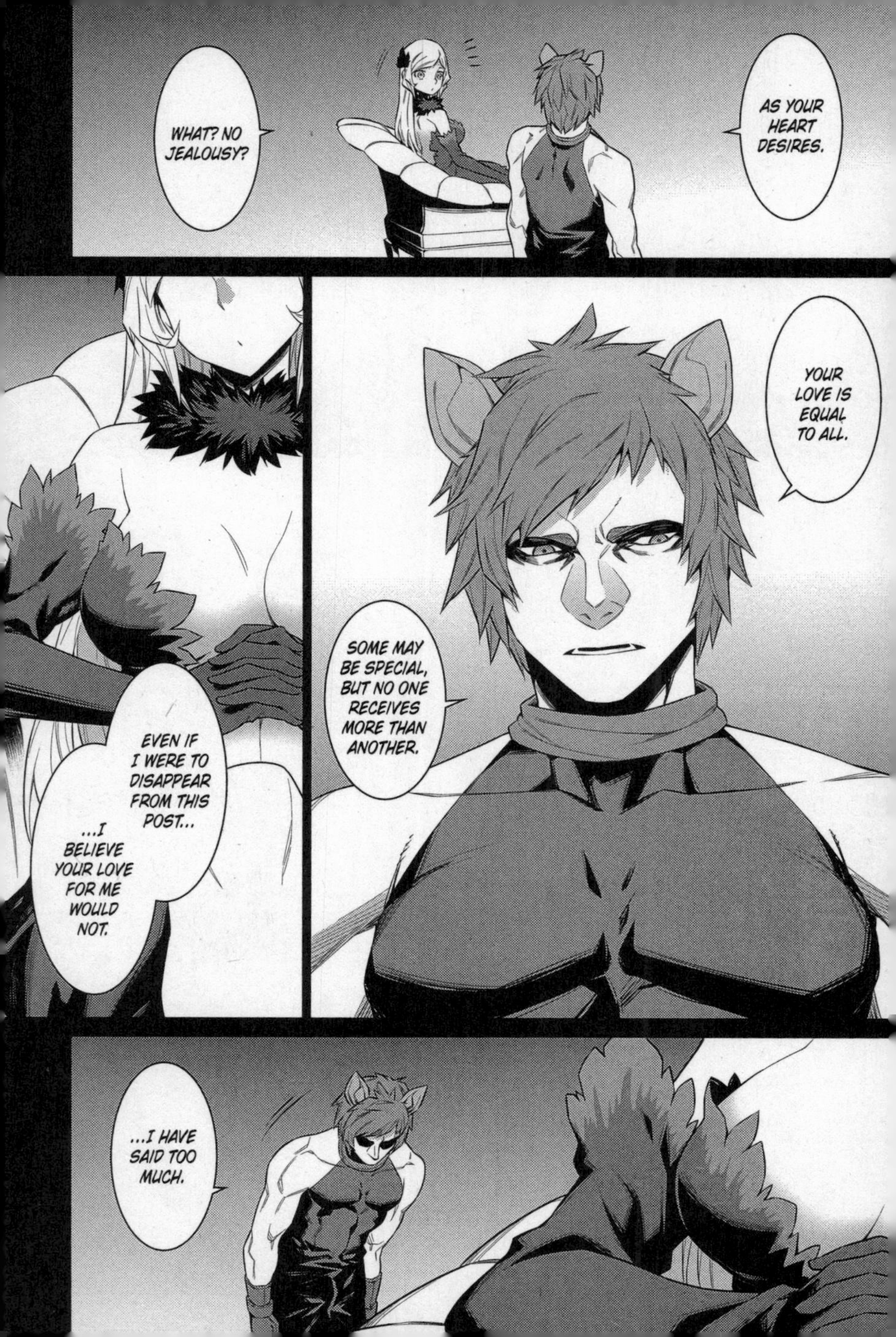
AS YOUR HEART DESIRES.
WHAT? NO JEALOUSY?
YOUR LOVE IS EQUAL TO ALL.
SOME MAY BE SPECIAL, BUT NO ONE RECEIVES MORE THAN ANOTHER.
EVEN IF I WERE TO DISAPPEAR FROM THIS POST...
...I BELIEVE YOUR LOVE FOR ME WOULD NOT.
...I HAVE SAID TOO MUCH.

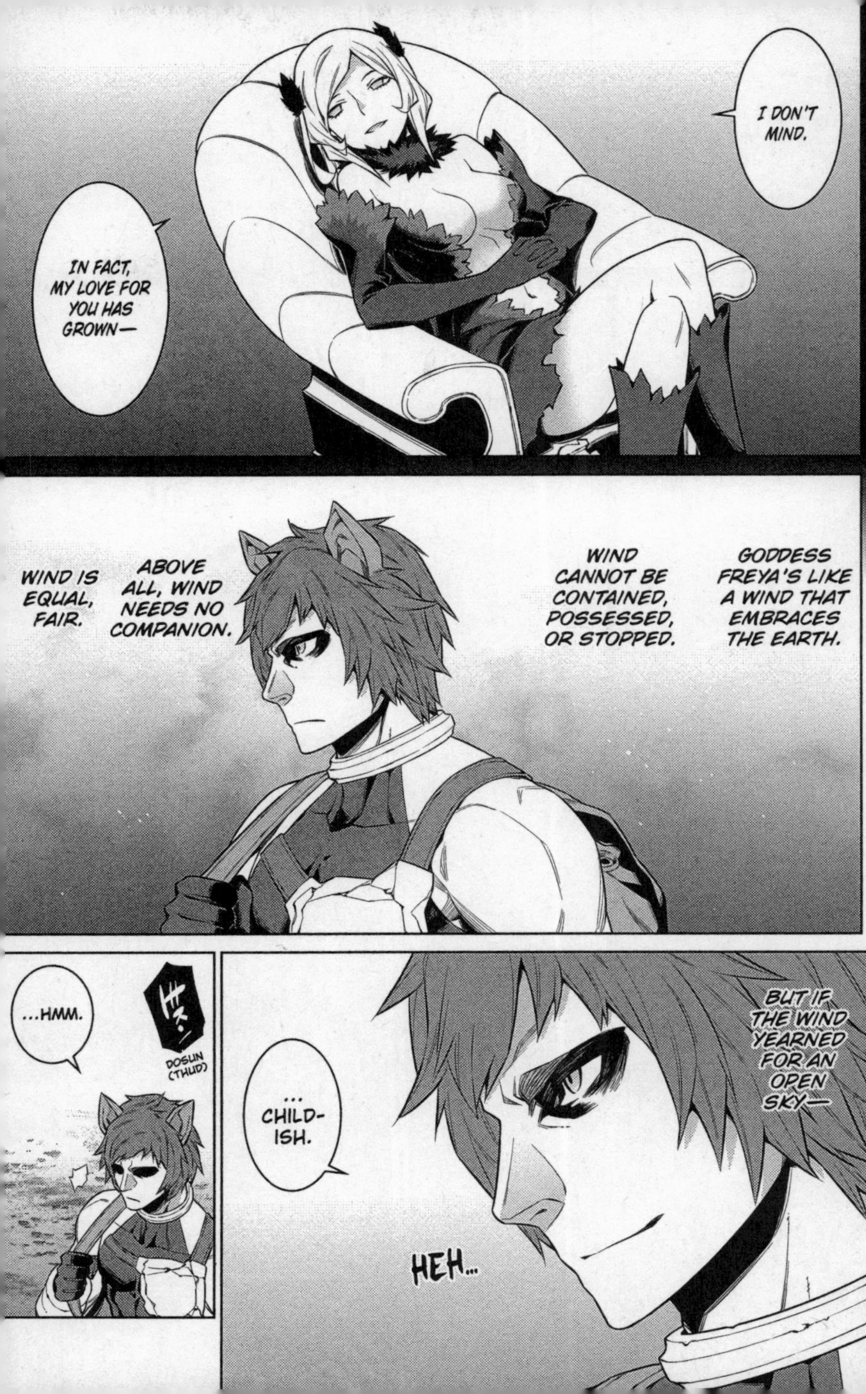
I DON'T MIND.
IN FACT, MY LOVE FOR YOU HAS GROWN—
GODDESS FREYA'S LIKE A WIND THAT EMBRACES THE EARTH.
WIND CANNOT BE CONTAINED, POSSESSED, OR STOPPED.
ABOVE ALL, WIND NEEDS NO COMPANION.
WIND IS EQUAL, FAIR.
BUT IF THE WIND YEARNED FOR AN OPEN SKY—
... CHILD-ISH.
HEH...
...HMM.
DOSUN (THUD)

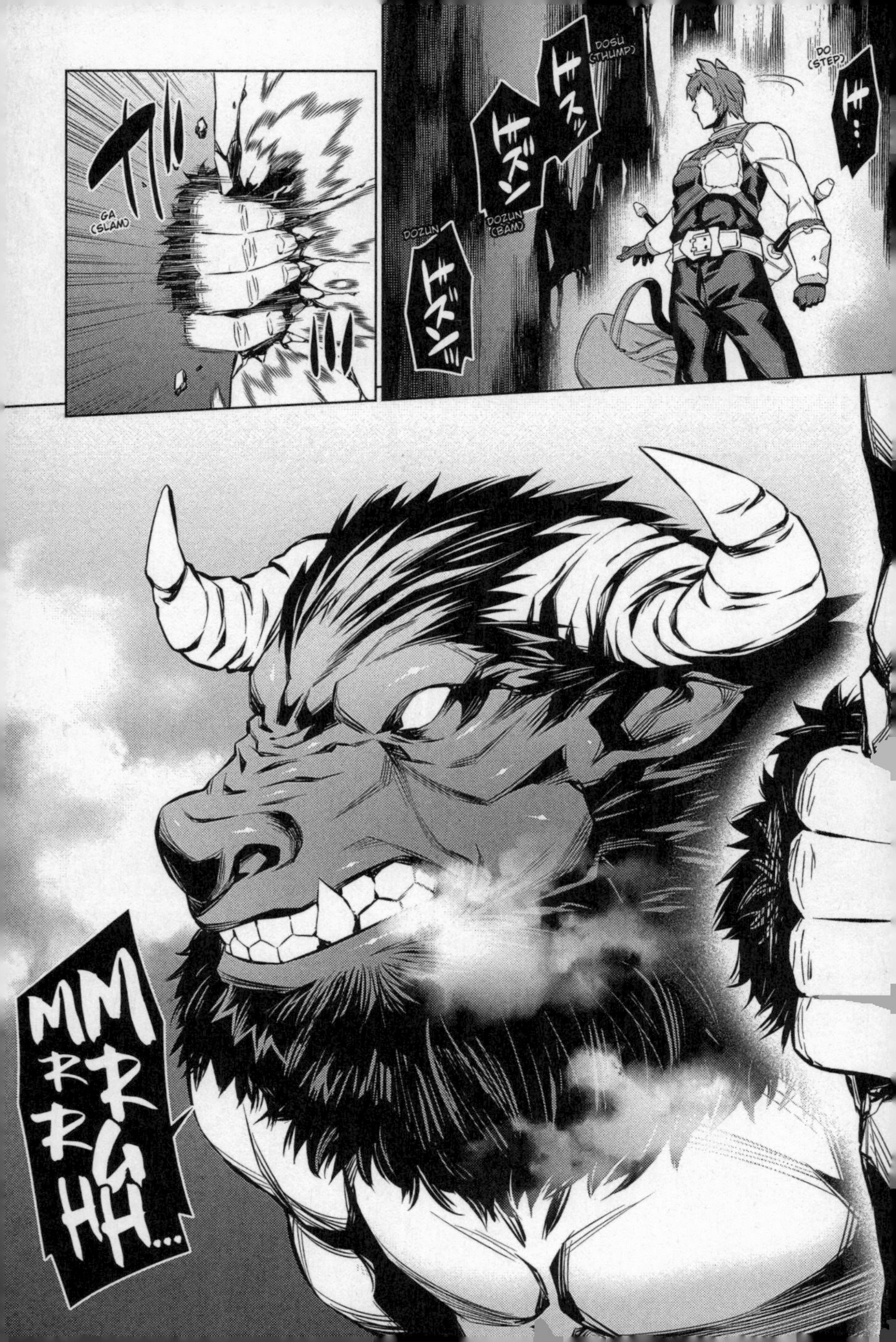

DO (STEP)
DOSU (THUMP)
DOZUN (BAM)
DOZUN
GA (SLAM)
MMRRRUHH...

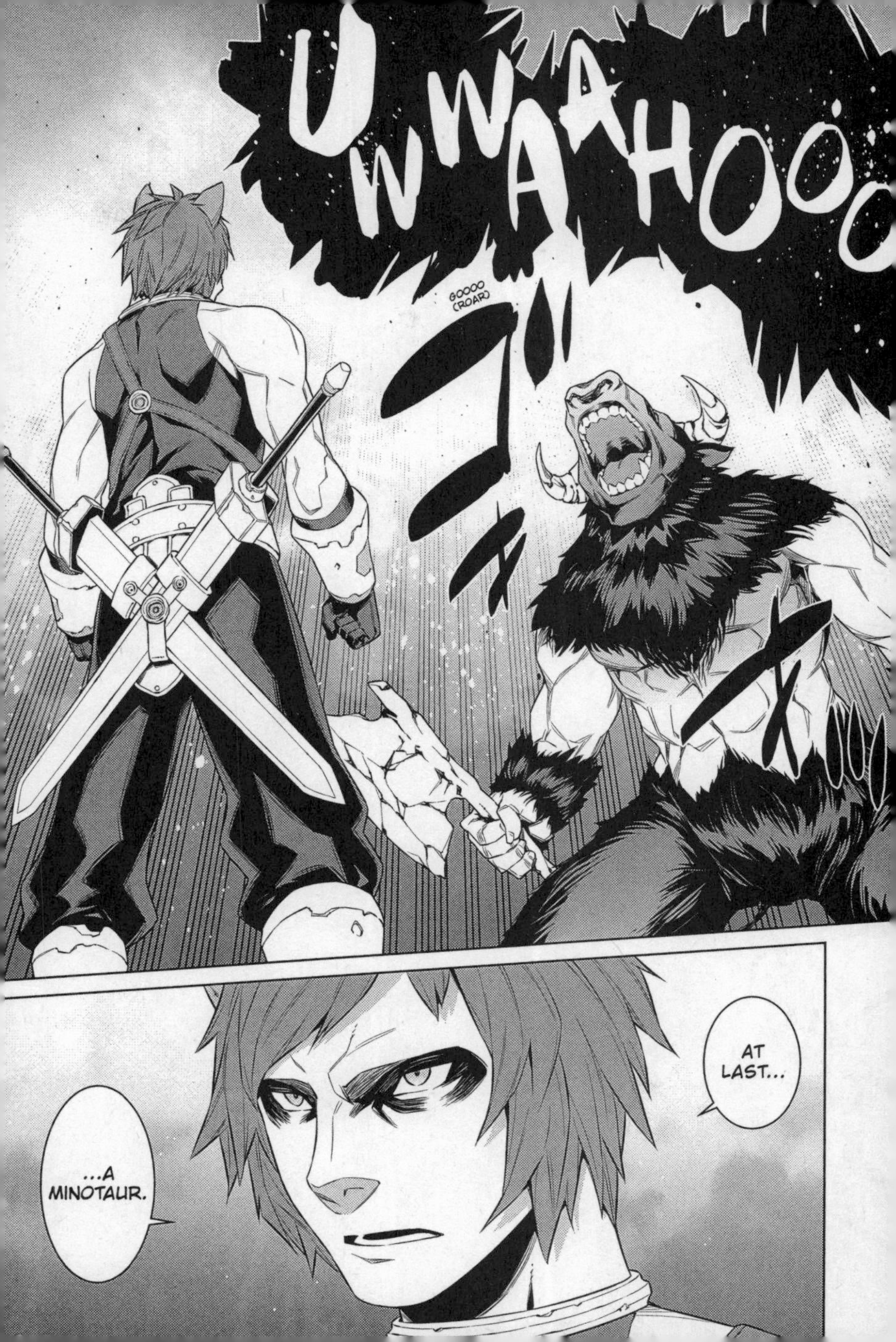
UWAAAHOOO
GOOOO (ROAR)
AT LAST...
...A MINOTAUR.

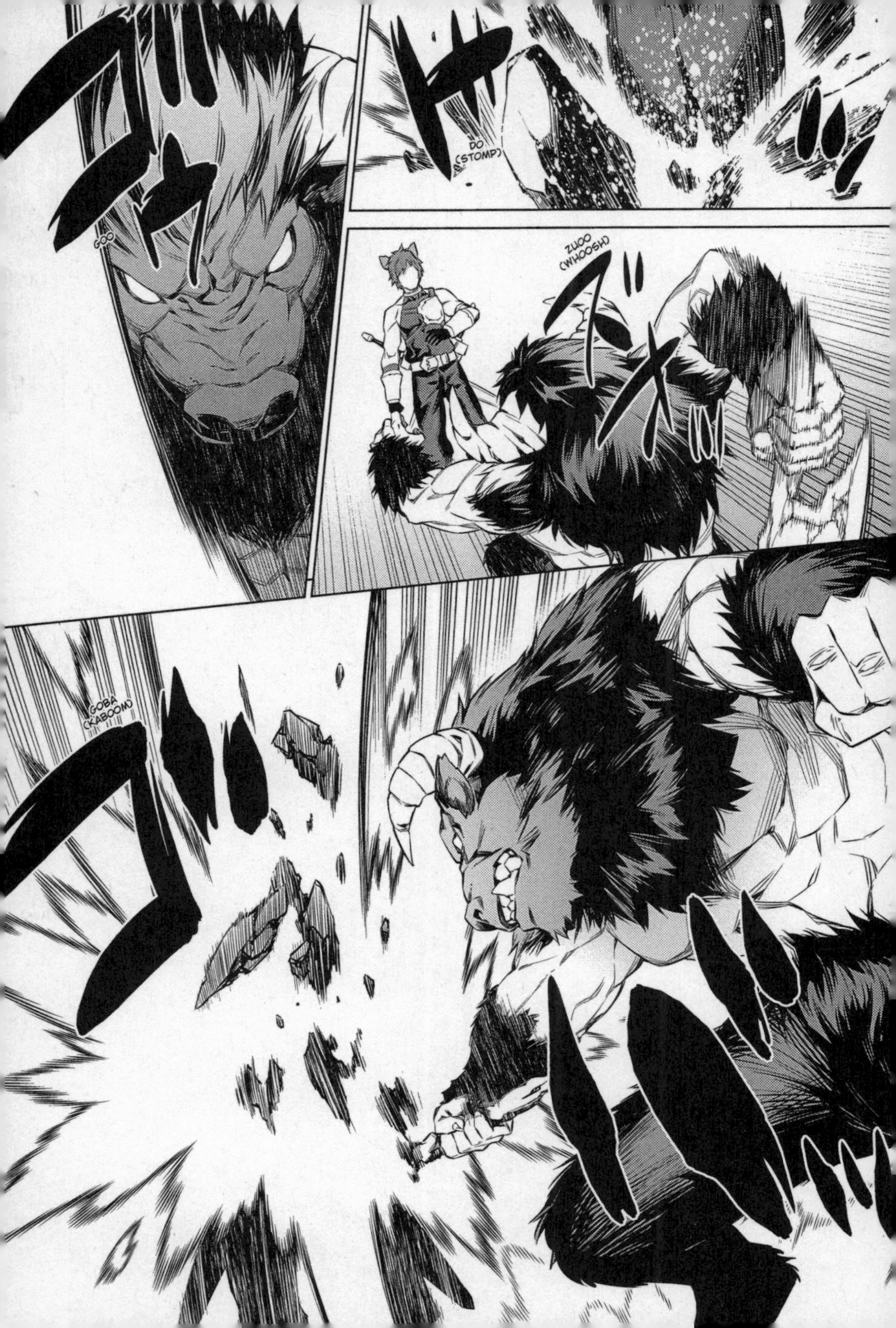
DO (STOMP)
ZUOO (WHOOSH)
GOO
GOBA (KABOOM)

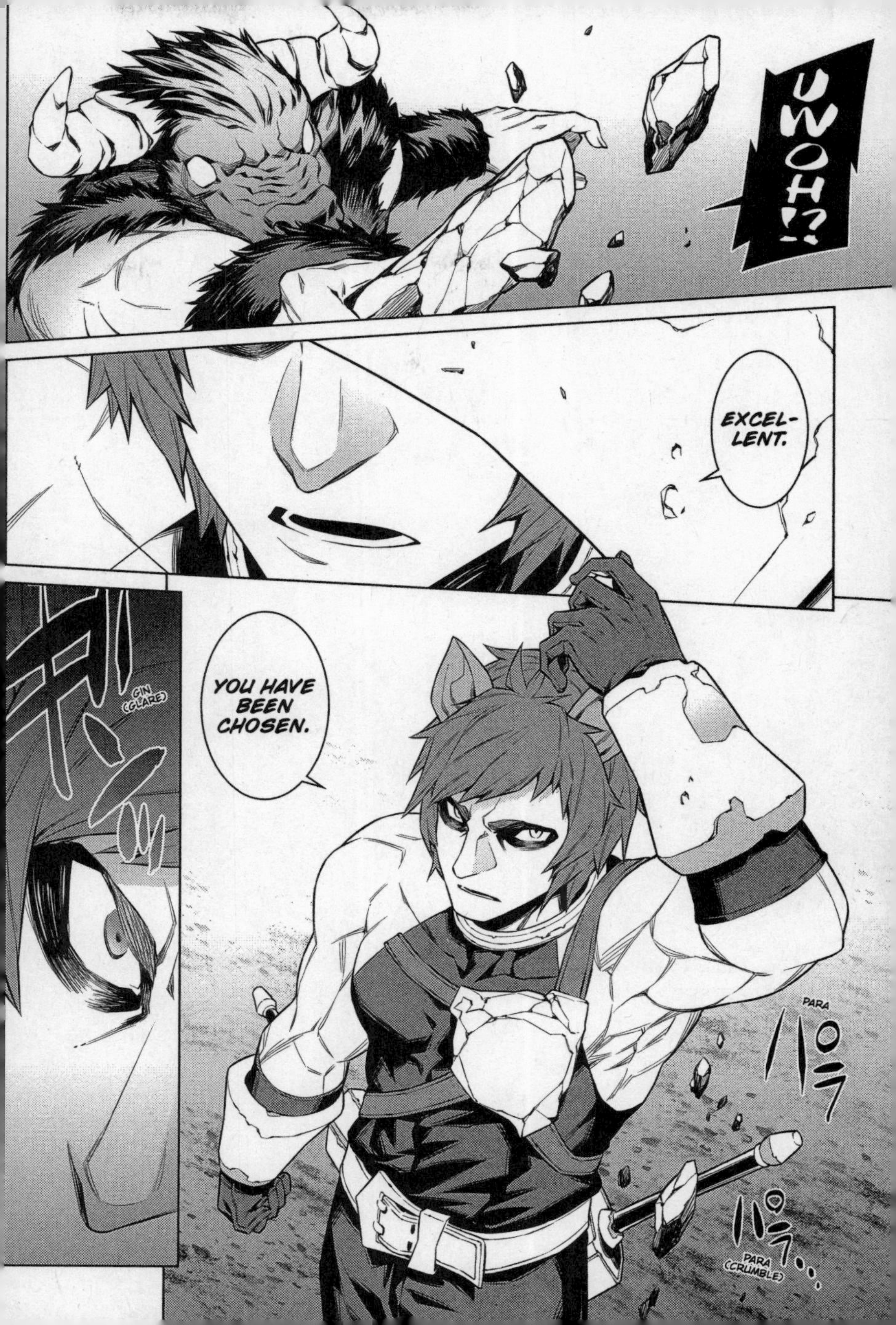
UWOH!?
EXCEL-LENT.
YOU HAVE BEEN CHOSEN.
PARA
PARA (CRUMBLE)
GIN (GLARE)

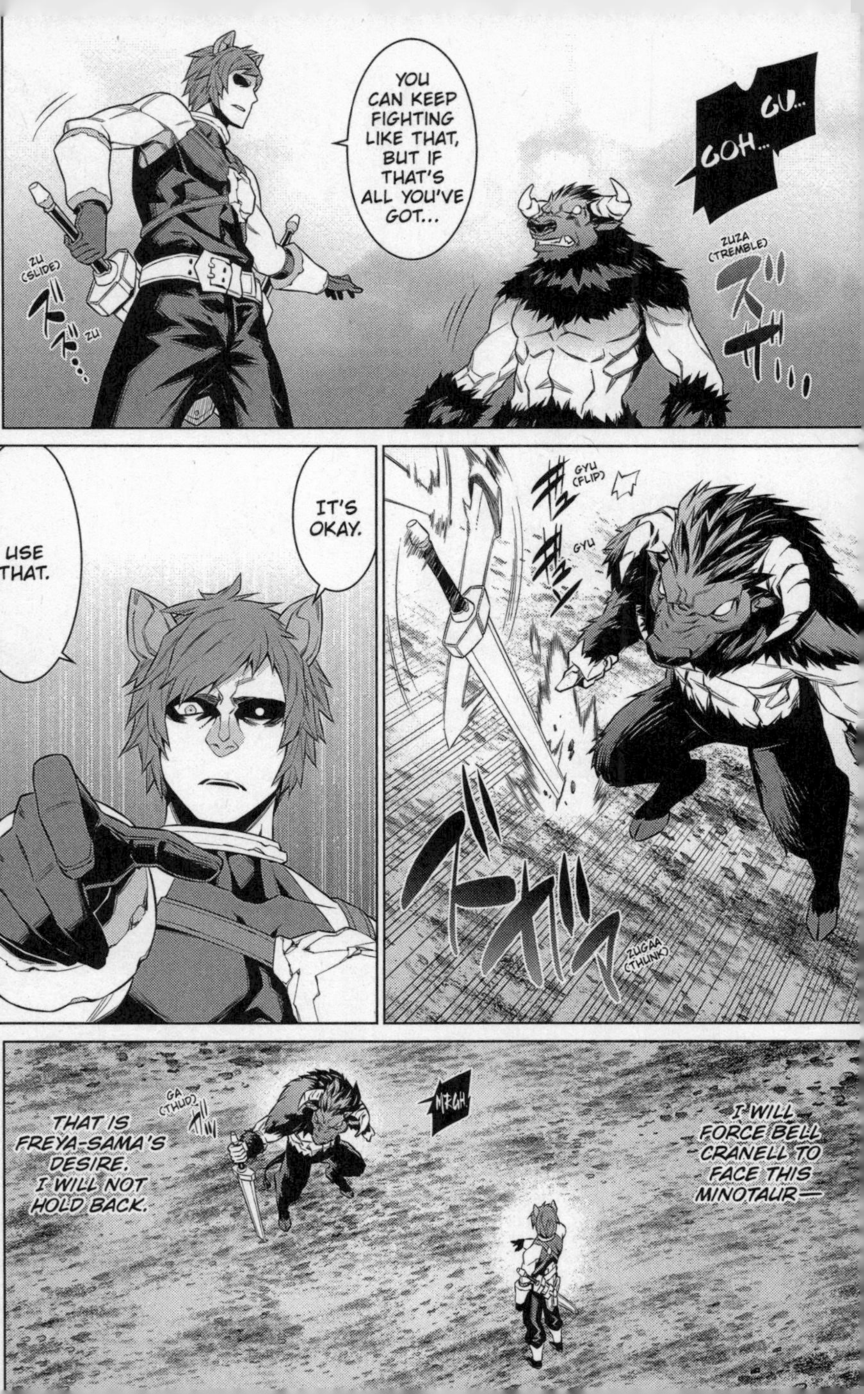
GU... GOH...
ZUZA (TREMBLE)
YOU CAN KEEP FIGHTING LIKE THAT, BUT IF THAT'S ALL YOU'VE GOT...
ZU (SLIDE)
ZU
GYU (FLIP)
GYU
ZUGAA (THUNK)
IT'S OKAY.
USE THAT.
I WILL FORCE BELL CRANELL TO FACE THIS MINOTAUR—
MRGH.
GA (THUD)
THAT IS FREYA-SAMA'S DESIRE. I WILL NOT HOLD BACK.

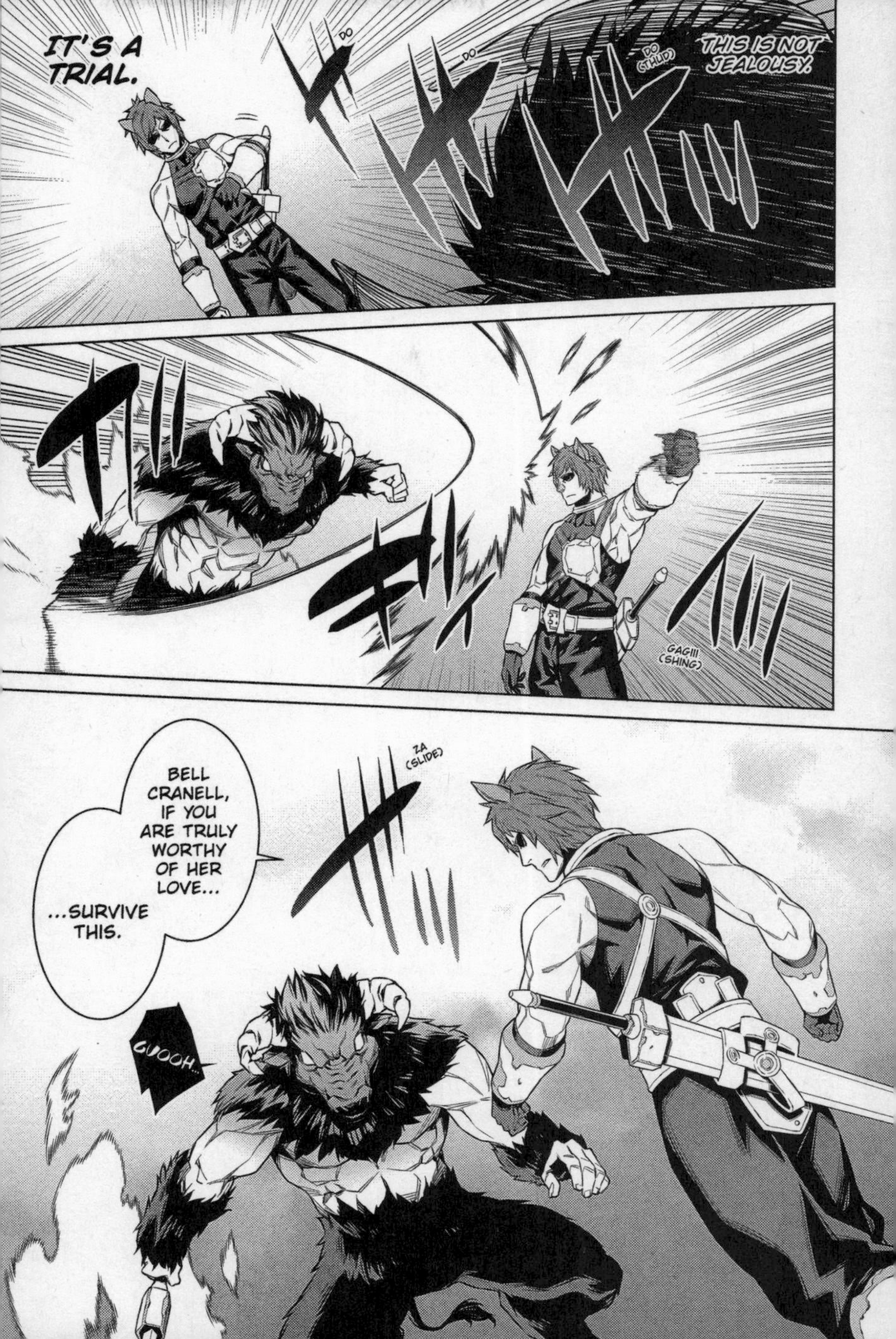
THIS IS NOT JEALOUSY.
DO (THUD)
DO
DO
IT'S A TRIAL.
GAGIII (SHING)
ZA (SLIDE)
BELL CRANELL, IF YOU ARE TRULY WORTHY OF HER LOVE...
...SURVIVE THIS.
GUOOH...

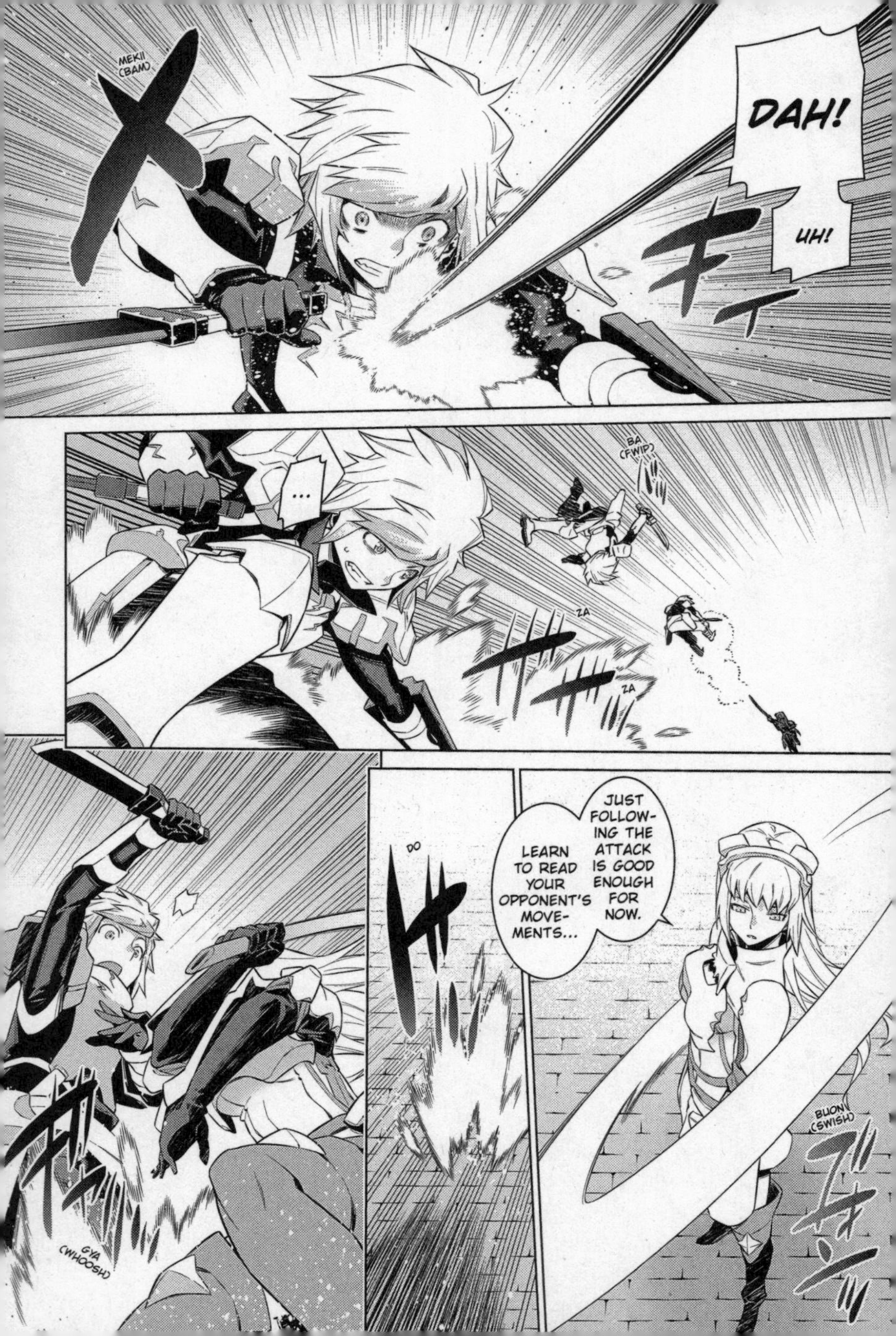

DAH!
UH!
MEKII (BAM)
BA (FWIP)
ZA
ZA
...
JUST FOLLOWING THE ATTACK IS GOOD ENOUGH FOR NOW.
LEARN TO READ YOUR OPPONENT'S MOVEMENTS...
BUON (SWISH)
DO
GYA (WHOOSH)

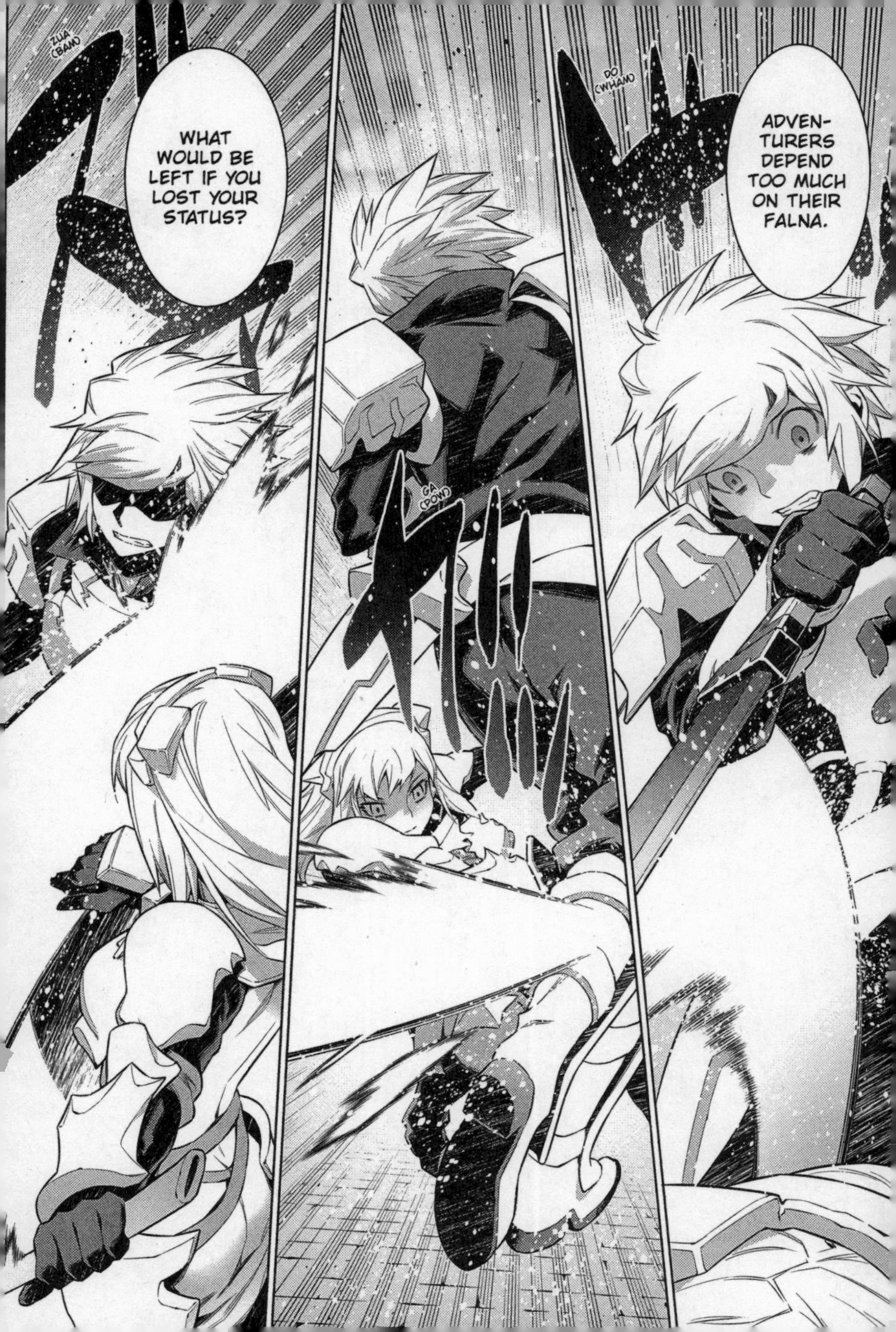
ADVEN-TURERS DEPEND TOO MUCH ON THEIR FALNA.
DO (WHAM)
GA (POW)
WHAT WOULD BE LEFT IF YOU LOST YOUR STATUS?
ZUA (BAM)

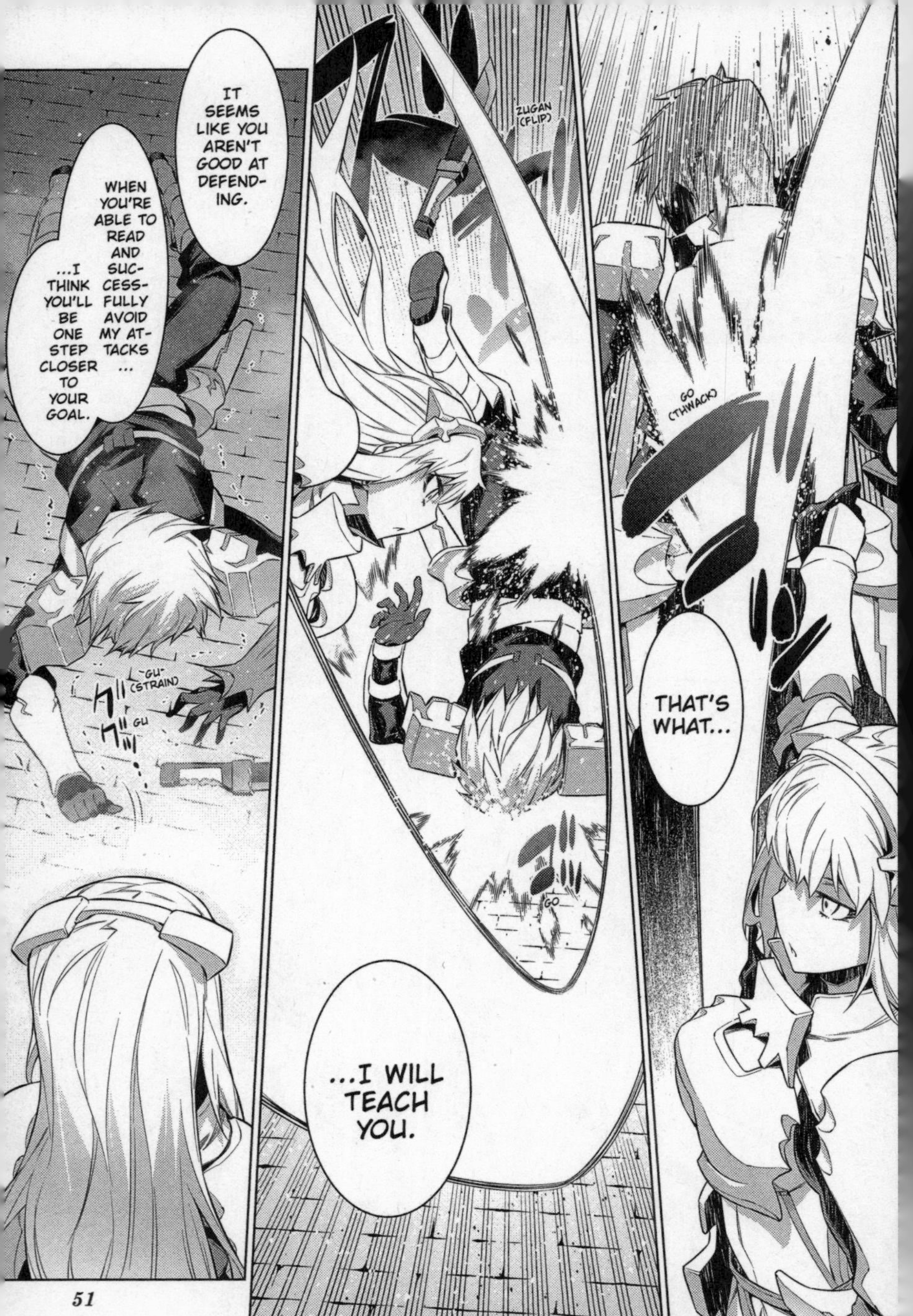
GO (THWACK)
THAT'S WHAT...
ZUGAN (FLIP)
GO
...I WILL TEACH YOU.
IT SEEMS LIKE YOU AREN'T GOOD AT DEFEND-ING.
WHEN YOU'RE ABLE TO READ AND SUC-CESS-FULLY AVOID MY AT-TACKS ...
...I THINK YOU'LL BE ONE STEP CLOSER TO YOUR GOAL.
GU (STRAIN)
GU

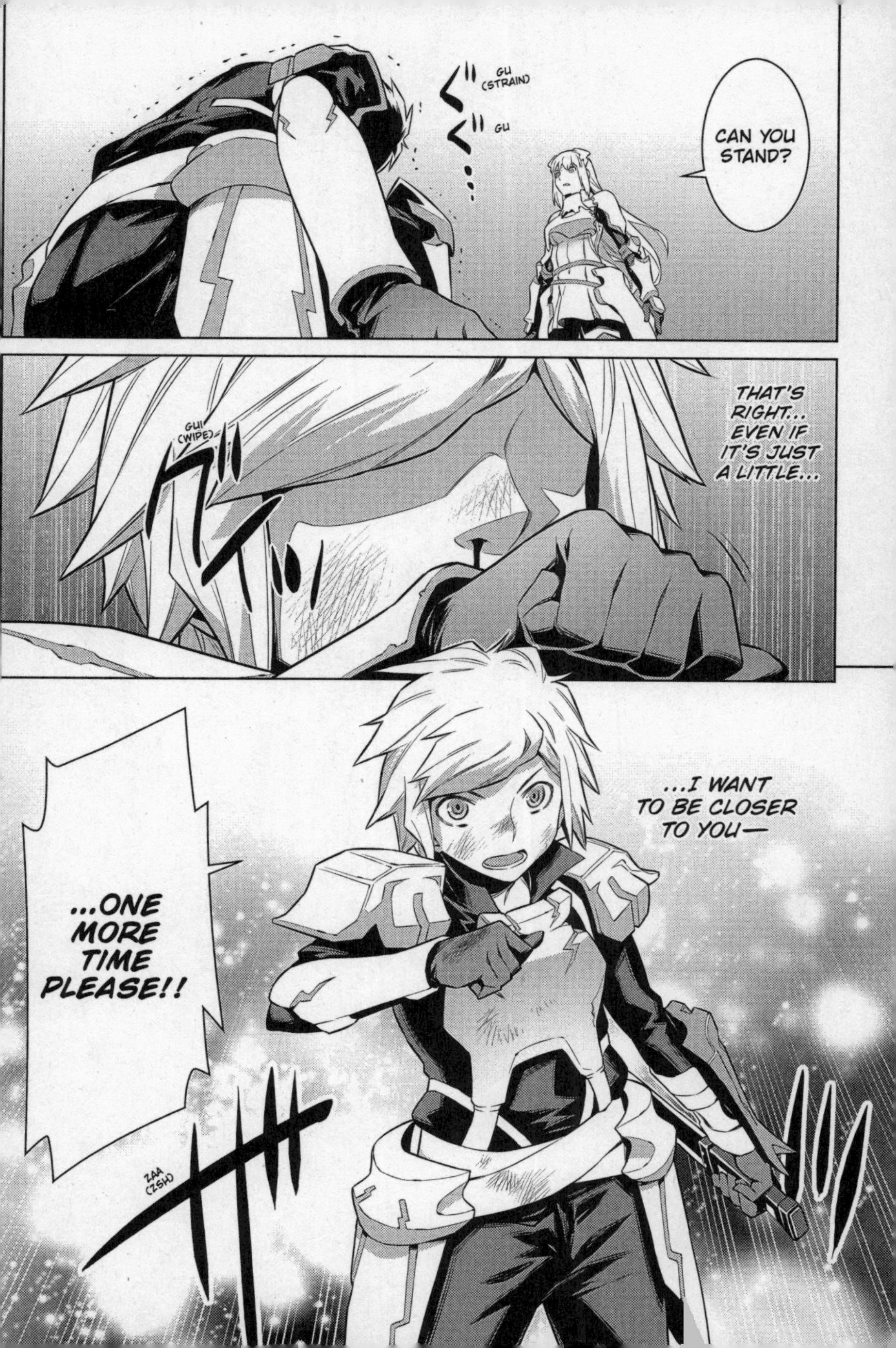
CAN YOU STAND?
GU (STRAIN)
GU
THAT'S RIGHT... EVEN IF IT'S JUST A LITTLE...
GUI (WIPE)
...I WANT TO BE CLOSER TO YOU—
...ONE MORE TIME PLEASE!!
ZAA (ZSH)

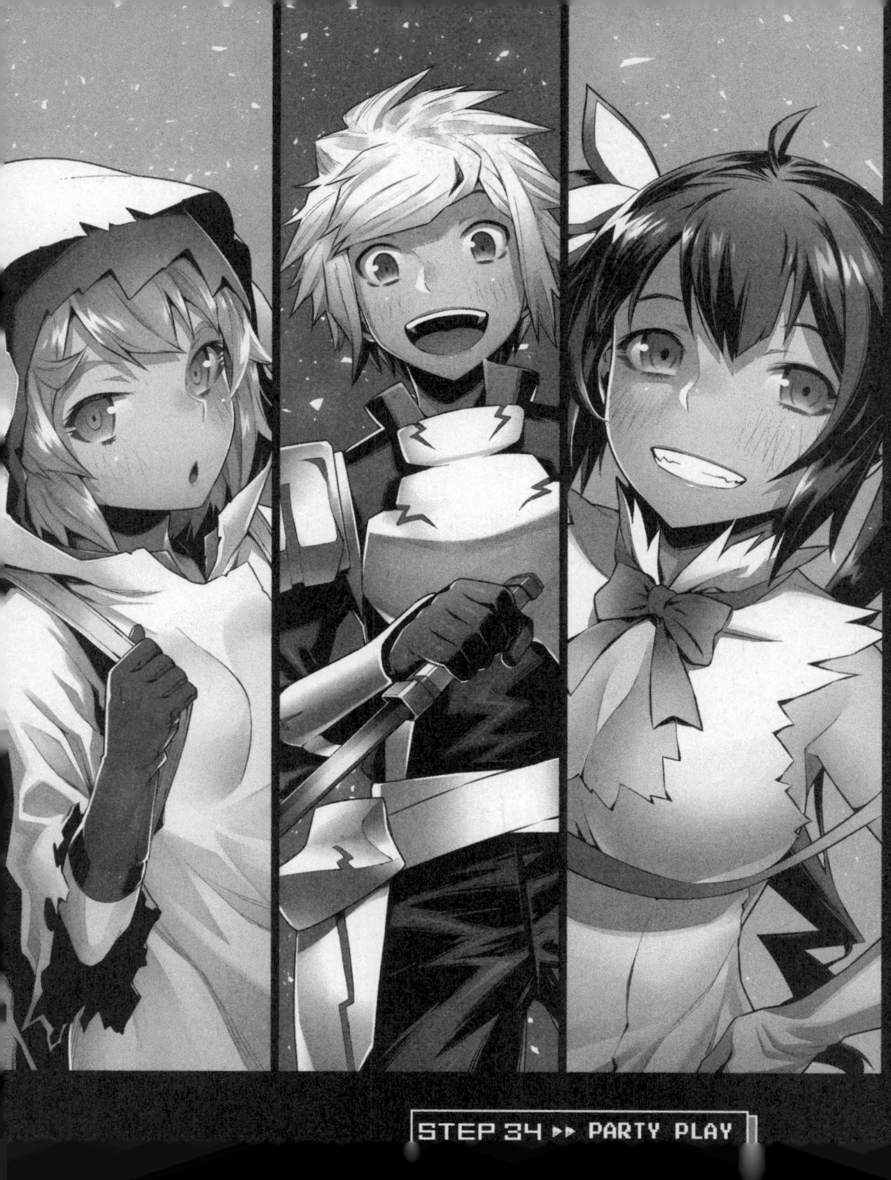
STEP 34 ▸▸ PARTY PLAY

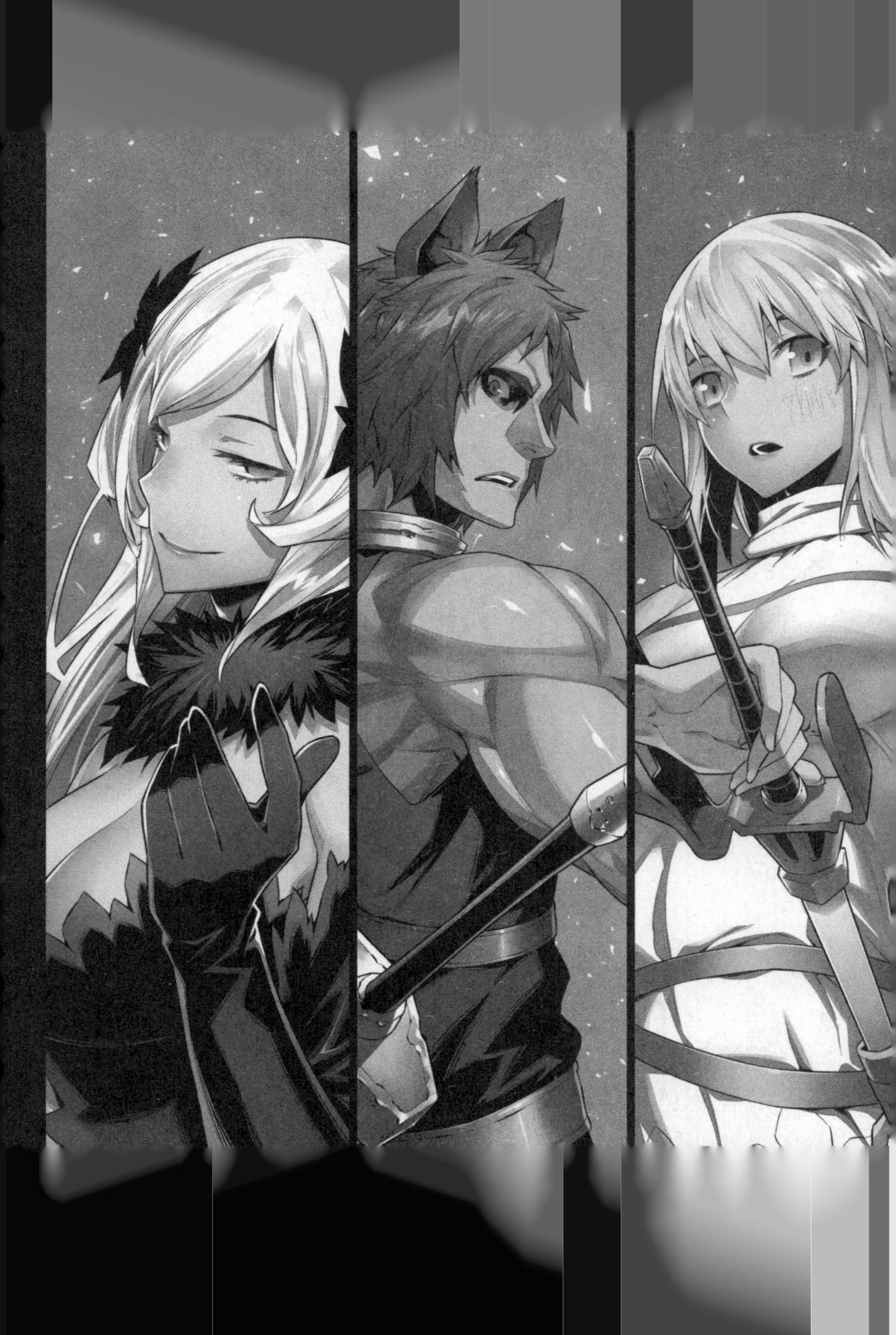

Is it WRONG to TRY to PICK UP GIRLS in a DUNGEON?

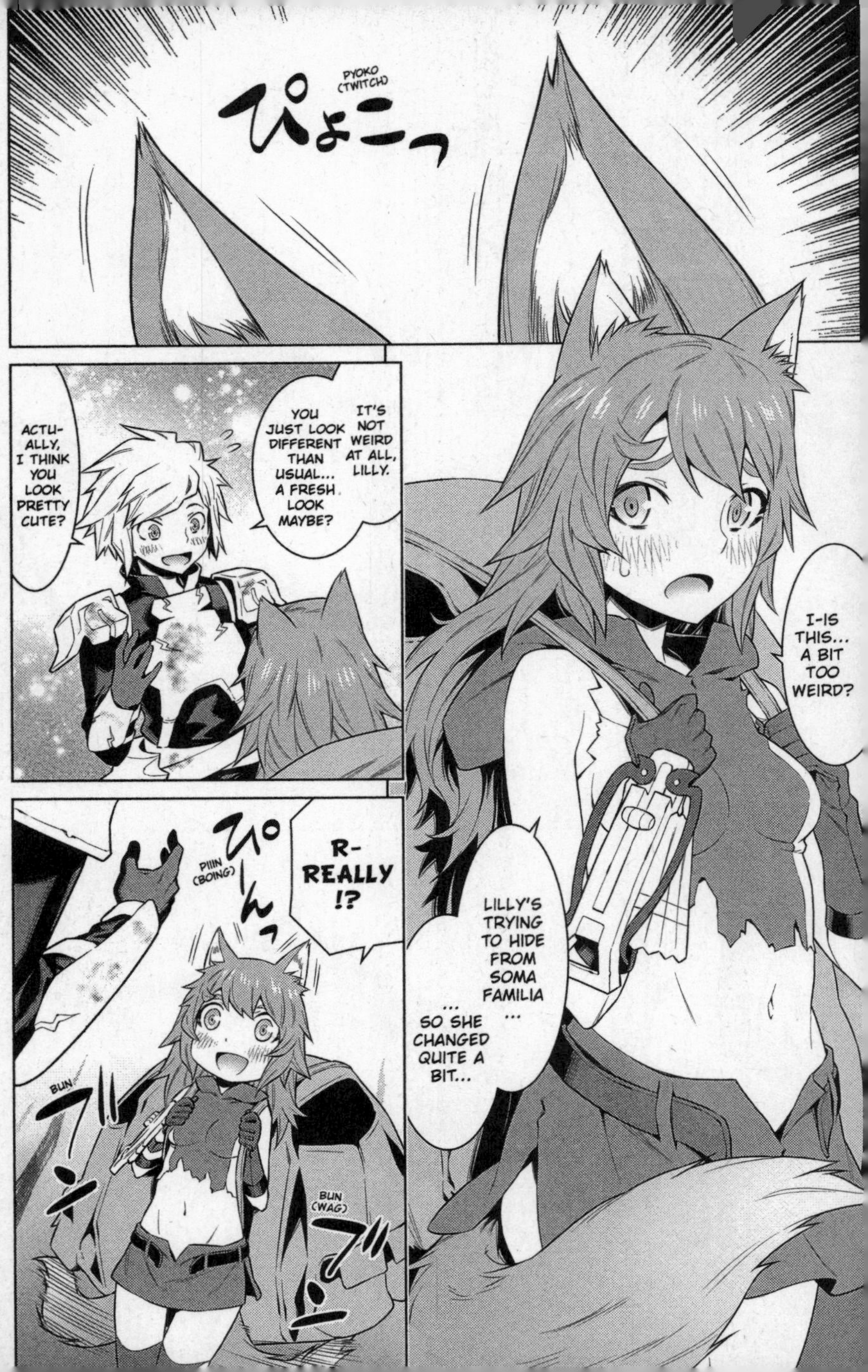
PYOKO (TWITCH)
ぴょこっ
I-IS THIS... A BIT TOO WEIRD?
LILLY'S TRYING TO HIDE FROM SOMA FAMILIA... SO SHE CHANGED QUITE A BIT...
IT'S NOT WEIRD AT ALL, LILLY.
YOU JUST LOOK DIFFERENT THAN USUAL... A FRESH LOOK MAYBE?
ACTU-ALLY, I THINK YOU LOOK PRETTY CUTE?
R-REALLY!?
ぴーんっ
PIIIN (BOING)
BUN
BUN (WAG)

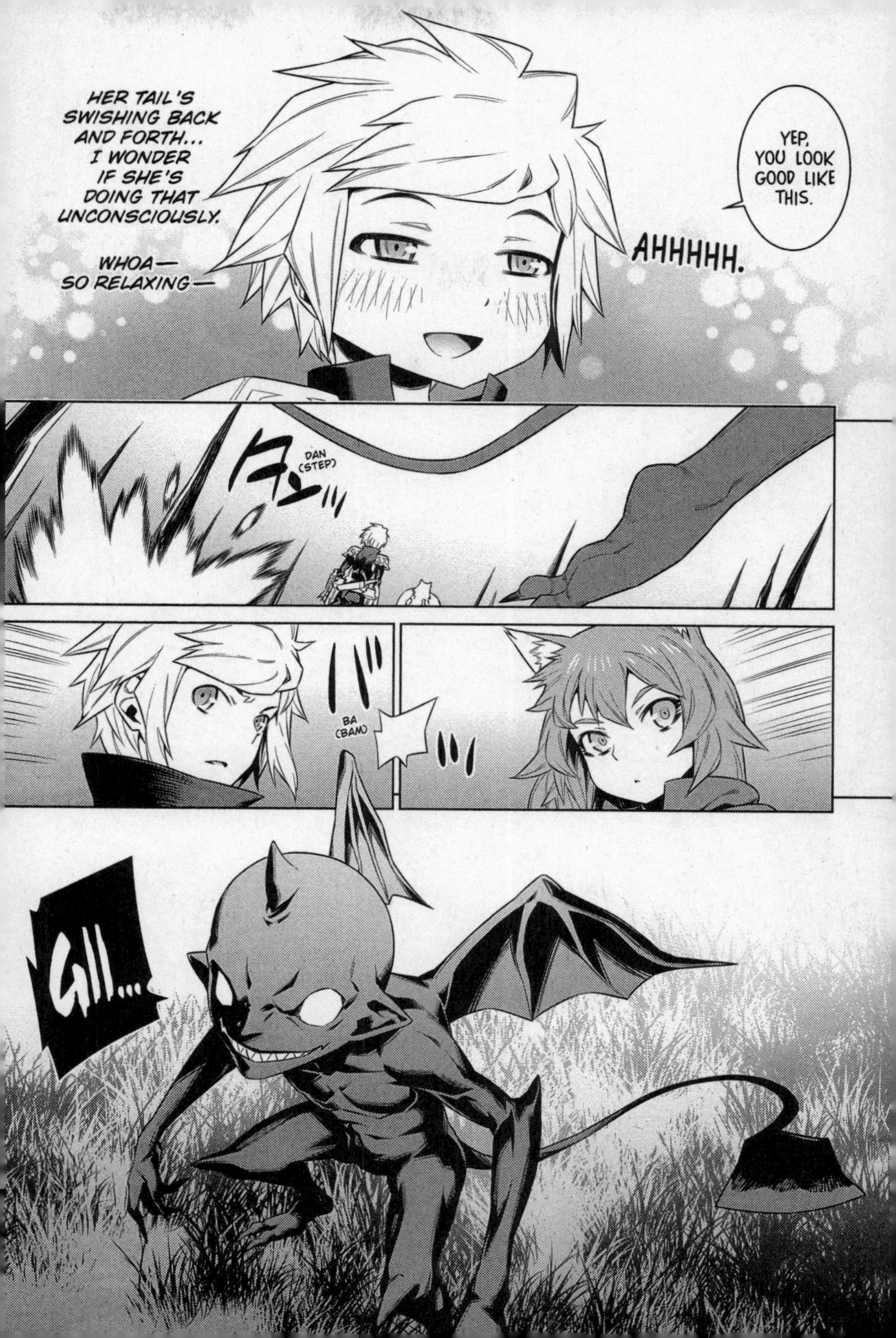
YEP, YOU LOOK GOOD LIKE THIS.
AHHHHH.
HER TAIL'S SWISHING BACK AND FORTH... I WONDER IF SHE'S DOING THAT UNCONSCIOUSLY.
WHOA— SO RELAXING—
DAN (STEP)
BA (BAM)
GII...

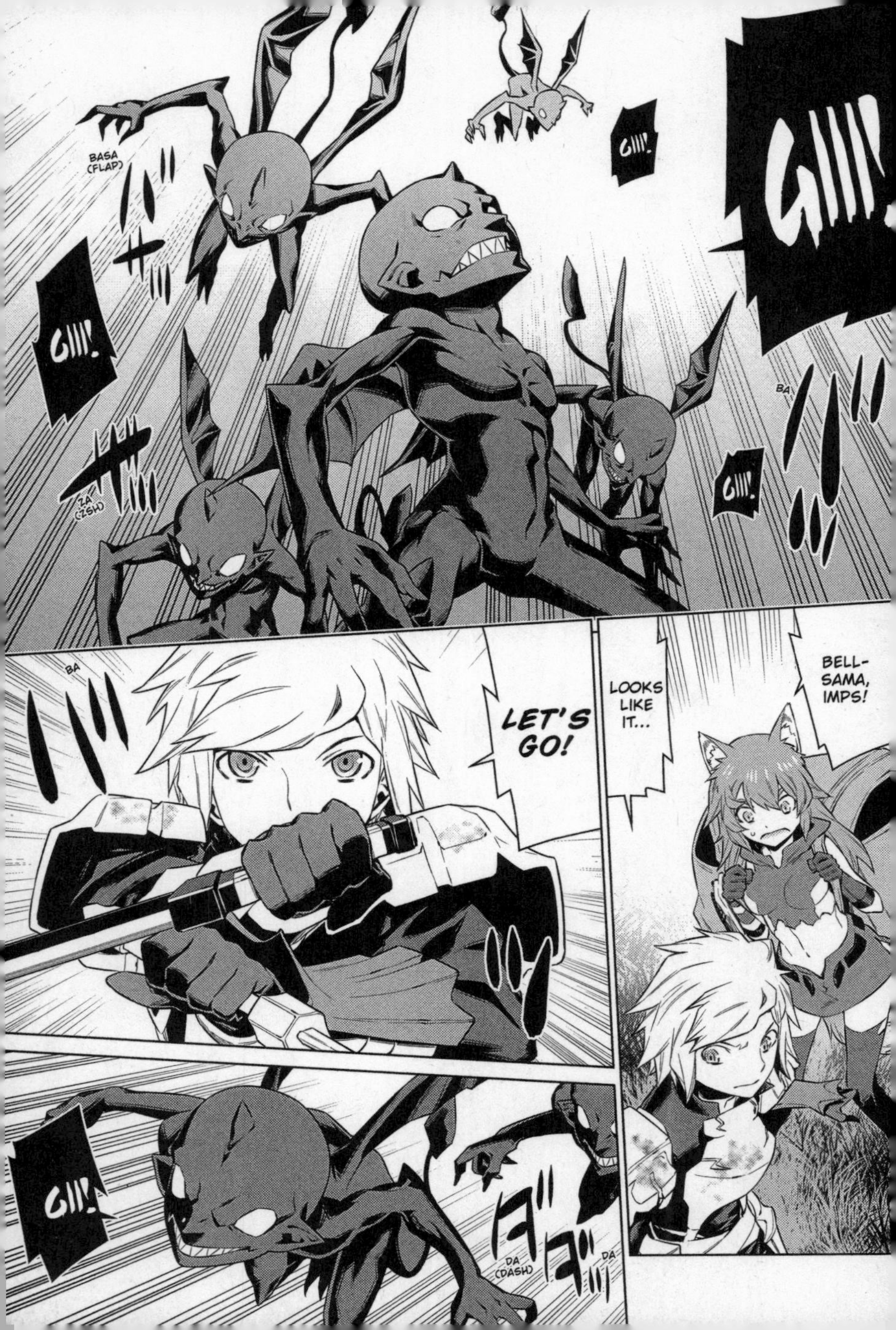
GIII!
GIII!
BA
GIII!
BASA (FLAP)
GIII!
ZA (ZSH)
BELL-SAMA, IMPS!
LOOKS LIKE IT...
LET'S GO!
BA
DA
DA (DASH)
GIII!

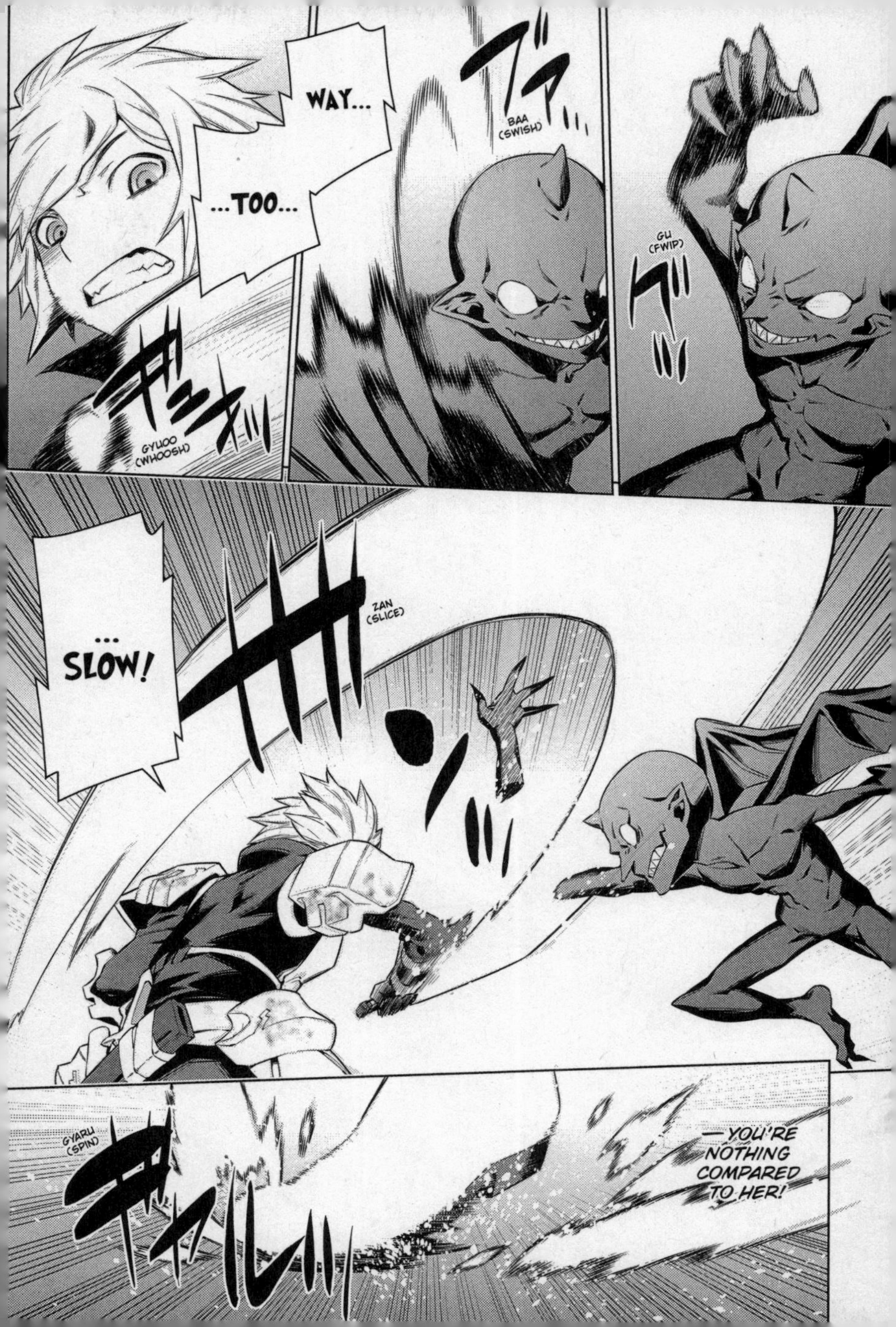
GU
(FWIP)
BAA
(SWISH)
WAY...
...TOO...
GYUOO
(WHOOSH)
ZAN
(SLICE)
...
SLOW!
—YOU'RE NOTHING COMPARED TO HER!
GYARU
(SPIN)

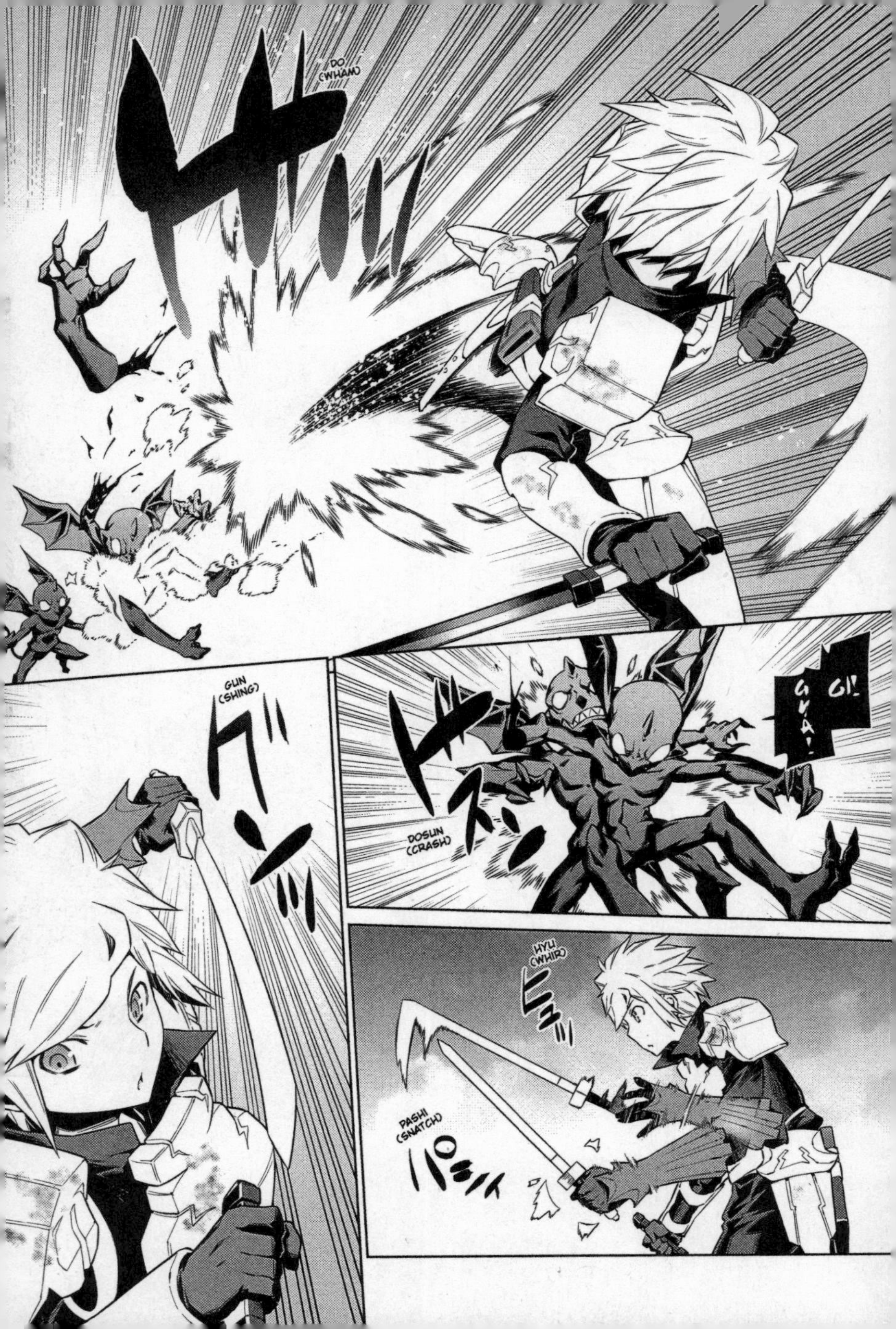
DO (WHAM)
GI!
GUA!
DOSUN (CRASH)
HYU (WHIR)
PASHI (SNATCH)
GUN (SHING)

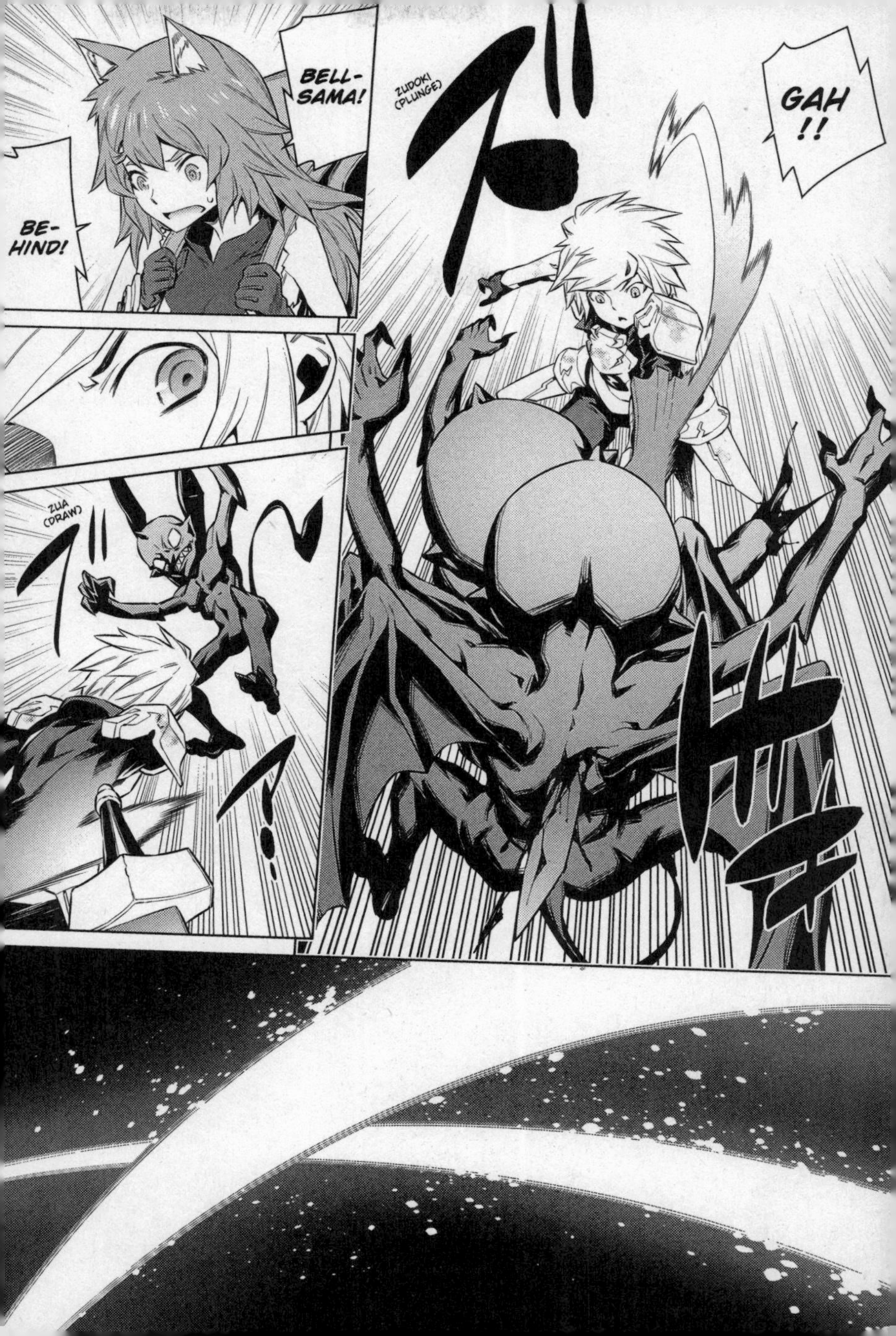
GAH!!
ZUDOKI (PLUNGE)
BELL-SAMA!
BE-HIND!
ZUA (DRAW)

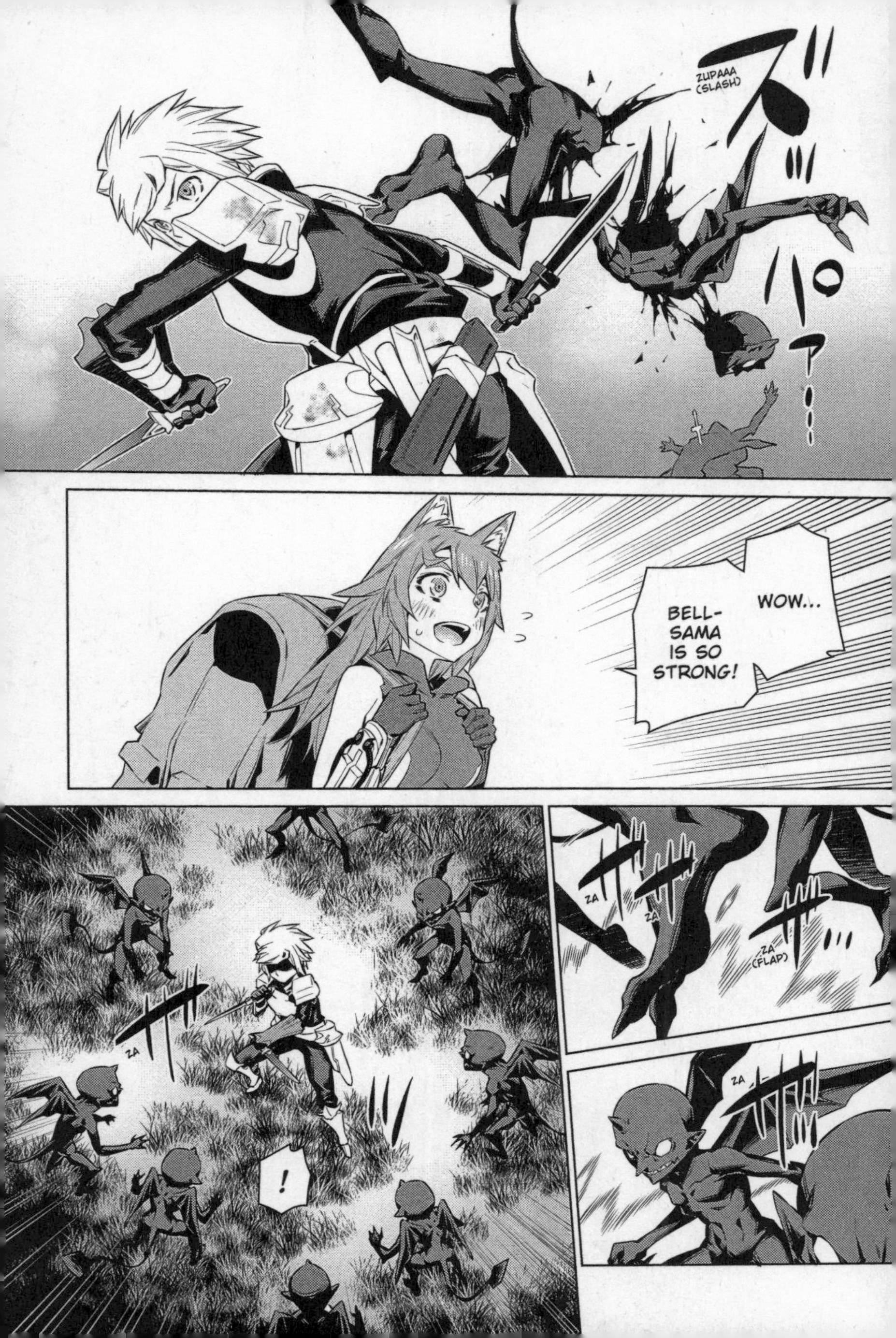
ZUPAAA (SLASH)
WOW... BELL-SAMA IS SO STRONG!
ZA
ZA
ZA (FLAP)
ZA
ZA
!

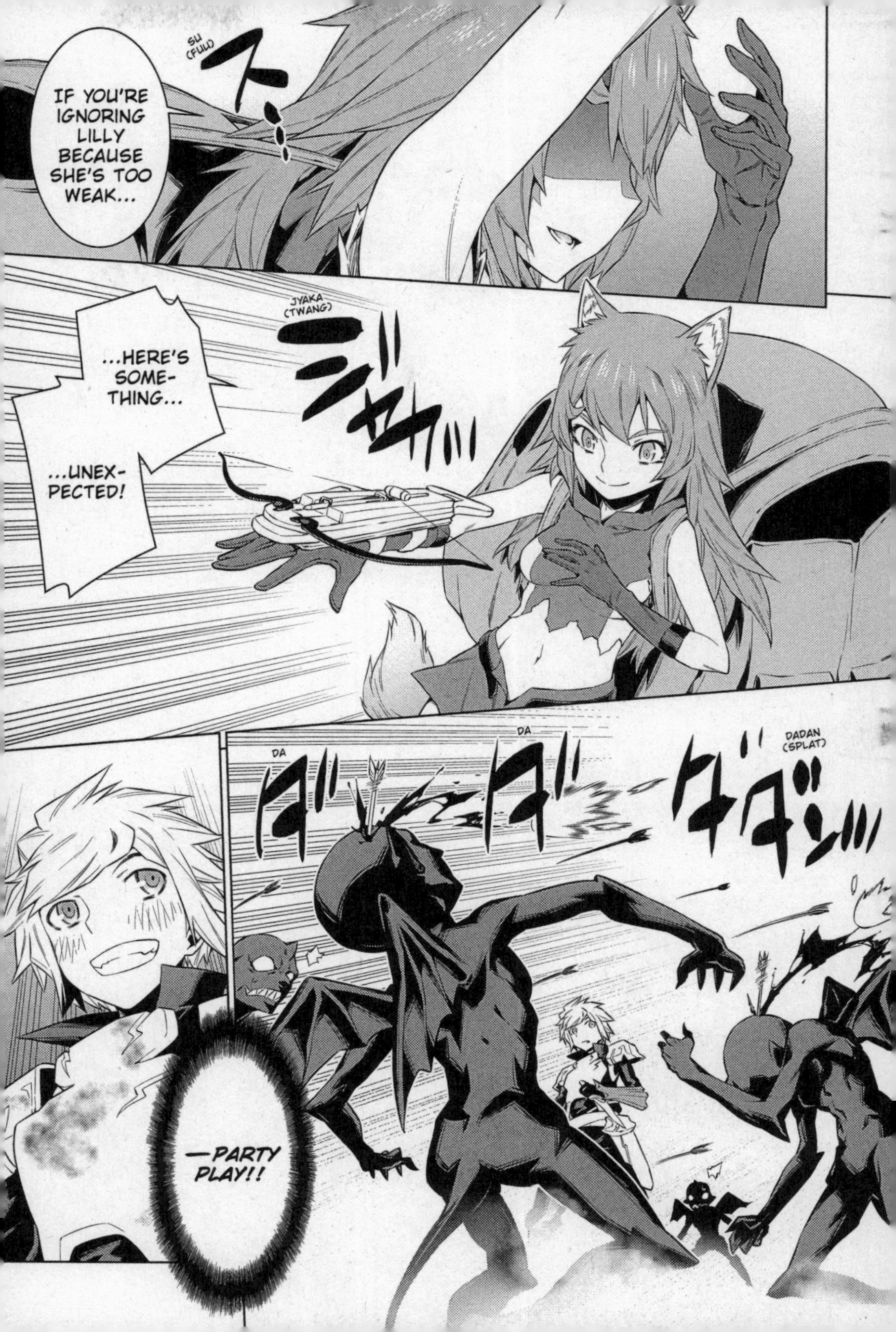
SU (FUU)
IF YOU'RE IGNORING LILLY BECAUSE SHE'S TOO WEAK...
JYAKA (TWANG)
...HERE'S SOME-THING...
...UNEX-PECTED!
DADAN (SPLAT)
DA
DA
—PARTY PLAY!!

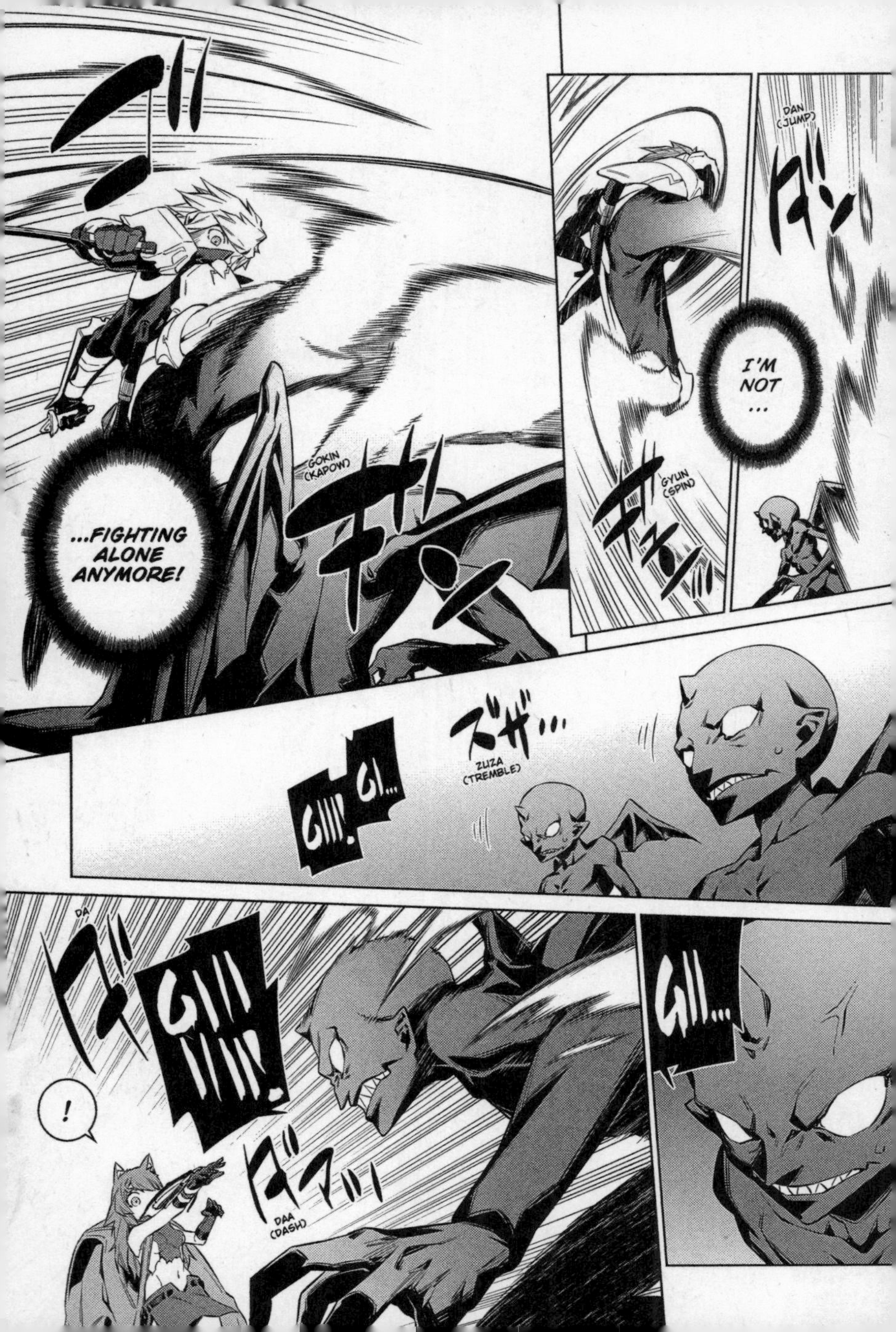
DAN (JUMP)
I'M NOT ...
GYUN (SPIN)
GOKIN (KAPOW)
...FIGHTING ALONE ANYMORE!
ZUZA (TREMBLE)
GI...
GIII!
GII...
DA
GIIIIIII!
!
DAA (DASH)

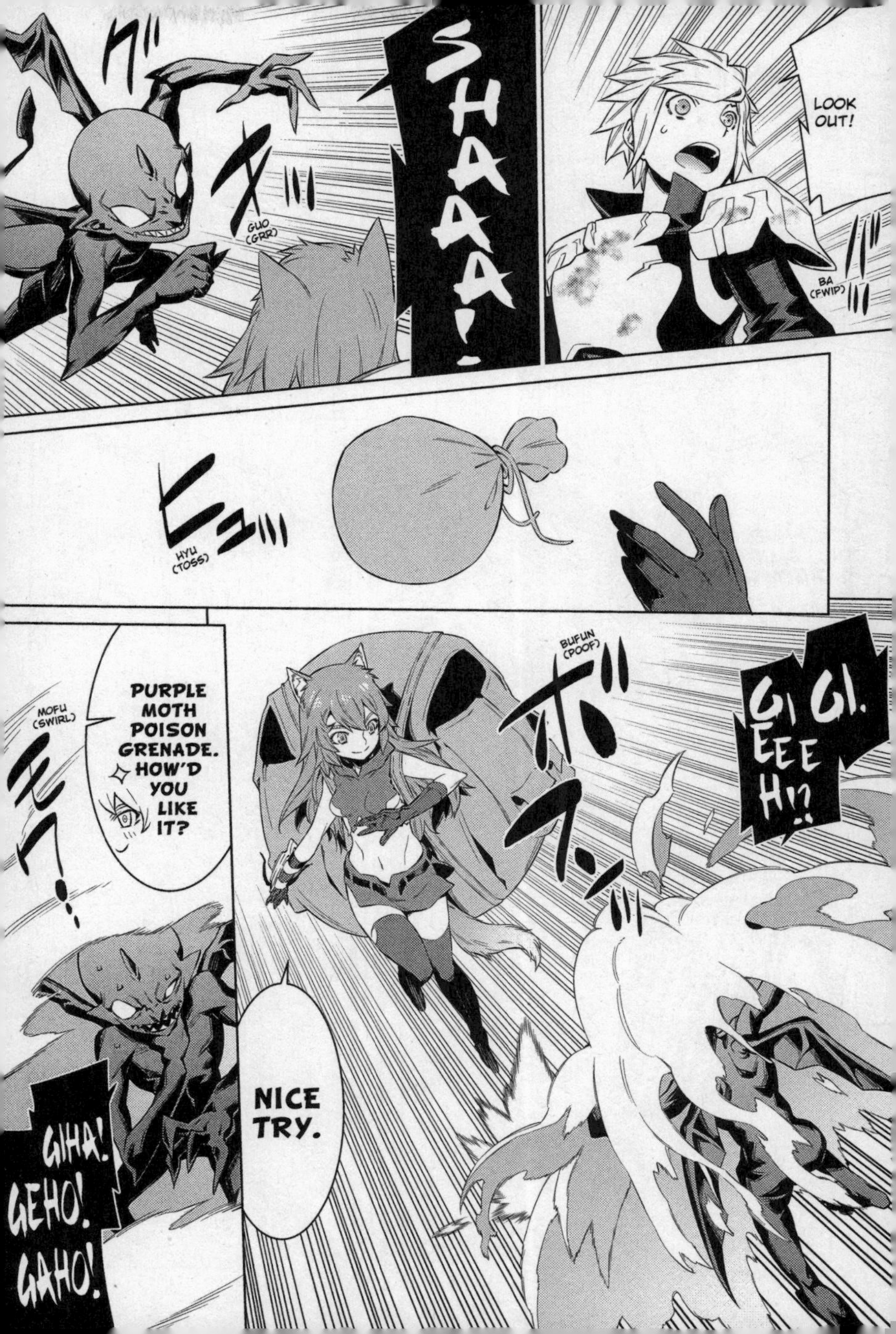
LOOK OUT!
BA (FWIP)
SHAAA!
GUO (GRR)
HYU (TOSS)
GI GI. EEEEH!?
BUFUN (POOF)
PURPLE MOTH POISON GRENADE. HOW'D YOU LIKE IT?
MOFU (SWIRL)
NICE TRY.
GIHA! GEHO! GAHO!

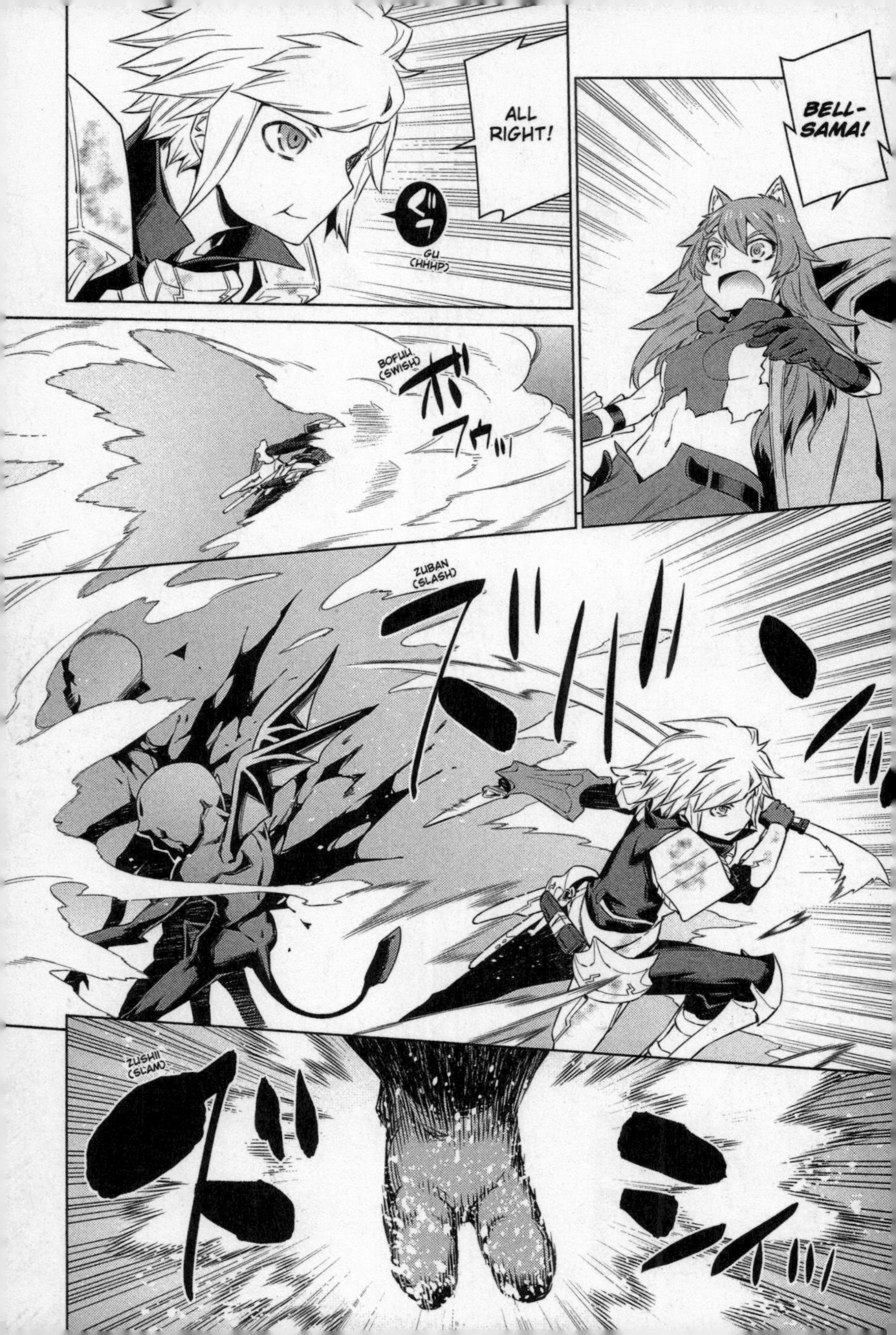
BELL-SAMA!
ALL RIGHT!
GU (HHHP)
BOFUU (SWISH)
ZUBAN (SLASH)
ZUSHII (SLAM)

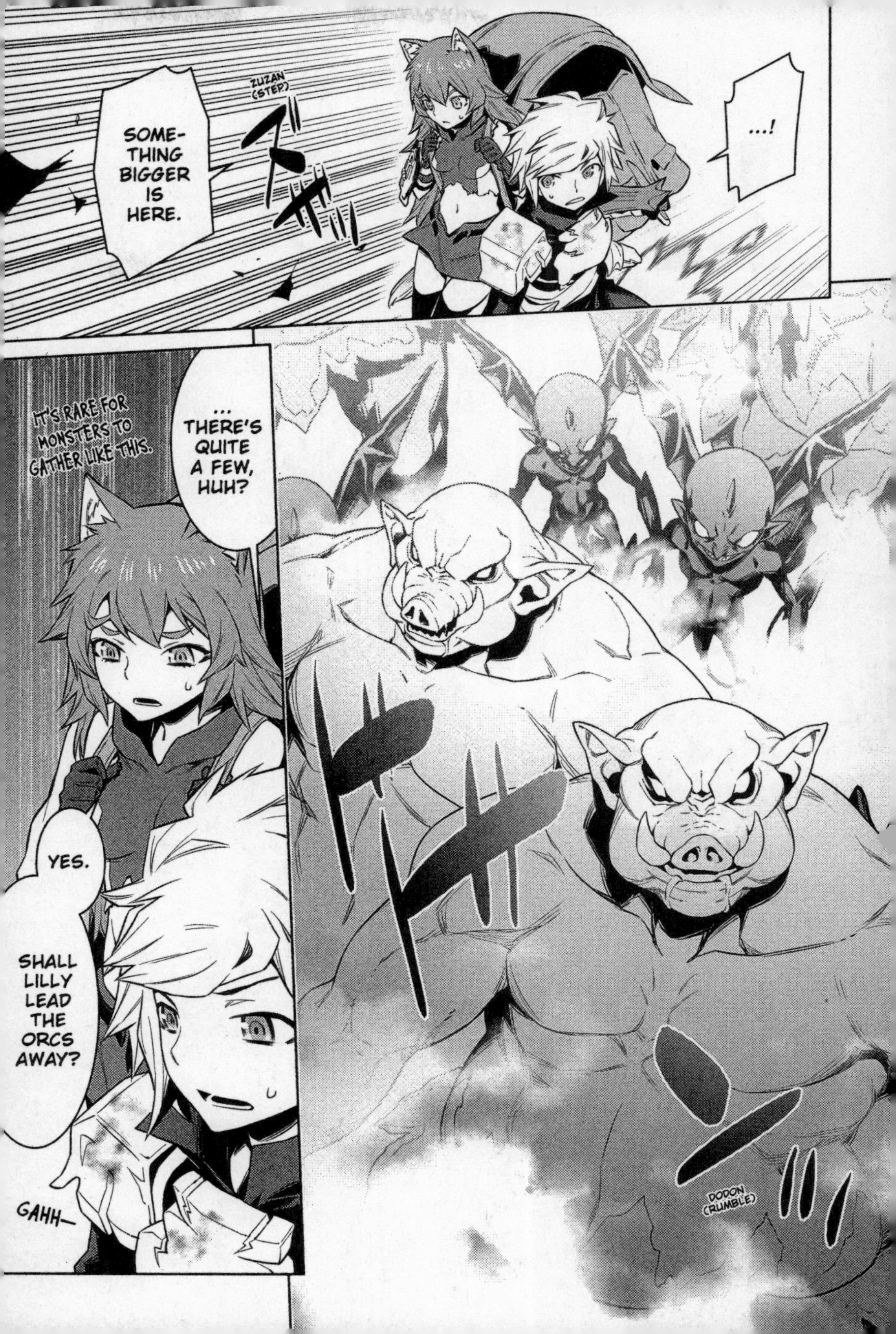
...!
ZUZAN (STEP)
SOME-THING BIGGER IS HERE.
DODON (RUMBLE)
... THERE'S QUITE A FEW, HUH?
IT'S RARE FOR MONSTERS TO GATHER LIKE THIS.
YES.
SHALL LILLY LEAD THE ORCS AWAY?
GAHH—

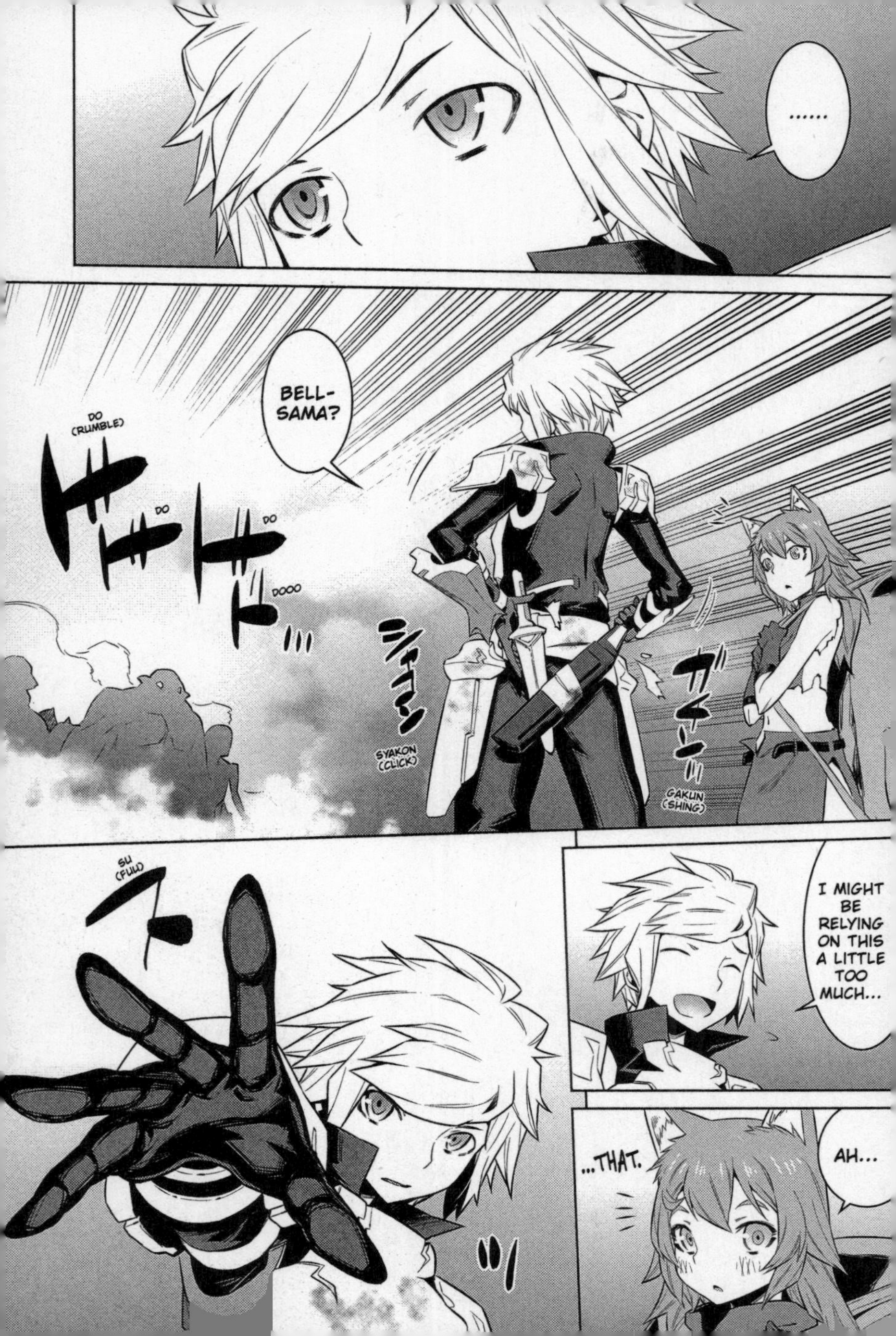
......
BELL-SAMA?
GAKUN (SHING)
SYAKON (CLICK)
DO (RUMBLE)
DO
DO
DOOO
I MIGHT BE RELYING ON THIS A LITTLE TOO MUCH...
AH...
...THAT.
SU (FUU)

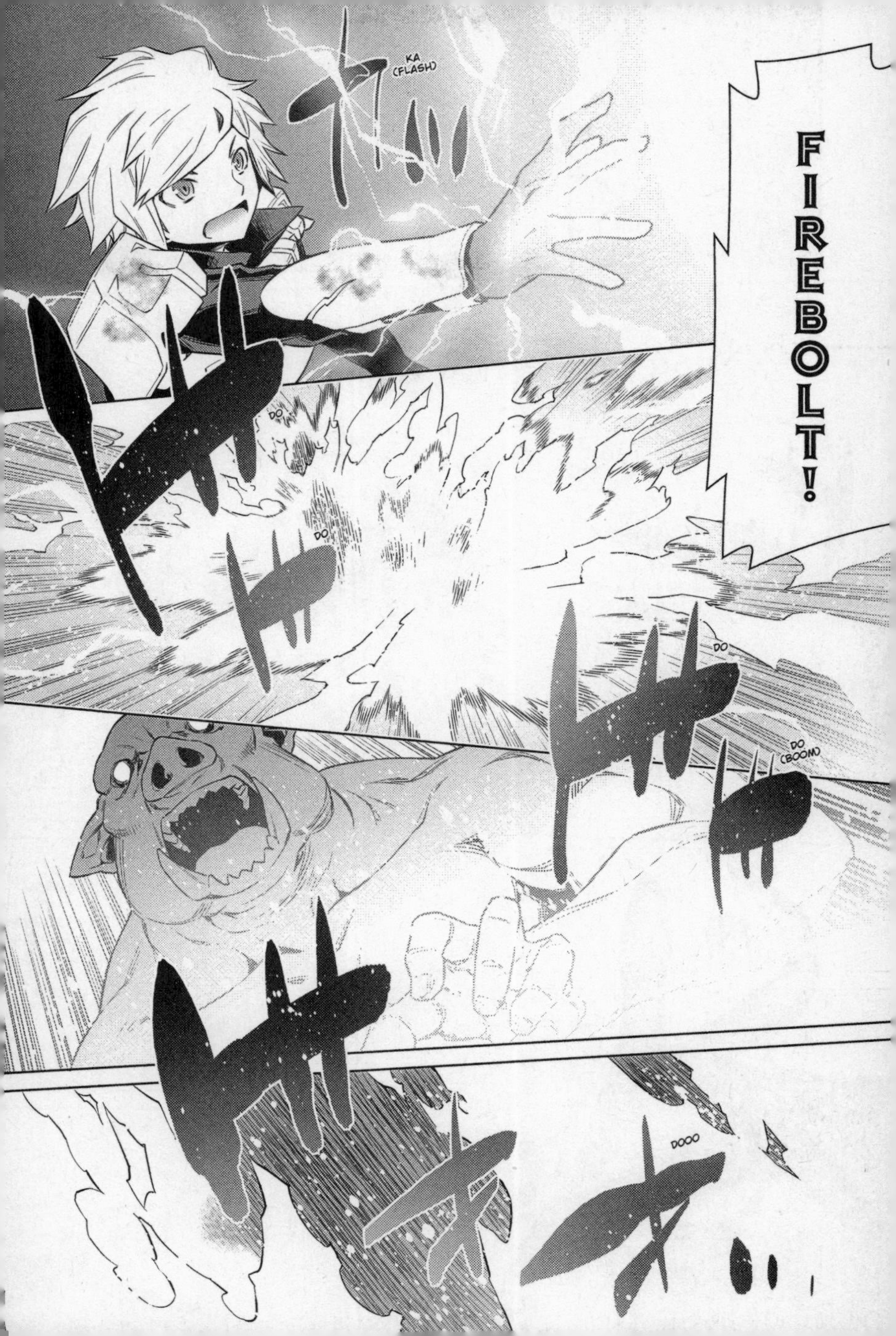
FIREBOLT!
KA
(FLASH)
DO
DO
DO
DO
(BOOM)
DOOO

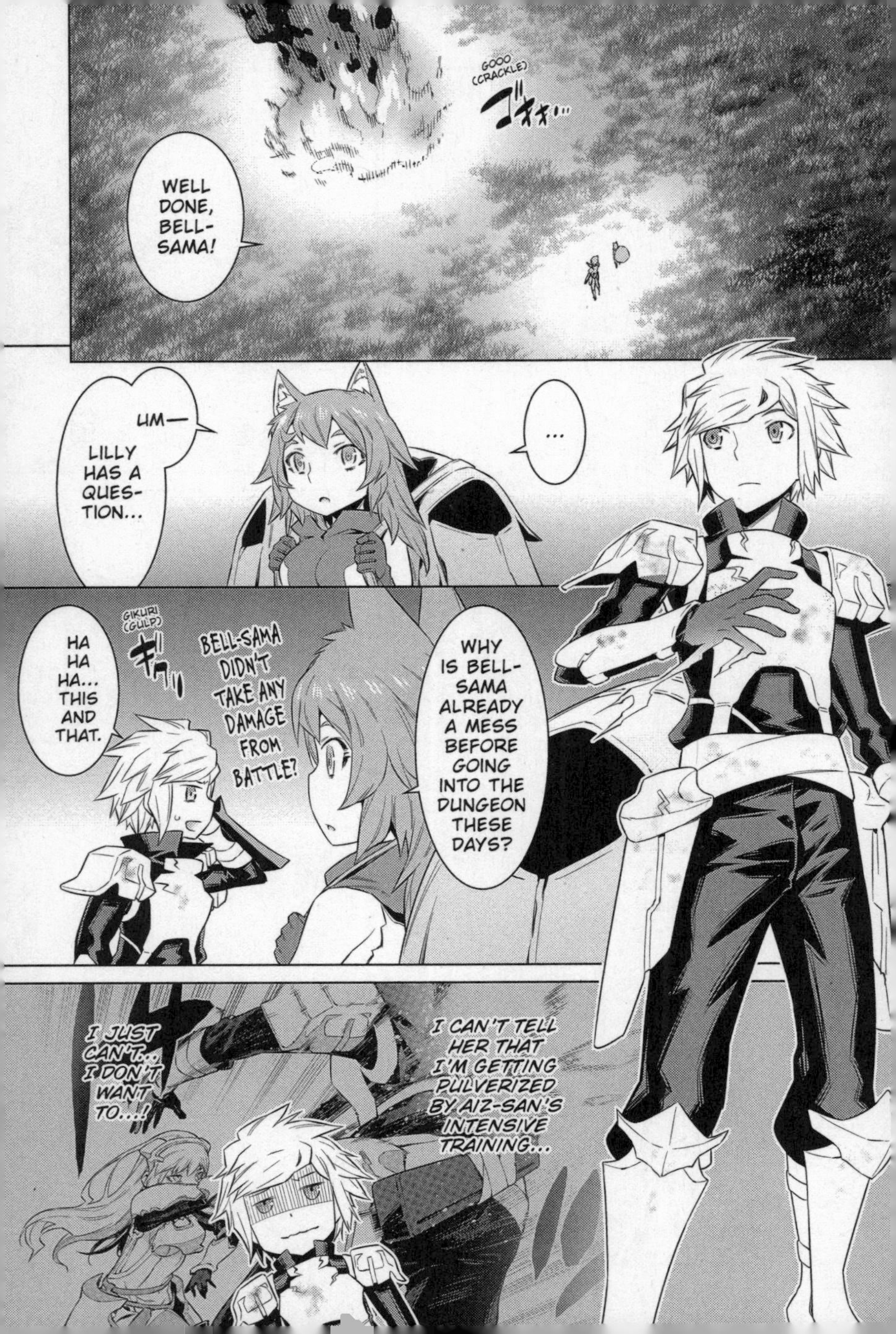
GOOO (CRACKLE)
ゴォォ…
WELL DONE, BELL-SAMA!
...
UM— LILLY HAS A QUESTION...
WHY IS BELL-SAMA ALREADY A MESS BEFORE GOING INTO THE DUNGEON THESE DAYS?
BELL-SAMA DIDN'T TAKE ANY DAMAGE FROM BATTLE?
GIKURI (GULP)
ギクッ
HA HA HA... THIS AND THAT.
I CAN'T TELL HER THAT I'M GETTING PULVERIZED BY AIZ-SAN'S INTENSIVE TRAINING...
I JUST CAN'T... I DON'T WANT TO...!

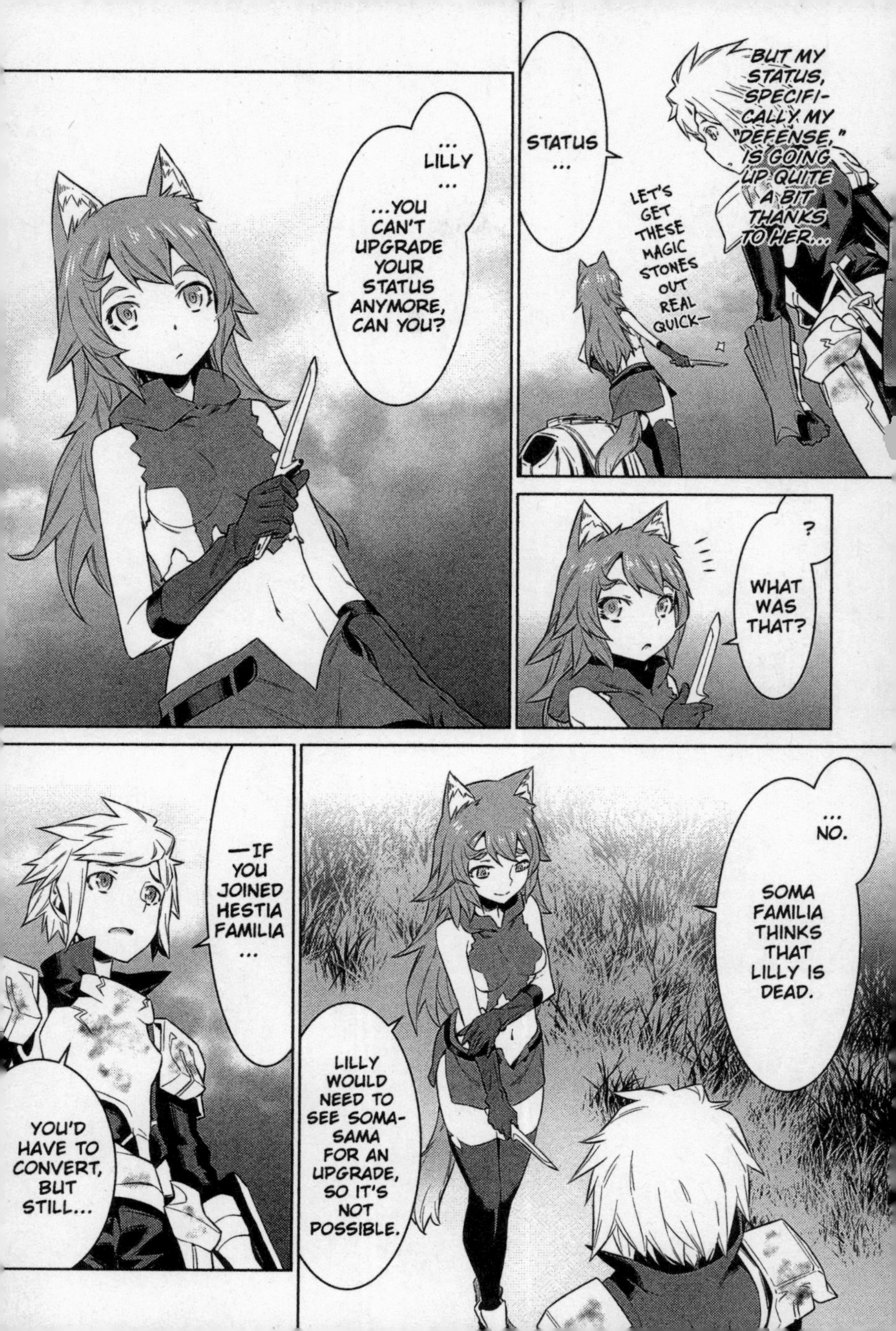

BUT MY STATUS, SPECIFICALLY MY "DEFENSE," IS GOING UP QUITE A BIT THANKS TO HER...
STATUS ...
LET'S GET THESE MAGIC STONES OUT REAL QUICK—
? WHAT WAS THAT?
... LILLY ... ...YOU CAN'T UPGRADE YOUR STATUS ANYMORE, CAN YOU?
... NO. SOMA FAMILIA THINKS THAT LILLY IS DEAD.
LILLY WOULD NEED TO SEE SOMA-SAMA FOR AN UPGRADE, SO IT'S NOT POSSIBLE.
—IF YOU JOINED HESTIA FAMILIA ...
YOU'D HAVE TO CONVERT, BUT STILL...

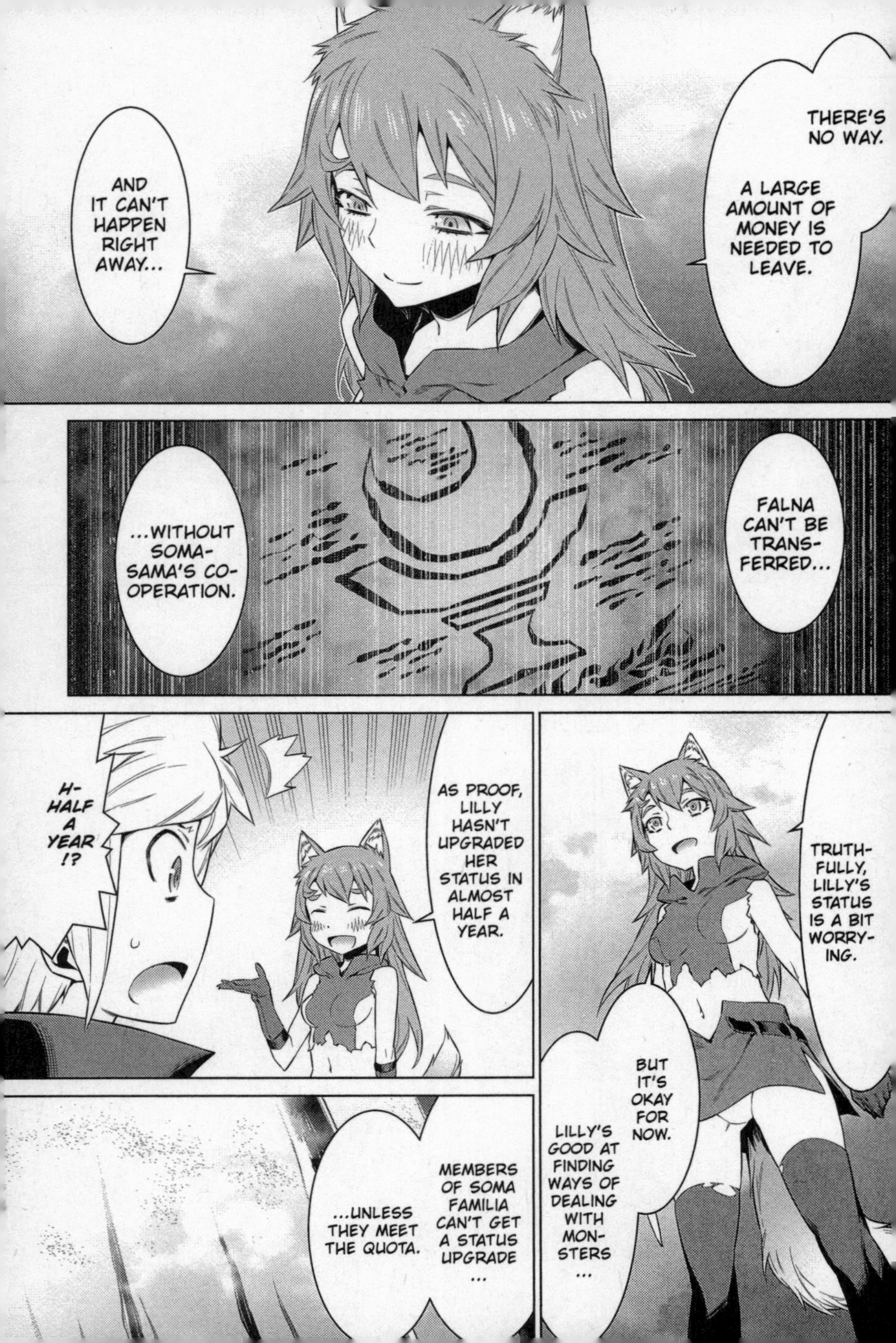
THERE'S NO WAY.
A LARGE AMOUNT OF MONEY IS NEEDED TO LEAVE.
AND IT CAN'T HAPPEN RIGHT AWAY...
FALNA CAN'T BE TRANS-FERRED...
...WITHOUT SOMA-SAMA'S CO-OPERATION.
TRUTH-FULLY, LILLY'S STATUS IS A BIT WORRY-ING.
BUT IT'S OKAY FOR NOW.
LILLY'S GOOD AT FINDING WAYS OF DEALING WITH MON-STERS...
AS PROOF, LILLY HASN'T UPGRADED HER STATUS IN ALMOST HALF A YEAR.
H-HALF A YEAR!?
MEMBERS OF SOMA FAMILIA CAN'T GET A STATUS UPGRADE...
...UNLESS THEY MEET THE QUOTA.

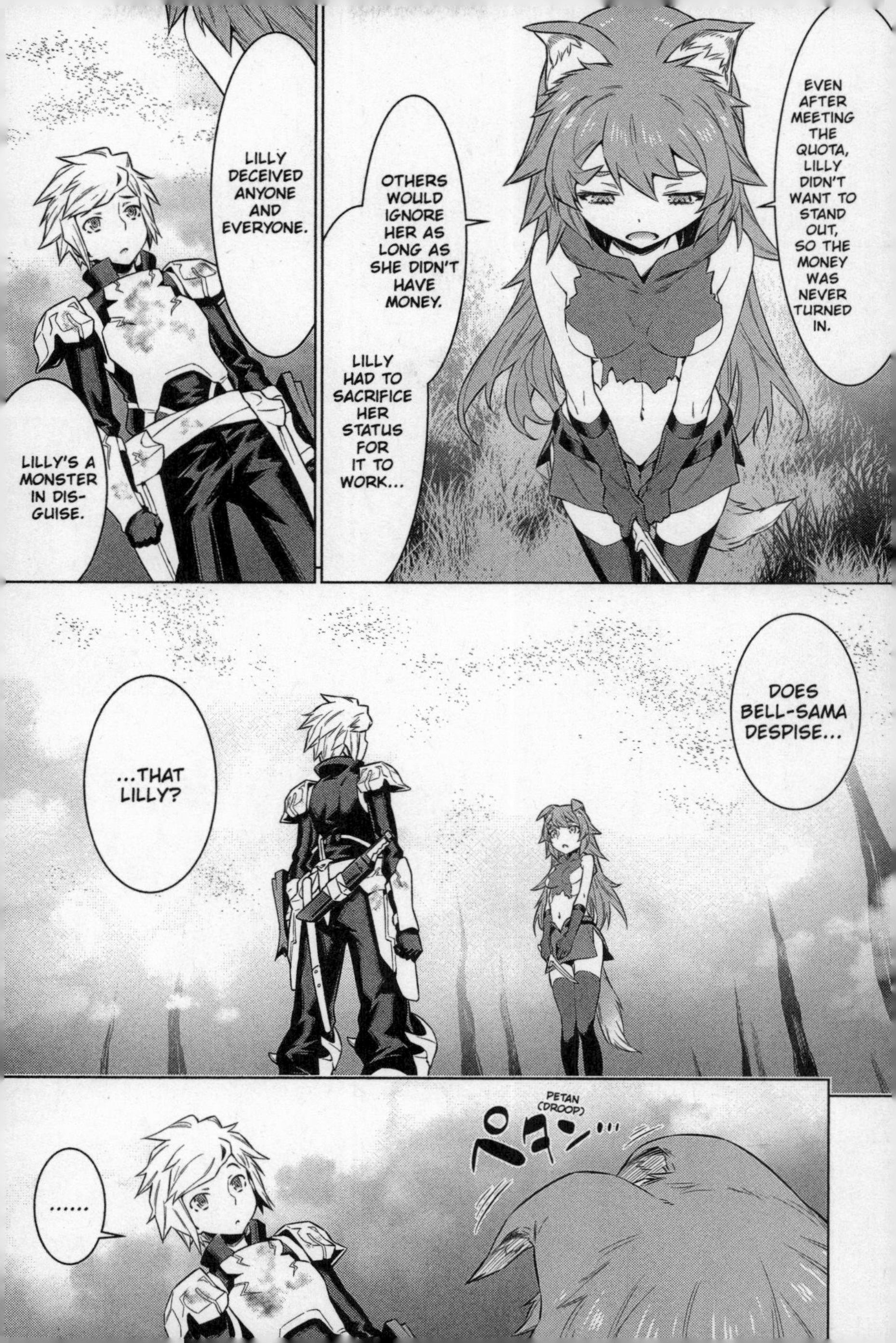
EVEN AFTER MEETING THE QUOTA, LILLY DIDN'T WANT TO STAND OUT, SO THE MONEY WAS NEVER TURNED IN.
OTHERS WOULD IGNORE HER AS LONG AS SHE DIDN'T HAVE MONEY.
LILLY HAD TO SACRIFICE HER STATUS FOR IT TO WORK...
LILLY DECEIVED ANYONE AND EVERYONE.
LILLY'S A MONSTER IN DIS-GUISE.
DOES BELL-SAMA DESPISE...
...THAT LILLY?
PETAN (DROOP)
......

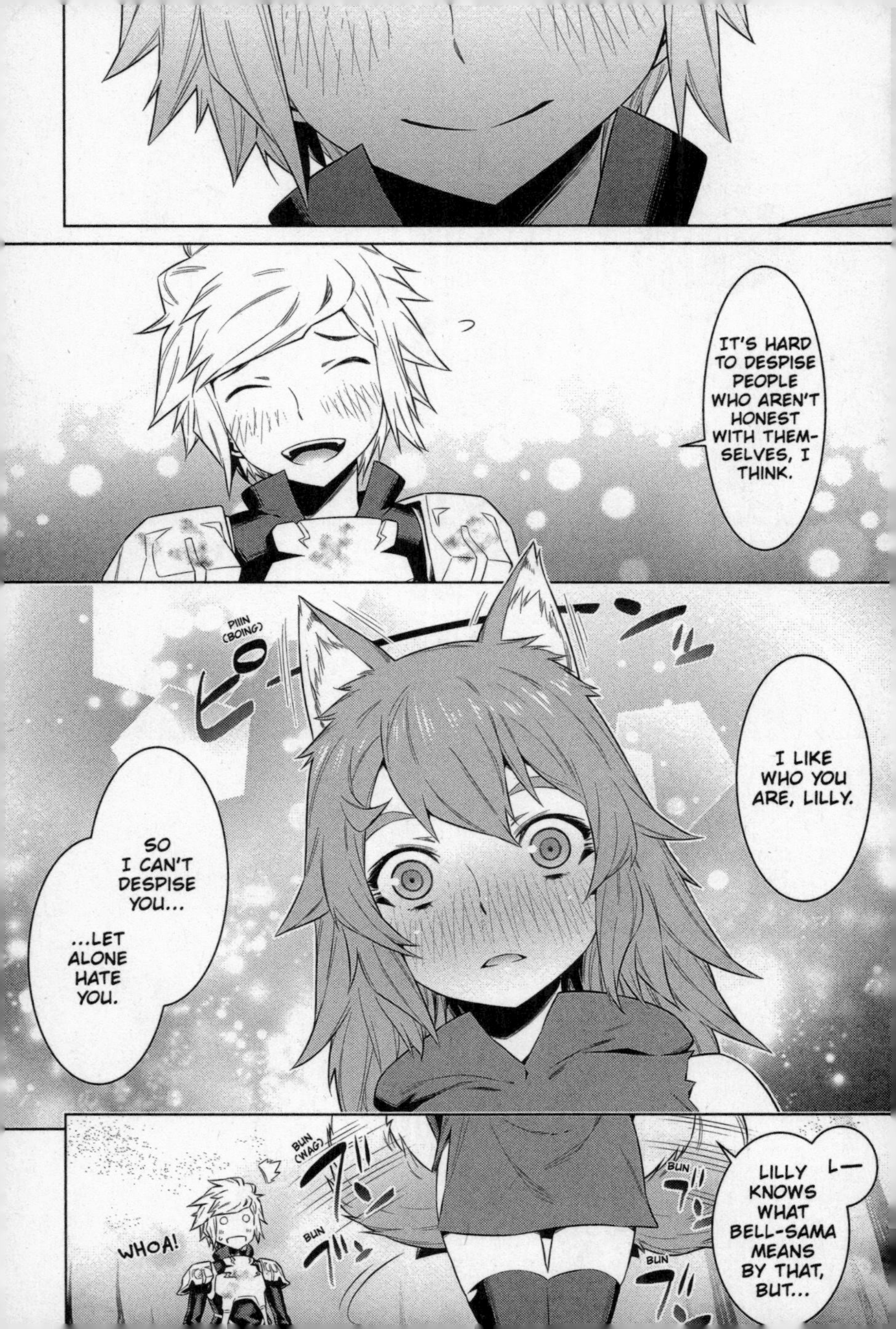
IT'S HARD TO DESPISE PEOPLE WHO AREN'T HONEST WITH THEM-SELVES, I THINK.
PIIIN (BOING)
I LIKE WHO YOU ARE, LILLY.
SO I CAN'T DESPISE YOU...
...LET ALONE HATE YOU.
LILLY KNOWS WHAT BELL-SAMA MEANS BY THAT, BUT...
BUN
BUN (WAG)
BUN
BUN
WHOA!

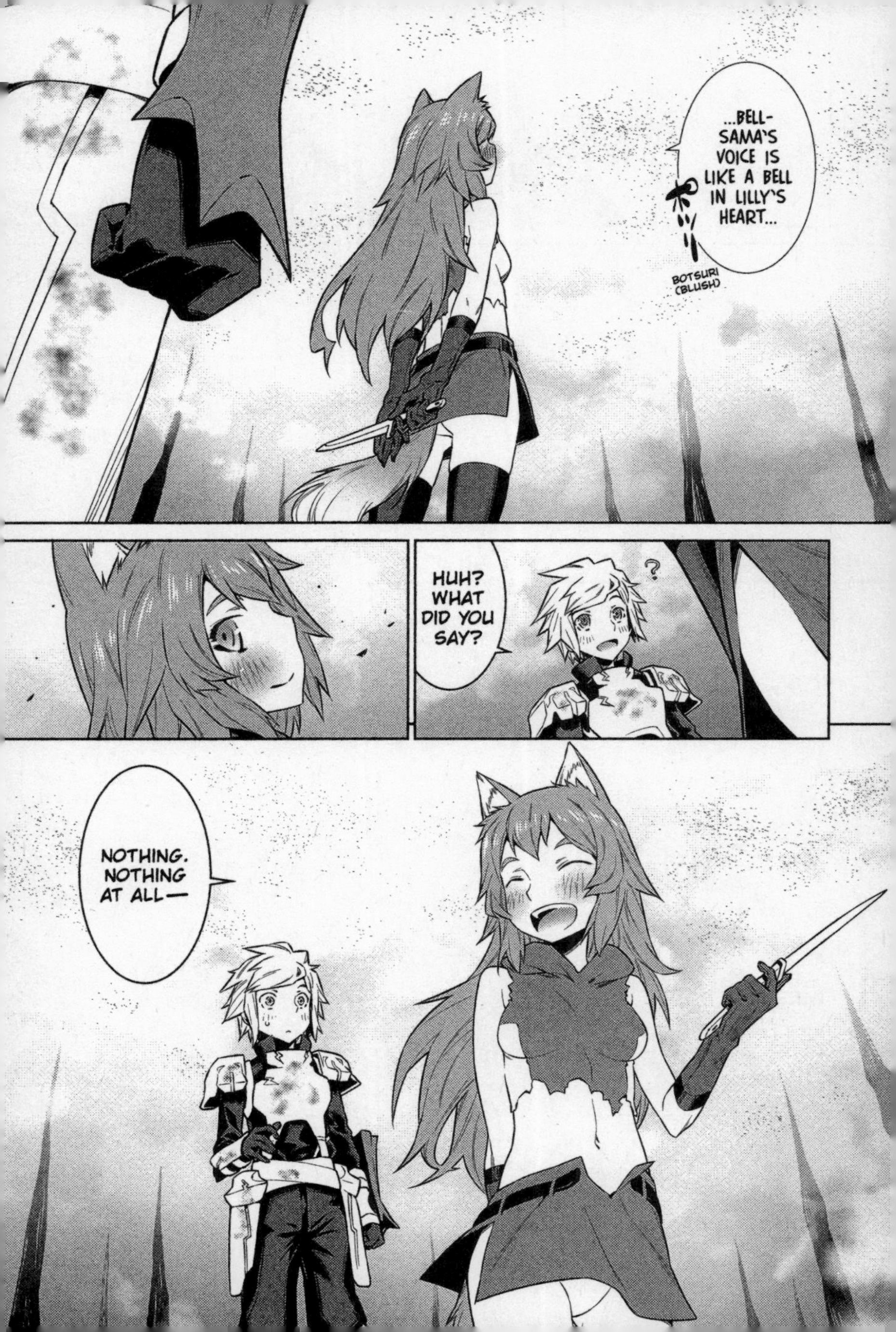
...BELL-SAMA'S VOICE IS LIKE A BELL IN LILLY'S HEART...
BOTSURI (BLUSH)
?
HUH? WHAT DID YOU SAY?
NOTHING. NOTHING AT ALL—

IS IT WRONG TO TRY TO PICK UP GIRLS IN A DUNGEON?

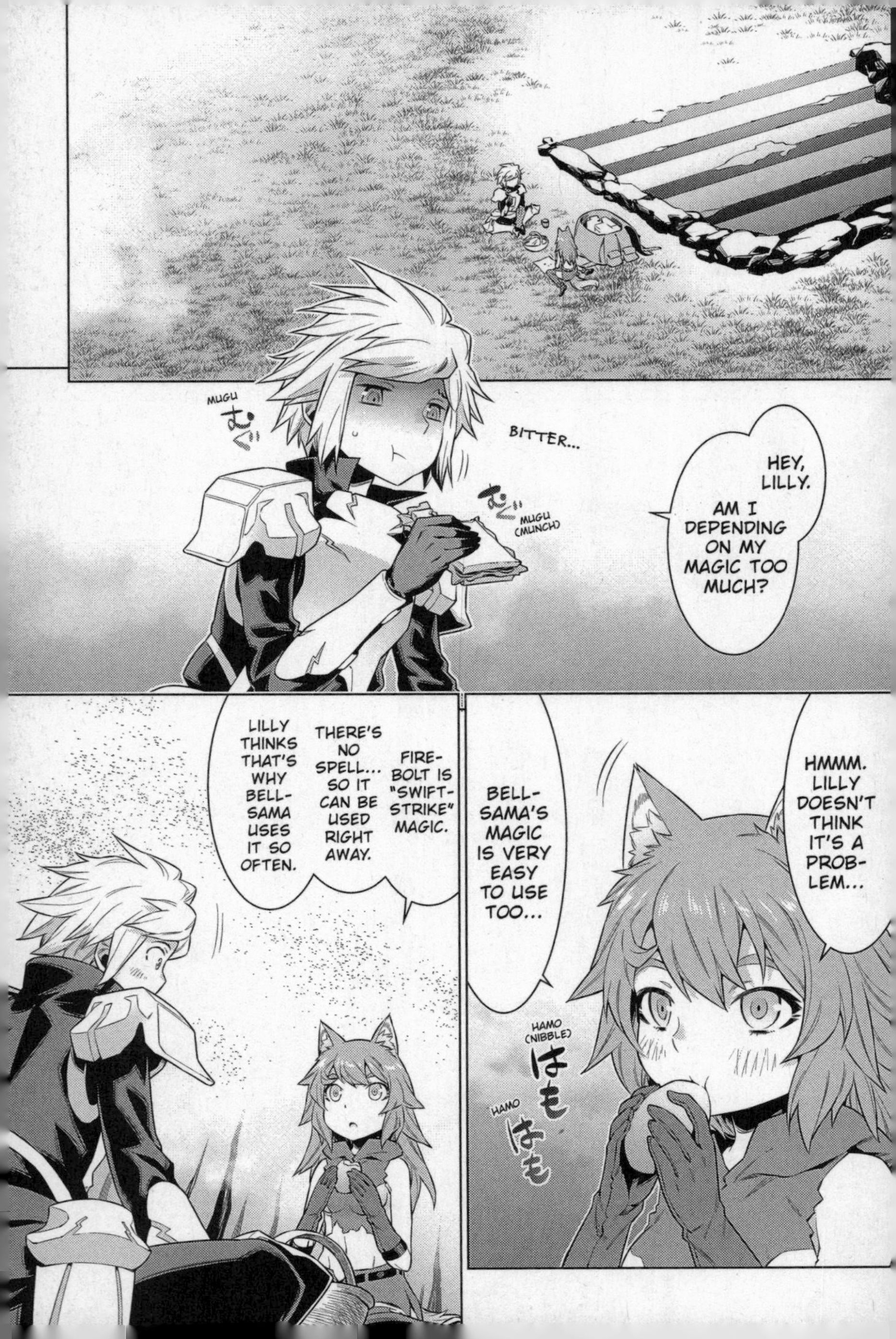
HEY, LILLY.
AM I DEPENDING ON MY MAGIC TOO MUCH?
BITTER...
むぐ MUGU (MUNCH)
むぐ MUGU
HMMM. LILLY DOESN'T THINK IT'S A PROB-LEM...
BELL-SAMA'S MAGIC IS VERY EASY TO USE TOO...
はも HAMO (NIBBLE)
はも HAMO
FIRE-BOLT IS "SWIFT-STRIKE" MAGIC.
THERE'S NO SPELL... SO IT CAN BE USED RIGHT AWAY.
LILLY THINKS THAT'S WHY BELL-SAMA USES IT SO OFTEN.

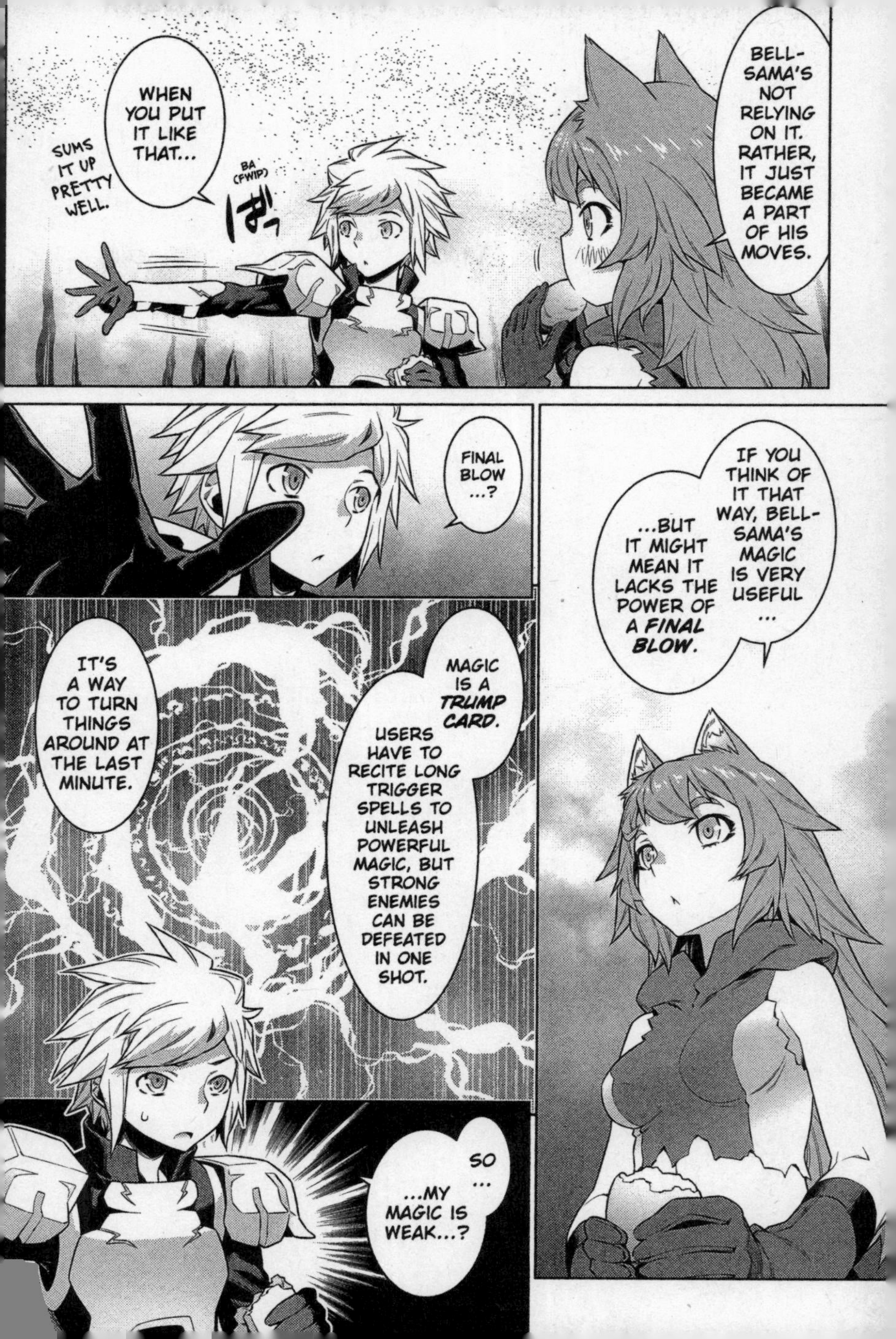
BELL-SAMA'S NOT RELYING ON IT. RATHER, IT JUST BECAME A PART OF HIS MOVES.
BA (FWIP)
ばっ
WHEN YOU PUT IT LIKE THAT...
SUMS IT UP PRETTY WELL.
IF YOU THINK OF IT THAT WAY, BELL-SAMA'S MAGIC IS VERY USEFUL...
...BUT IT MIGHT MEAN IT LACKS THE POWER OF A *FINAL BLOW*.
FINAL BLOW...?
MAGIC IS A *TRUMP CARD*.
USERS HAVE TO RECITE LONG TRIGGER SPELLS TO UNLEASH POWERFUL MAGIC, BUT STRONG ENEMIES CAN BE DEFEATED IN ONE SHOT.
IT'S A WAY TO TURN THINGS AROUND AT THE LAST MINUTE.
SO...
...MY MAGIC IS WEAK...?

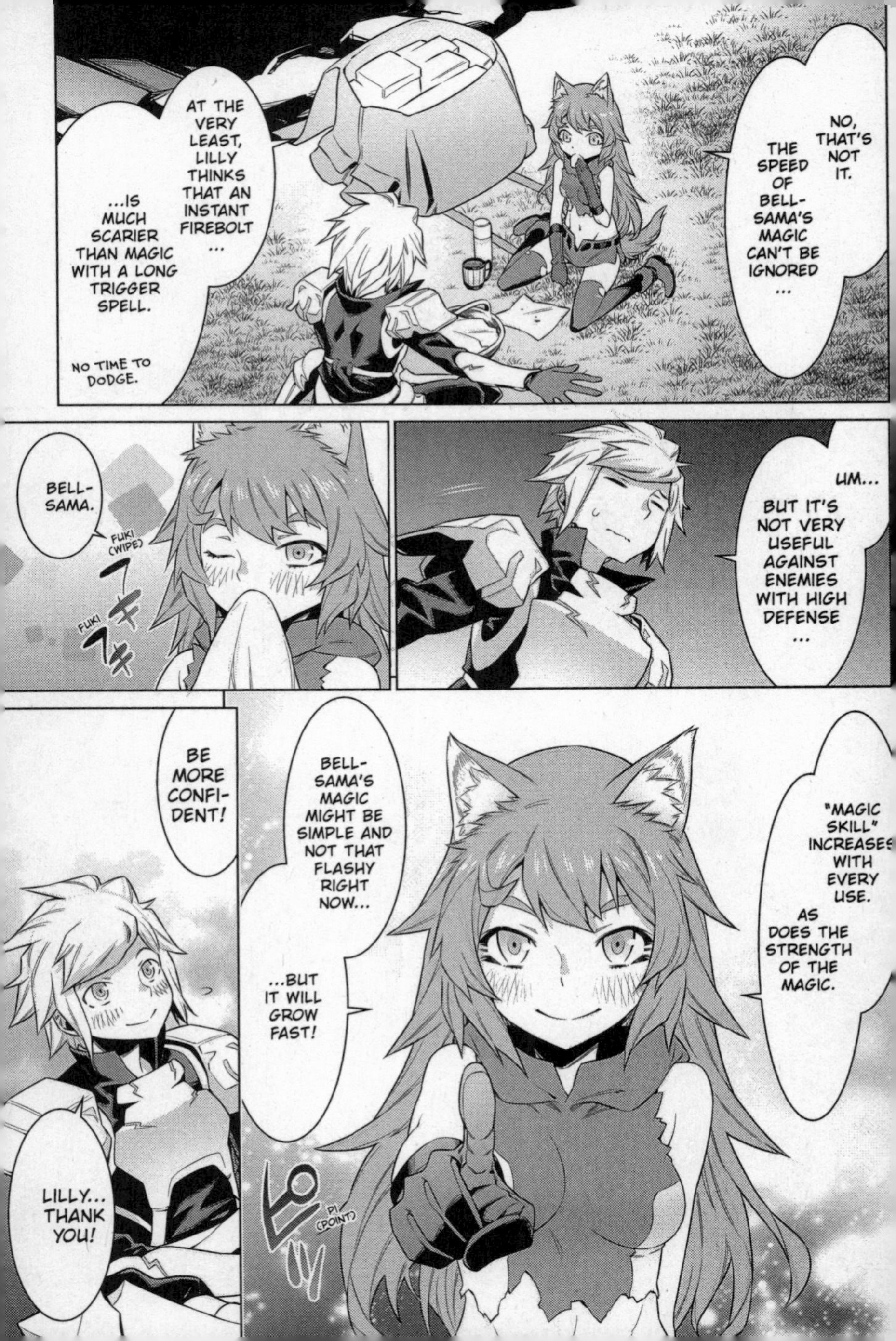
NO, THAT'S NOT IT.
THE SPEED OF BELL-SAMA'S MAGIC CAN'T BE IGNORED ...
AT THE VERY LEAST, LILLY THINKS THAT AN INSTANT FIREBOLT ...
...IS MUCH SCARIER THAN MAGIC WITH A LONG TRIGGER SPELL.
NO TIME TO DODGE.
UM...
BUT IT'S NOT VERY USEFUL AGAINST ENEMIES WITH HIGH DEFENSE ...
BELL-SAMA.
FUKI (WIPE)
FUKI
"MAGIC SKILL" INCREASES WITH EVERY USE.
AS DOES THE STRENGTH OF THE MAGIC.
BELL-SAMA'S MAGIC MIGHT BE SIMPLE AND NOT THAT FLASHY RIGHT NOW...
...BUT IT WILL GROW FAST!
PI (POINT)
BE MORE CONFIDENT!
LILLY... THANK YOU!

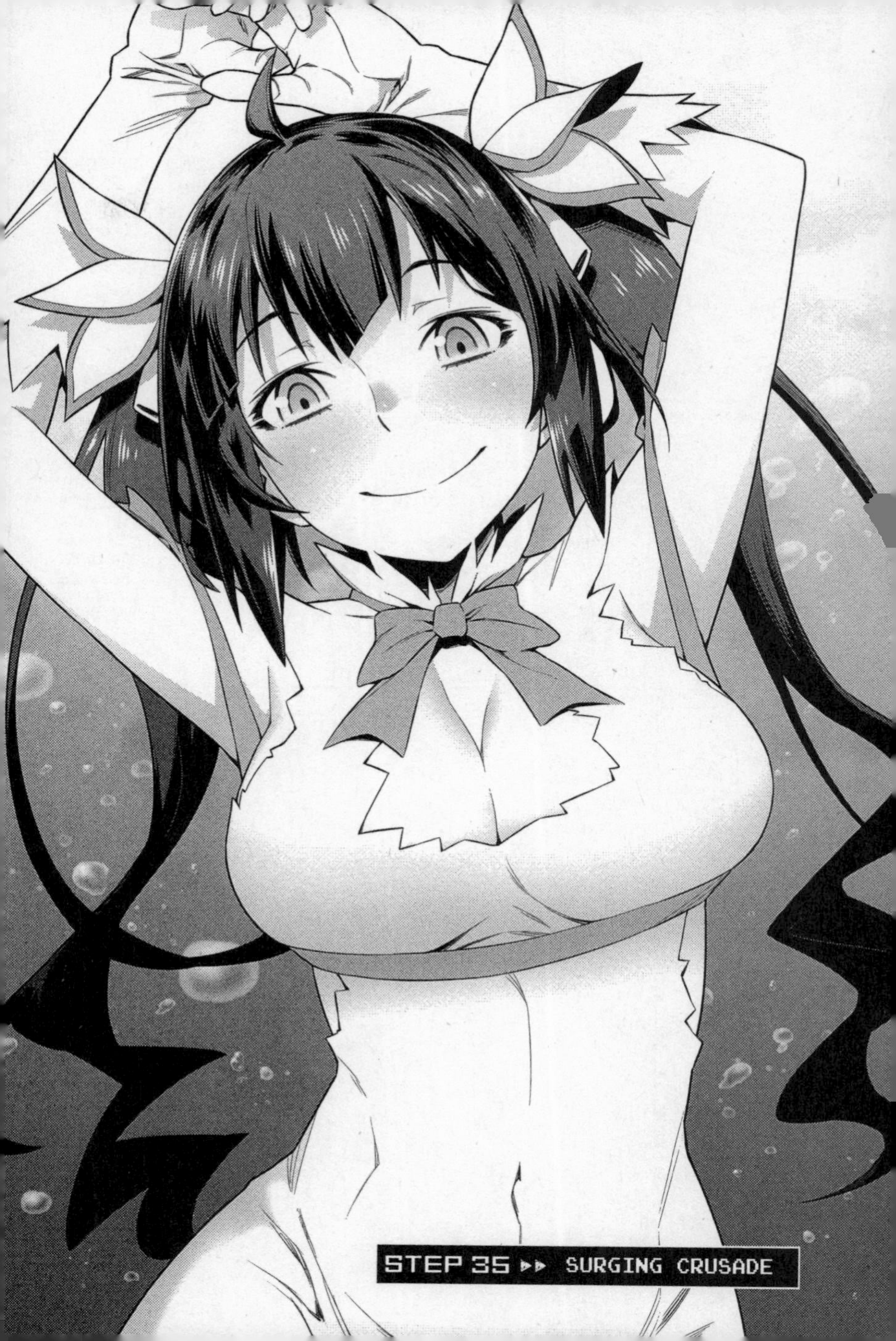

STEP 35 ▸▸ SURGING CRUSADE

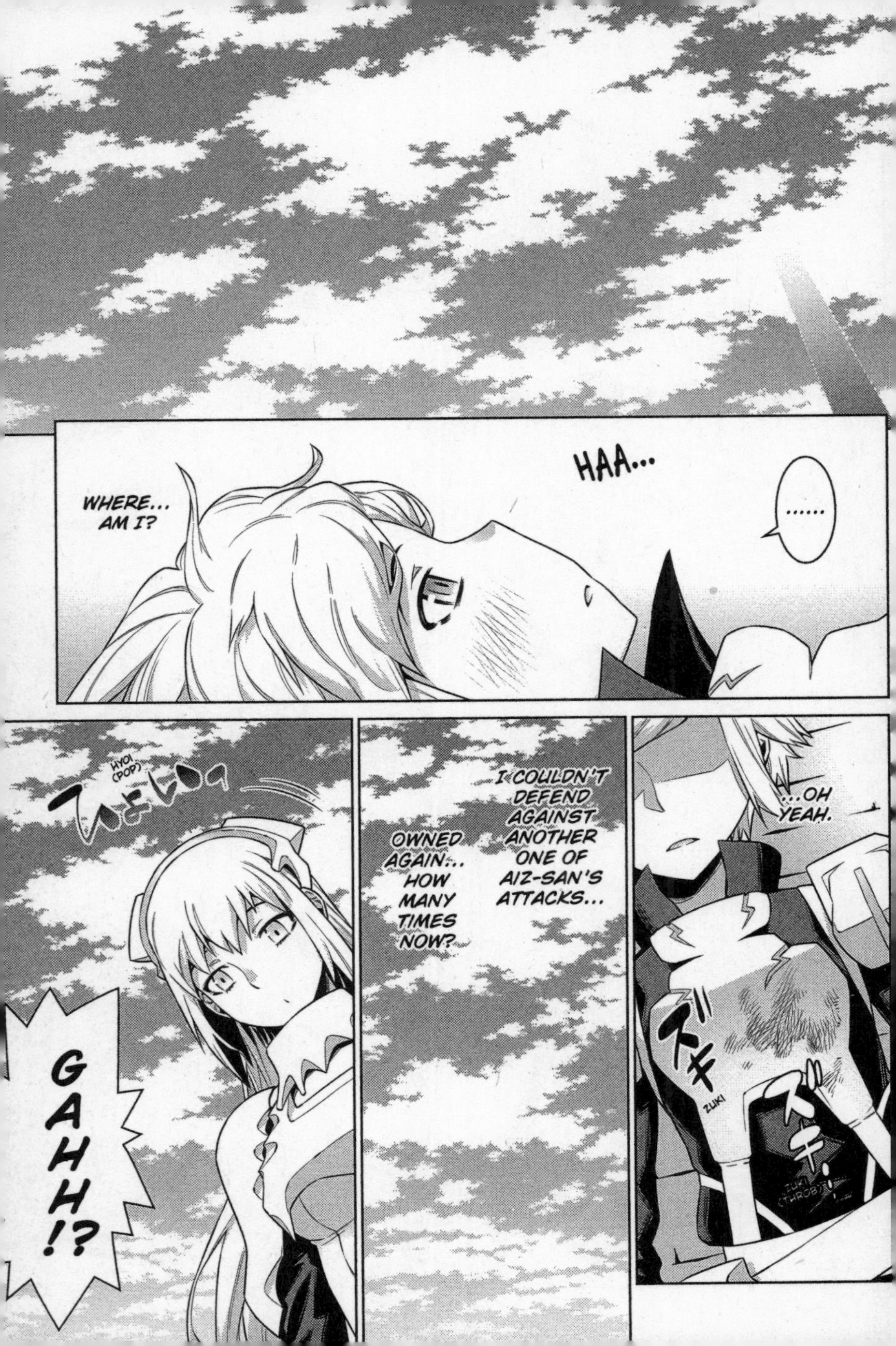
......
HAA...
WHERE... AM I?
...OH YEAH.
ZUKI
ZUKI (THROB)
I COULDN'T DEFEND AGAINST ANOTHER ONE OF AIZ-SAN'S ATTACKS...
OWNED AGAIN... HOW MANY TIMES NOW?
HYOI (POP)
GAHH!?

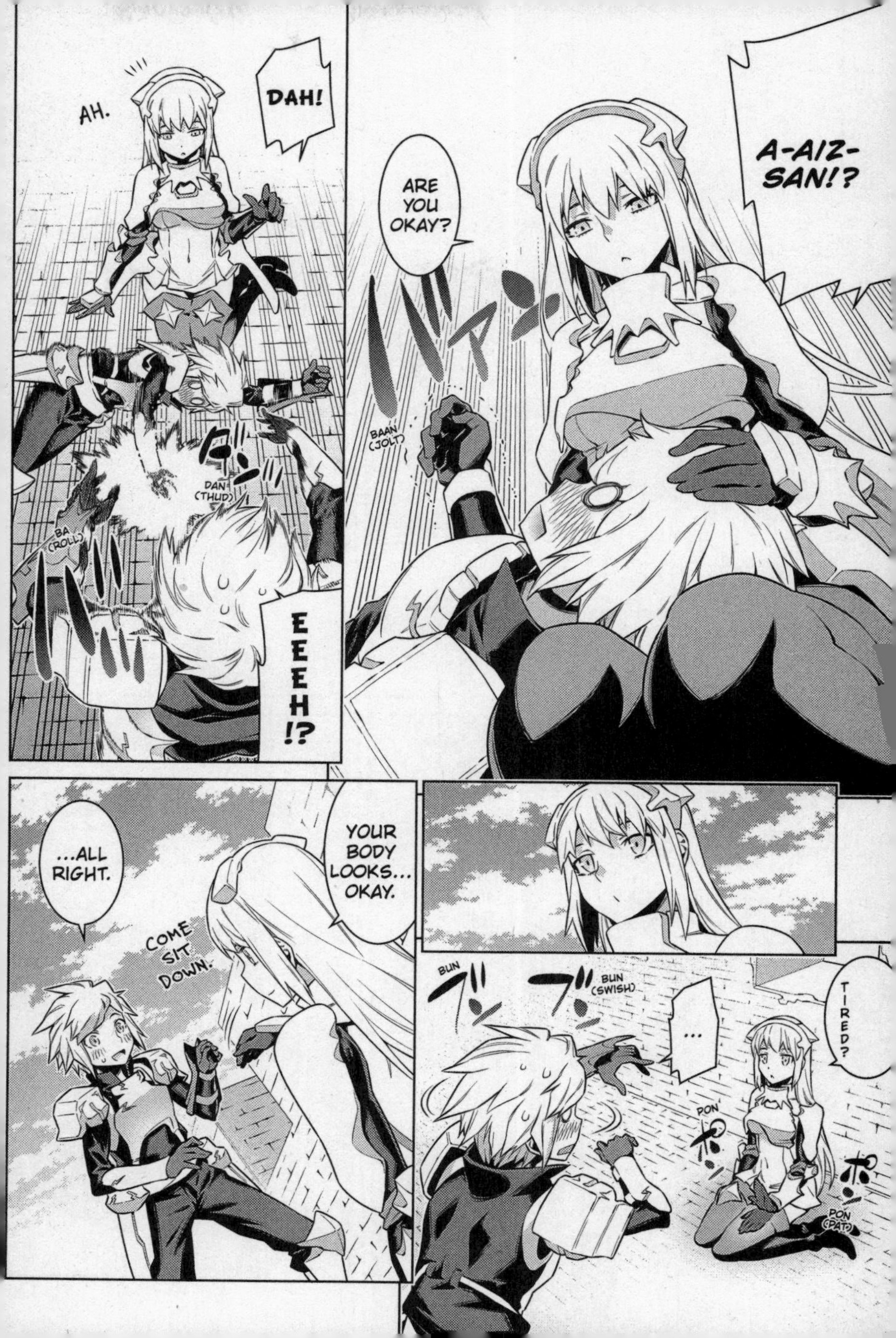
A-AIZ-SAN!?
ARE YOU OKAY?
BAAN (JOLT)
DAH!
AH.
DAN (THUD)
BA (ROLL)
EEEEH!?
TIRED?
...
BUN (SWISH)
BUN
PON
PON (PAT)
YOUR BODY LOOKS... OKAY.
...ALL RIGHT.
COME SIT DOWN.

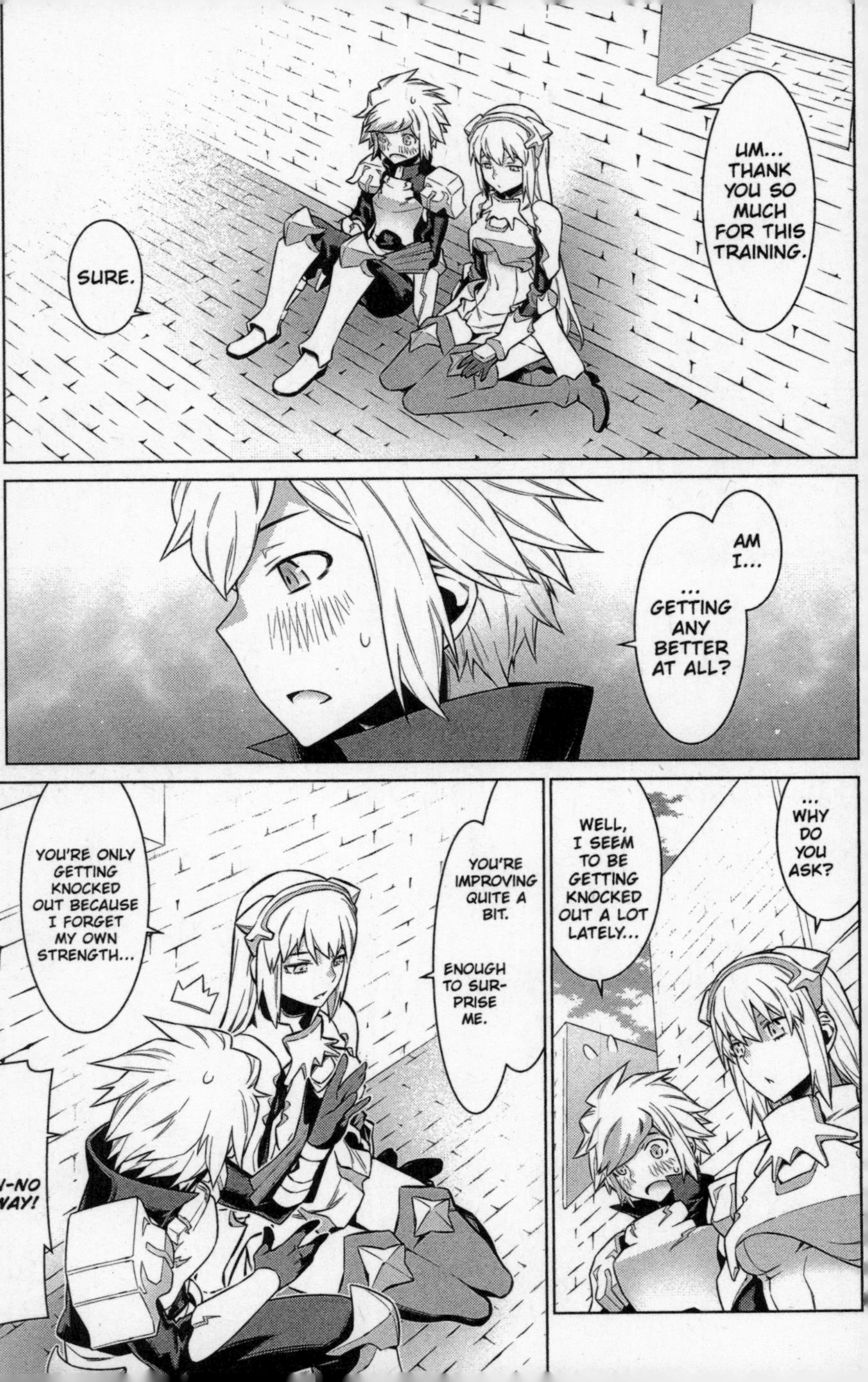
UM... THANK YOU SO MUCH FOR THIS TRAINING.
SURE.
AM I...
... GETTING ANY BETTER AT ALL?
... WHY DO YOU ASK?
WELL, I SEEM TO BE GETTING KNOCKED OUT A LOT LATELY...
YOU'RE IMPROVING QUITE A BIT.
ENOUGH TO SUR-PRISE ME.
YOU'RE ONLY GETTING KNOCKED OUT BECAUSE I FORGET MY OWN STRENGTH...
N-NO WAY!

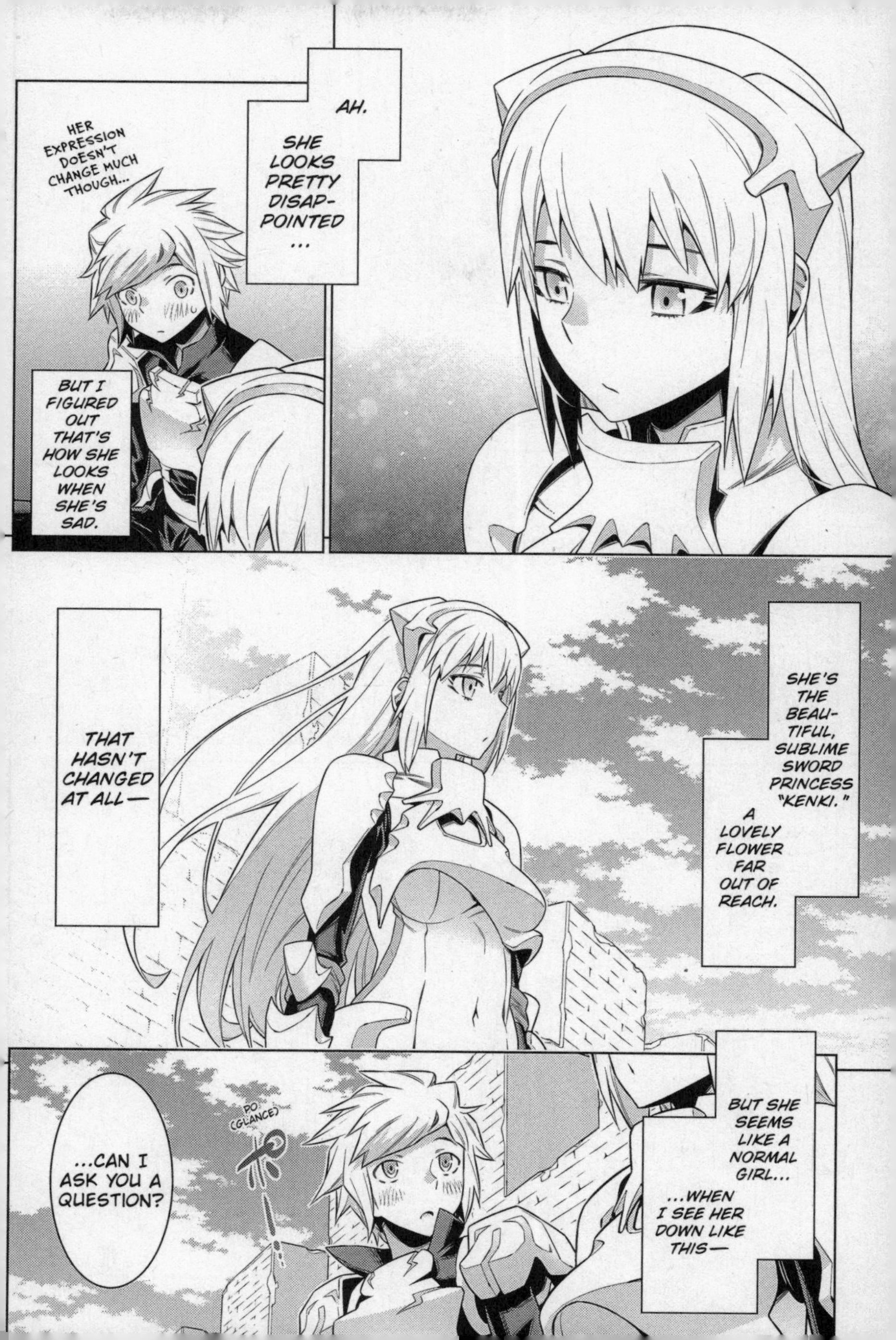
AH.
SHE LOOKS PRETTY DISAP-POINTED ...
HER EXPRESSION DOESN'T CHANGE MUCH THOUGH...
BUT I FIGURED OUT THAT'S HOW SHE LOOKS WHEN SHE'S SAD.
SHE'S THE BEAU-TIFUL, SUBLIME SWORD PRINCESS "KENKI."
A LOVELY FLOWER FAR OUT OF REACH.
THAT HASN'T CHANGED AT ALL—
BUT SHE SEEMS LIKE A NORMAL GIRL...
...WHEN I SEE HER DOWN LIKE THIS—
PO (GLANCE)
...CAN I ASK YOU A QUESTION?

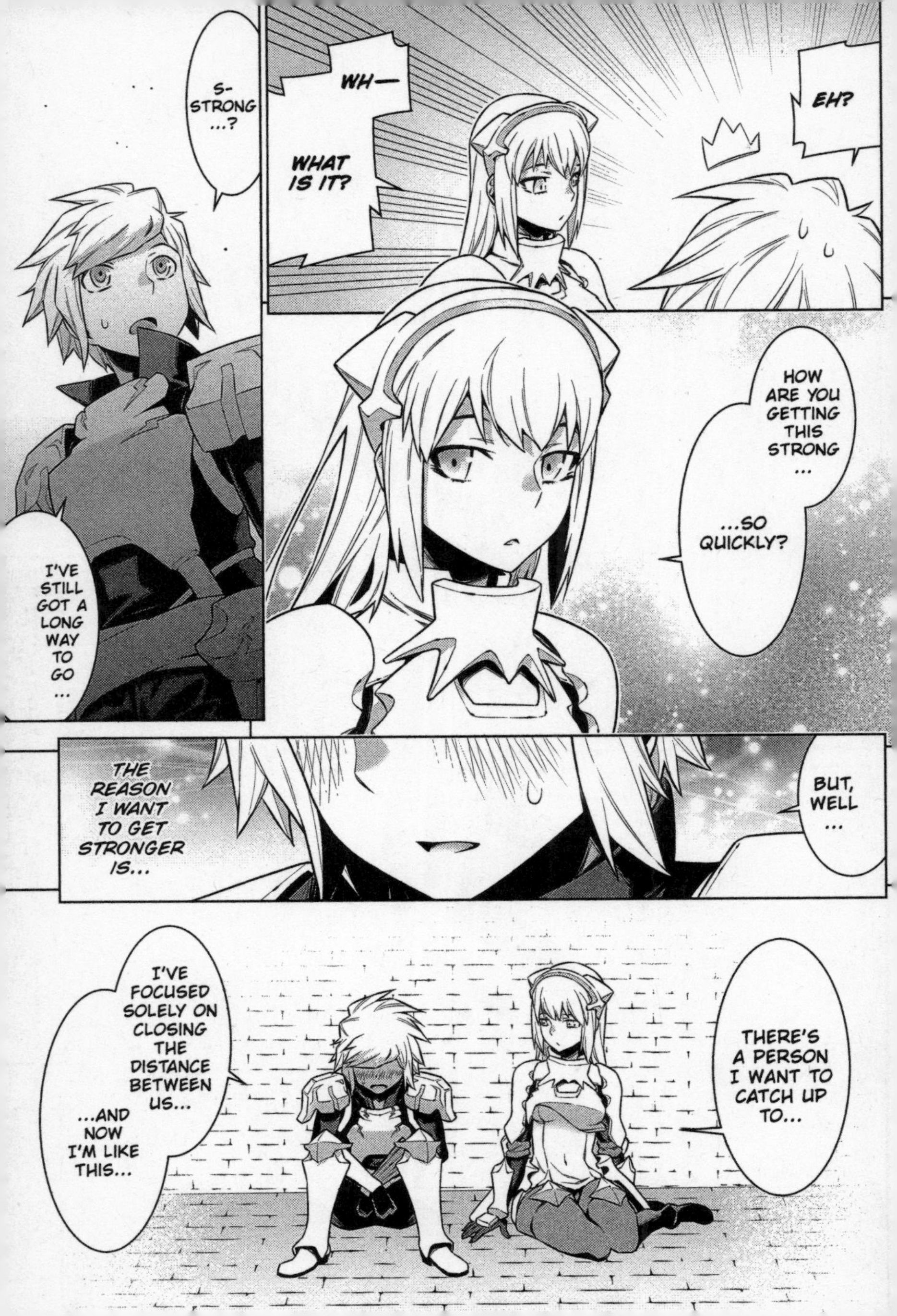
EH?
WH—
WHAT IS IT?
HOW ARE YOU GETTING THIS STRONG...
...SO QUICKLY?
S-STRONG...?
I'VE STILL GOT A LONG WAY TO GO...
BUT, WELL...
THE REASON I WANT TO GET STRONGER IS...
THERE'S A PERSON I WANT TO CATCH UP TO...
I'VE FOCUSED SOLELY ON CLOSING THE DISTANCE BETWEEN US...
...AND NOW I'M LIKE THIS...

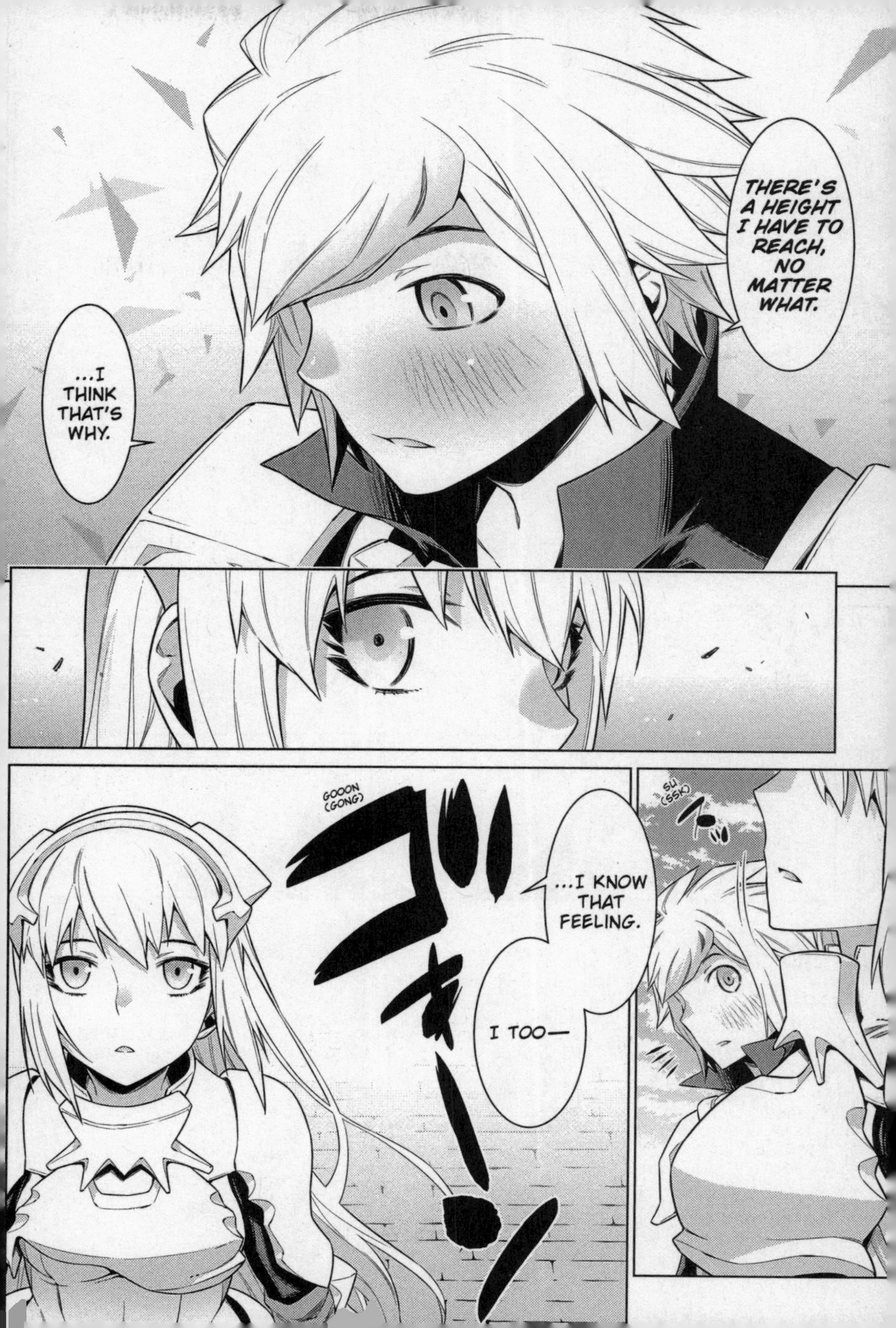
THERE'S A HEIGHT I HAVE TO REACH, NO MATTER WHAT.
...I THINK THAT'S WHY.
SU (SSK)
...I KNOW THAT FEELING.
GOOOON (GONG)
I TOO—

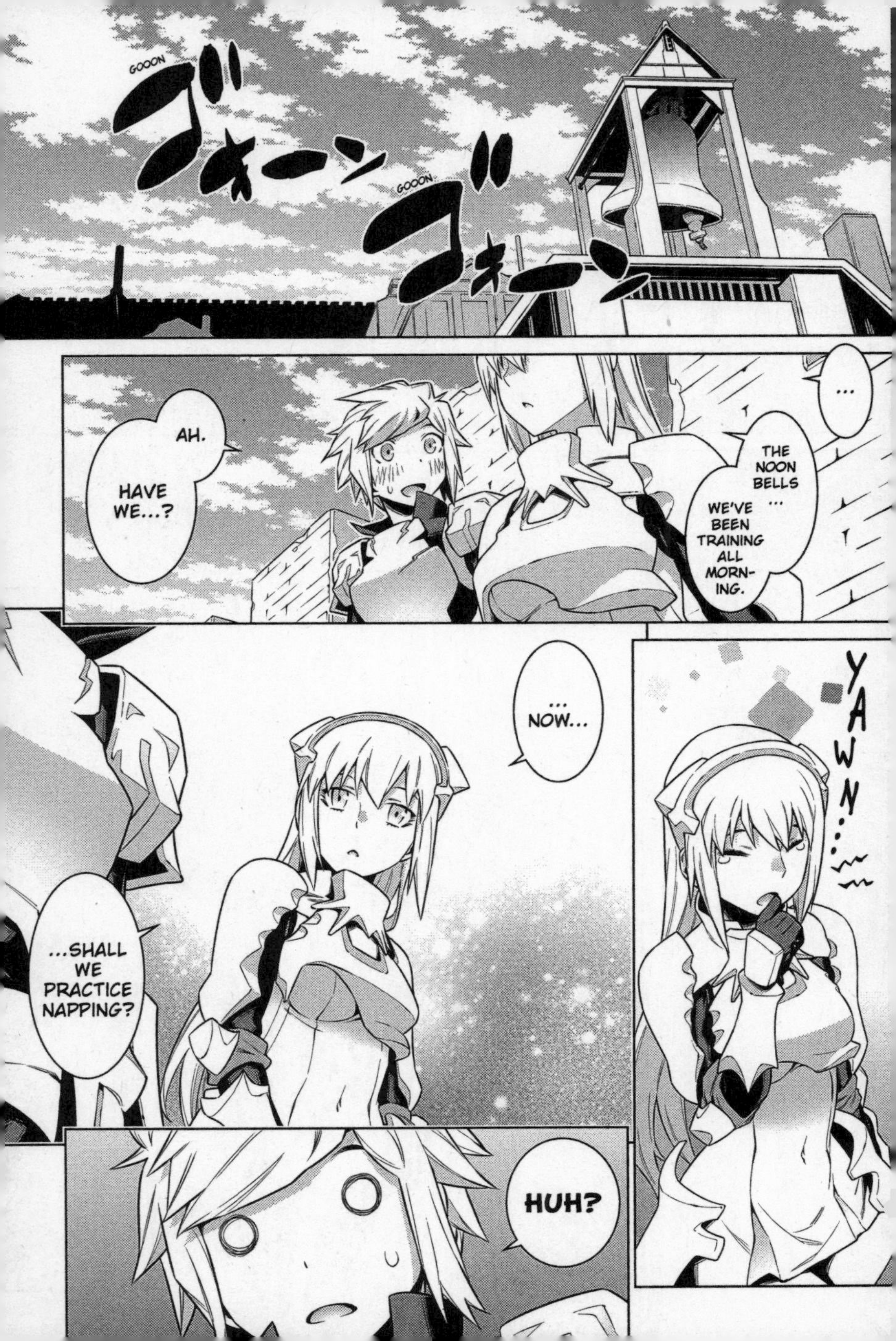
GOOON
GOOON
...
THE NOON BELLS ... WE'VE BEEN TRAINING ALL MORNING.
AH.
HAVE WE...?
YAWN...
... NOW...
...SHALL WE PRACTICE NAPPING?
HUH?

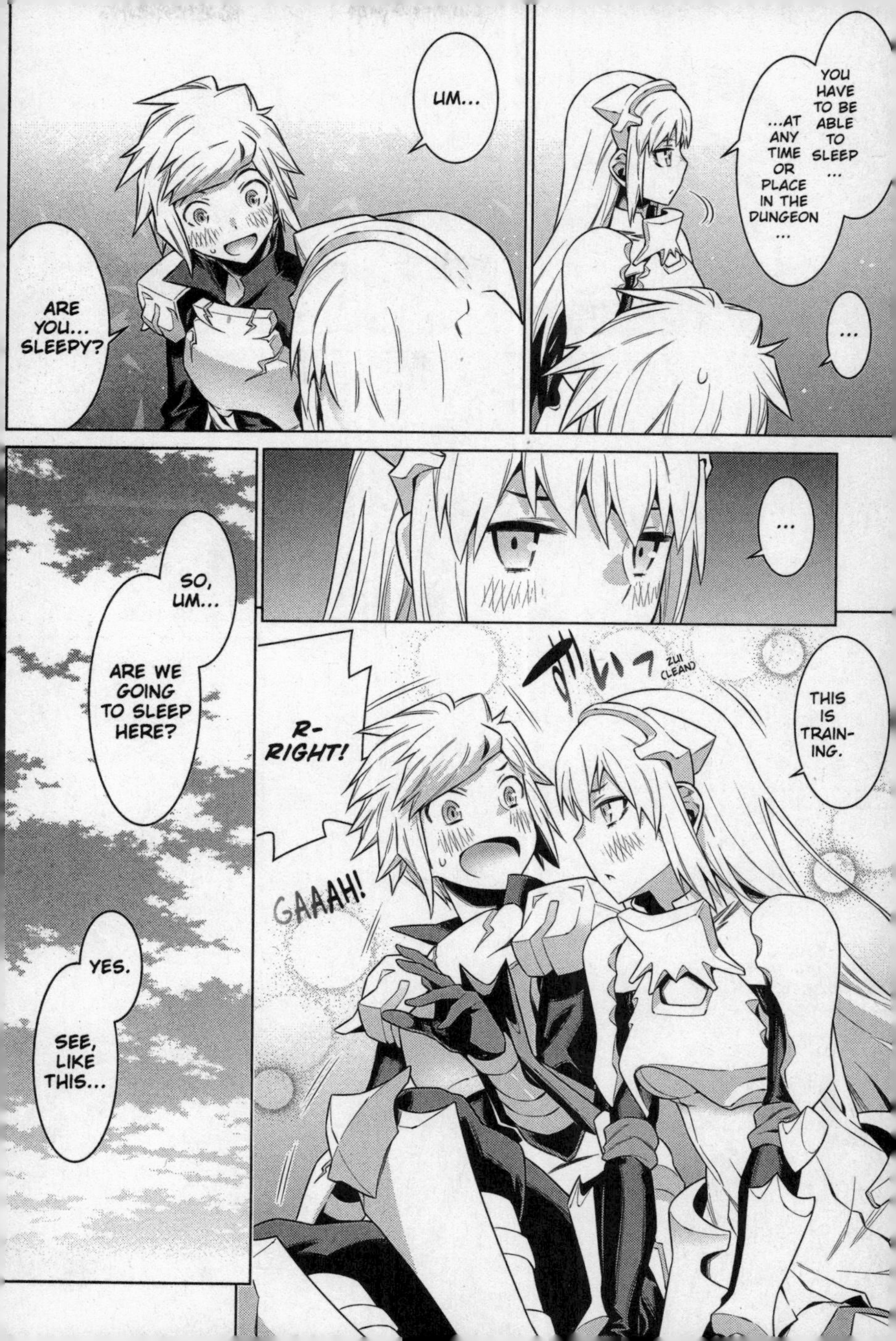
YOU HAVE TO BE ABLE TO SLEEP...
...AT ANY TIME OR PLACE IN THE DUNGEON...
...
UM...
ARE YOU... SLEEPY?
...
ZUI (CLEAN)
THIS IS TRAIN-ING.
R-RIGHT!
GAAAH!
SO, UM...
ARE WE GOING TO SLEEP HERE?
YES.
SEE, LIKE THIS...

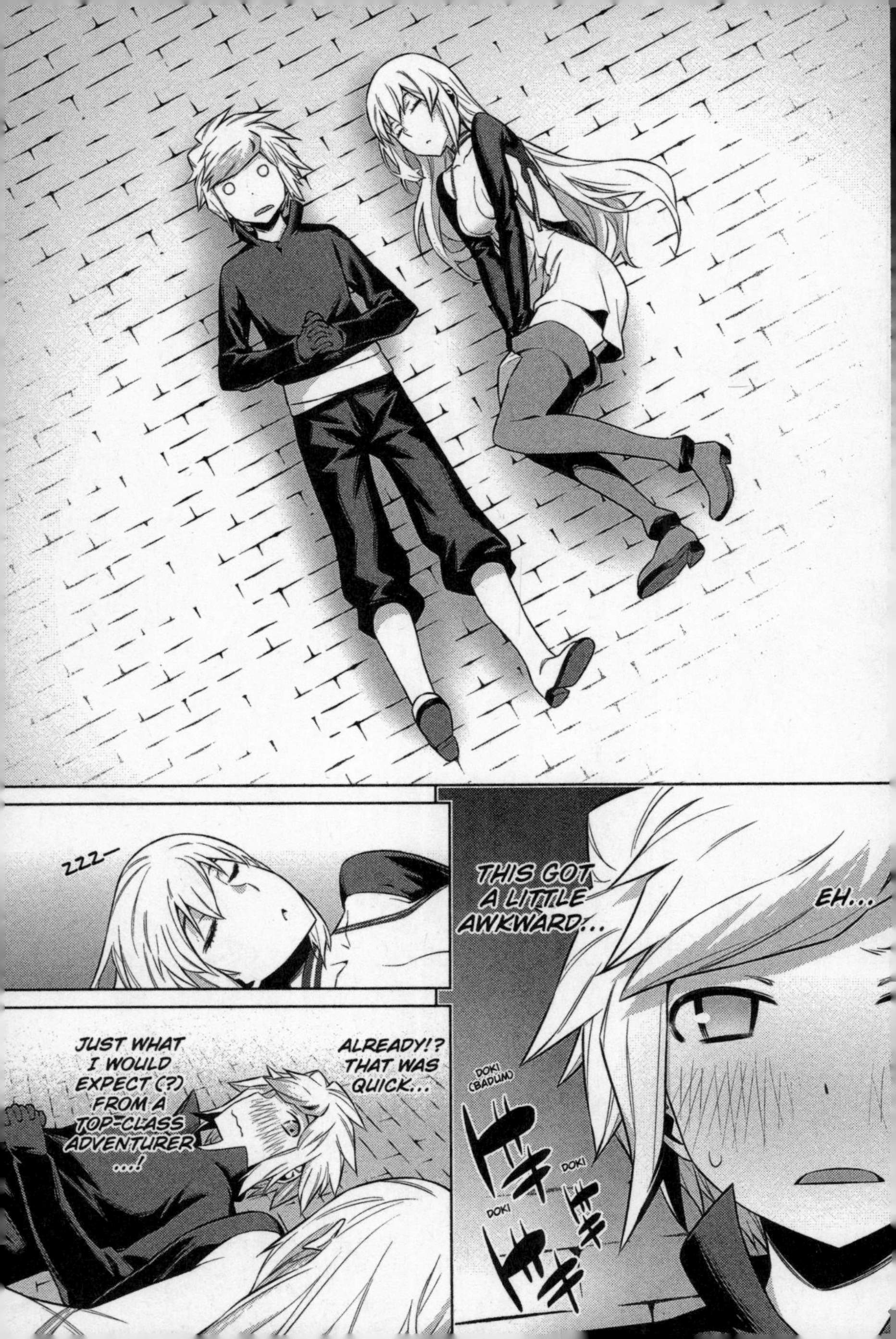
EH...
THIS GOT A LITTLE AWKWARD...
DOKI (BADUM)
DOKI
DOKI
ZZZ–
ALREADY!? THAT WAS QUICK...
JUST WHAT I WOULD EXPECT (?) FROM A TOP-CLASS ADVENTURER ...!

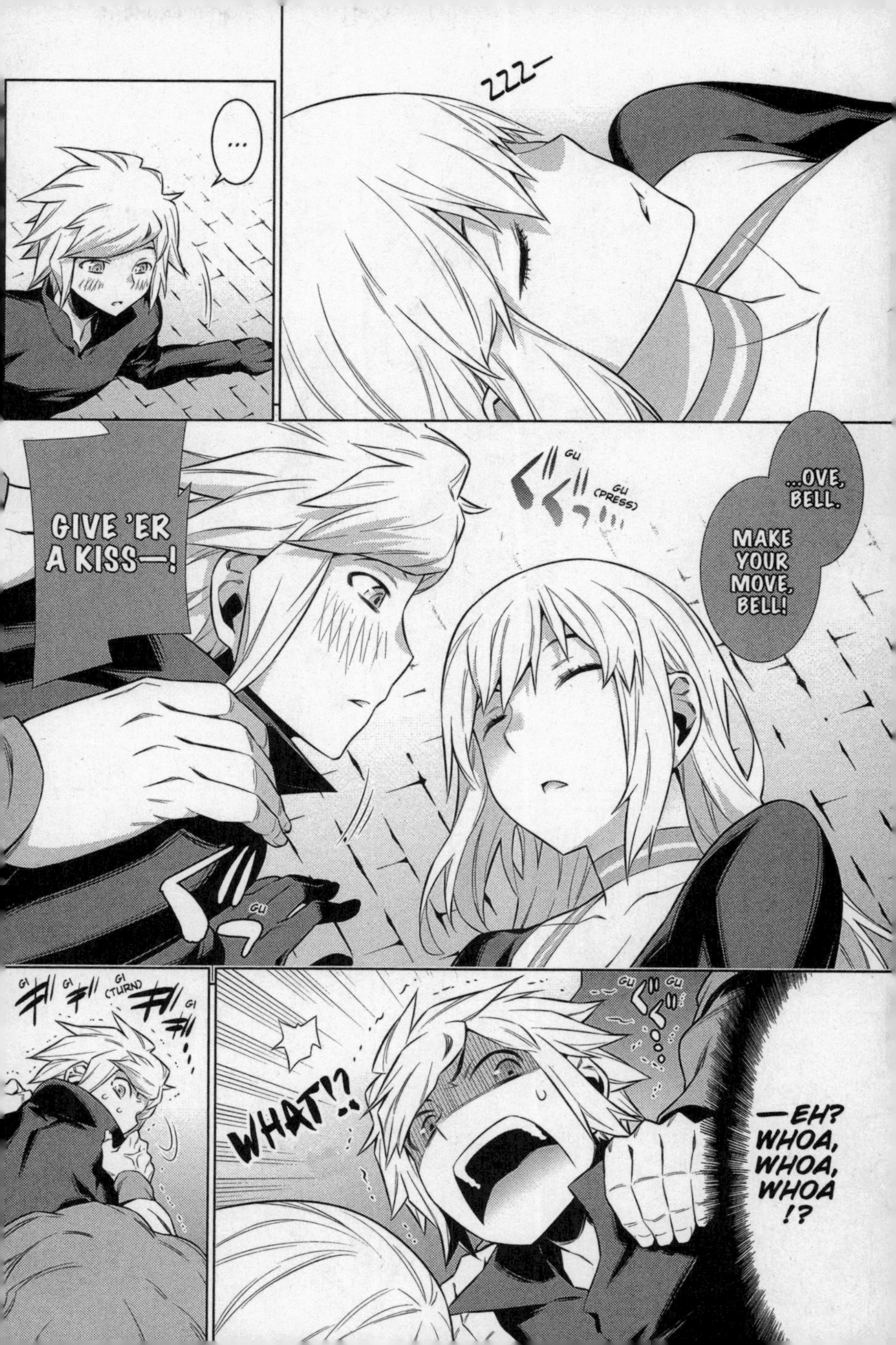
ZZZ—
...
...OVE, BELL.
MAKE YOUR MOVE, BELL!
GU GU (PRESS)
GIVE 'ER A KISS—!
GU
GU GU
—EH? WHOA, WHOA, WHOA!?
WHAT!?
GI GI GI (TURN) GI

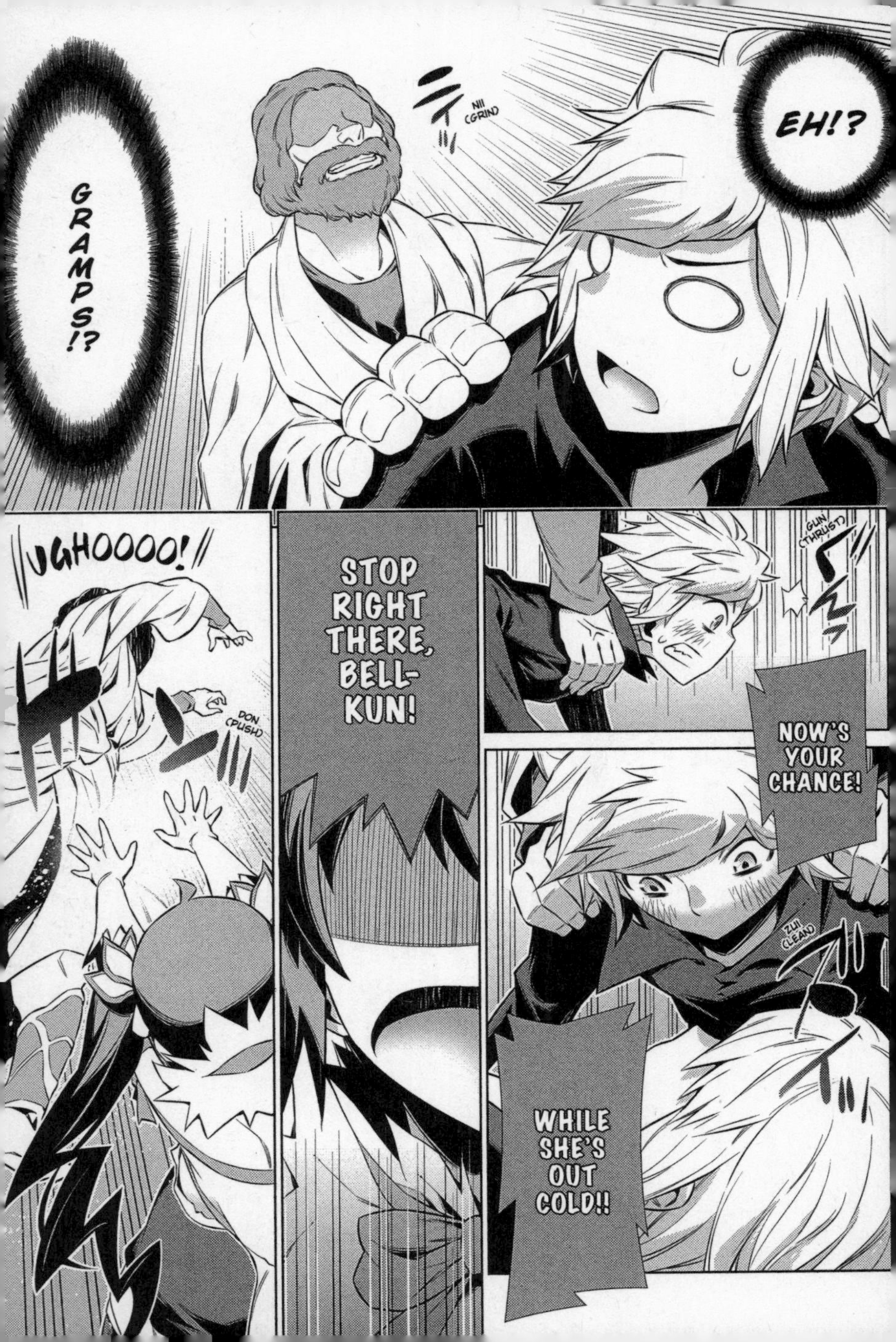
EH!?
NII (GRIN)
GRAMPS!?
GUN (THRUST)
NOW'S YOUR CHANCE!
ZUI (LEAN)
WHILE SHE'S OUT COLD!!
STOP RIGHT THERE, BELL-KUN!
UGHOOOO!
DON (PUSH)

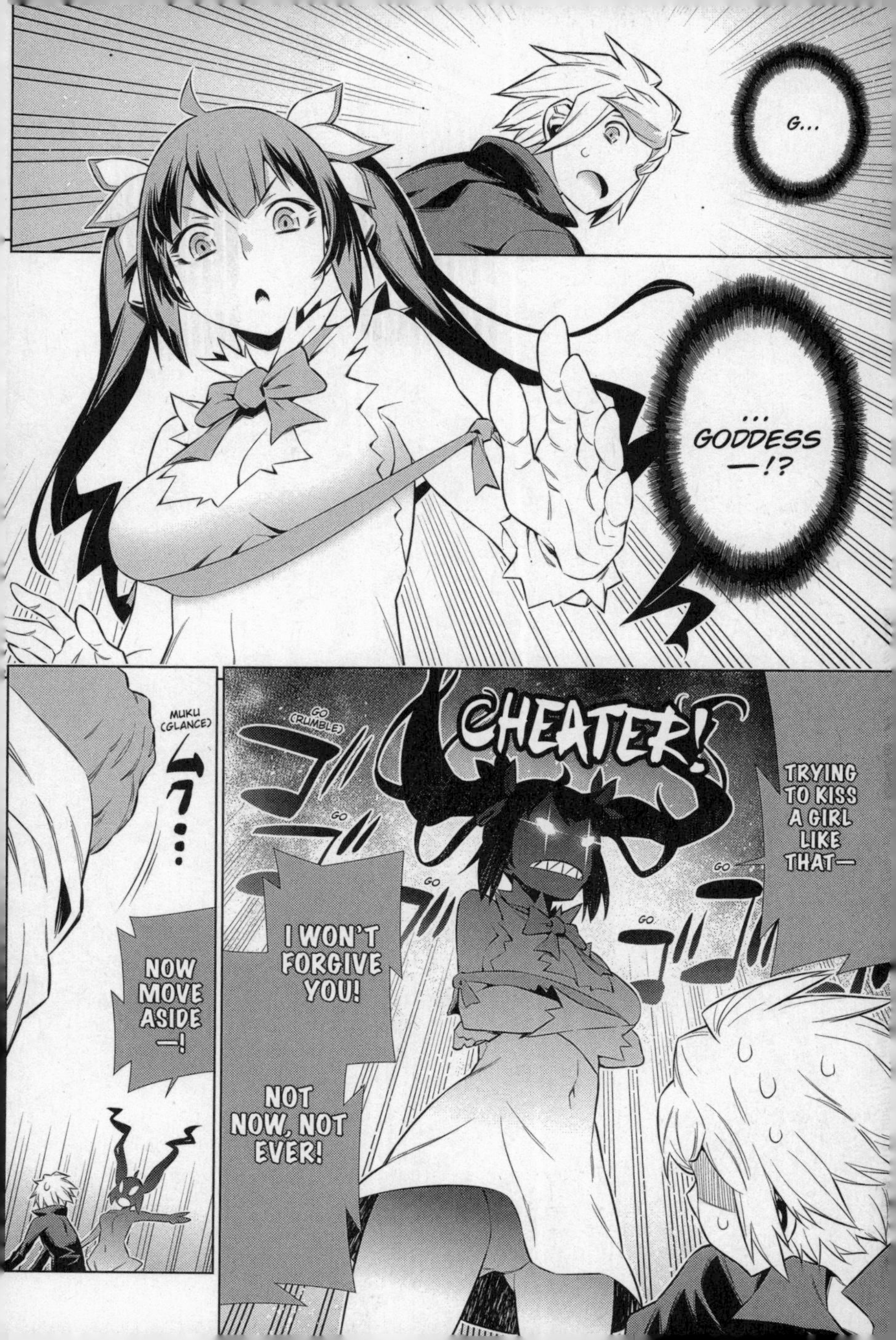
G...
...GODDESS—!?
CHEATER!
TRYING TO KISS A GIRL LIKE THAT—
GO (RUMBLE)
GO
GO
GO
GO
I WON'T FORGIVE YOU!
NOT NOW, NOT EVER!
MUKU (GLANCE)
NOW MOVE ASIDE—!

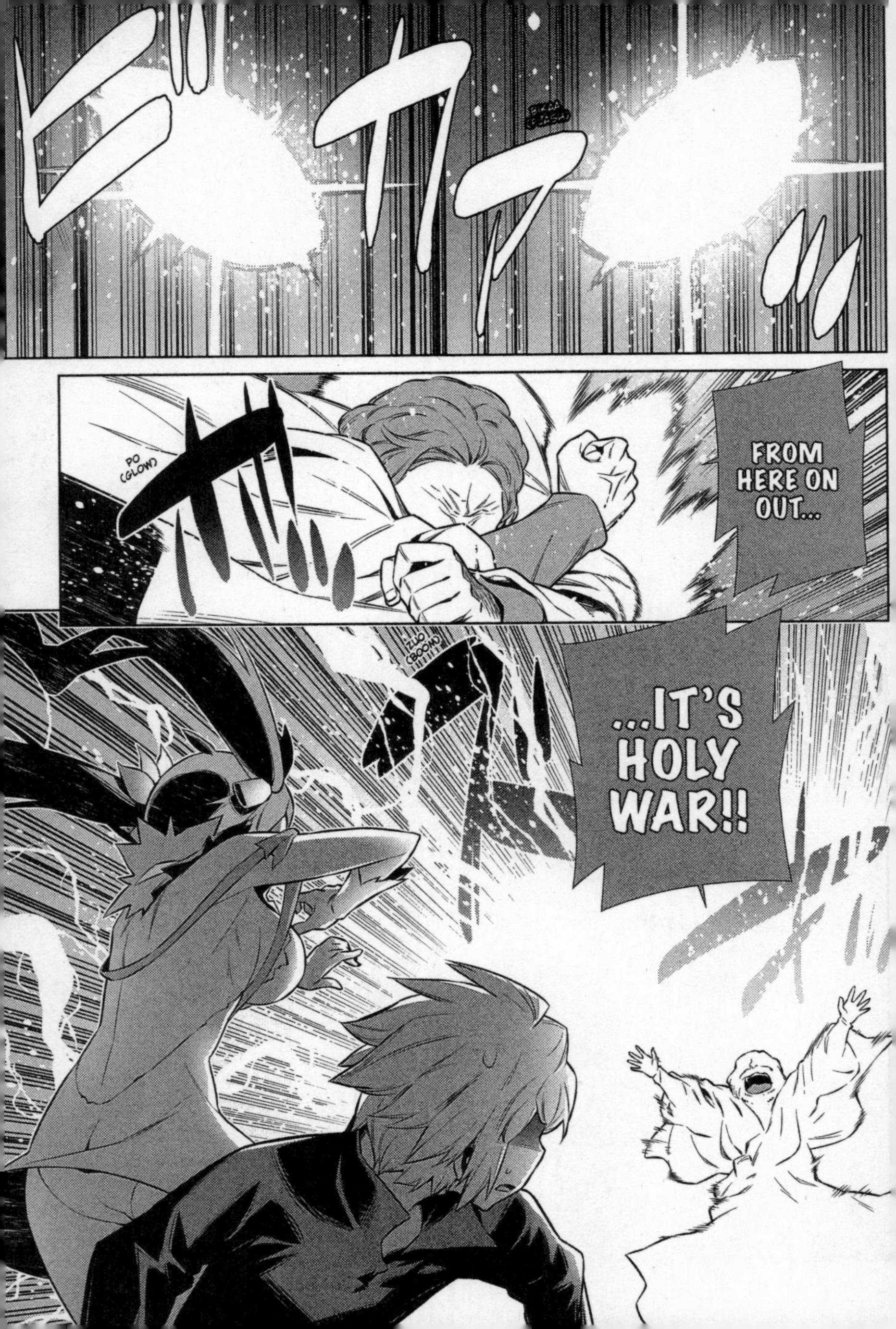
PIKAA (FLASH)
FROM HERE ON OUT...
PO (GLOW)
ZUO (BOOM)
...IT'S HOLY WAR!!

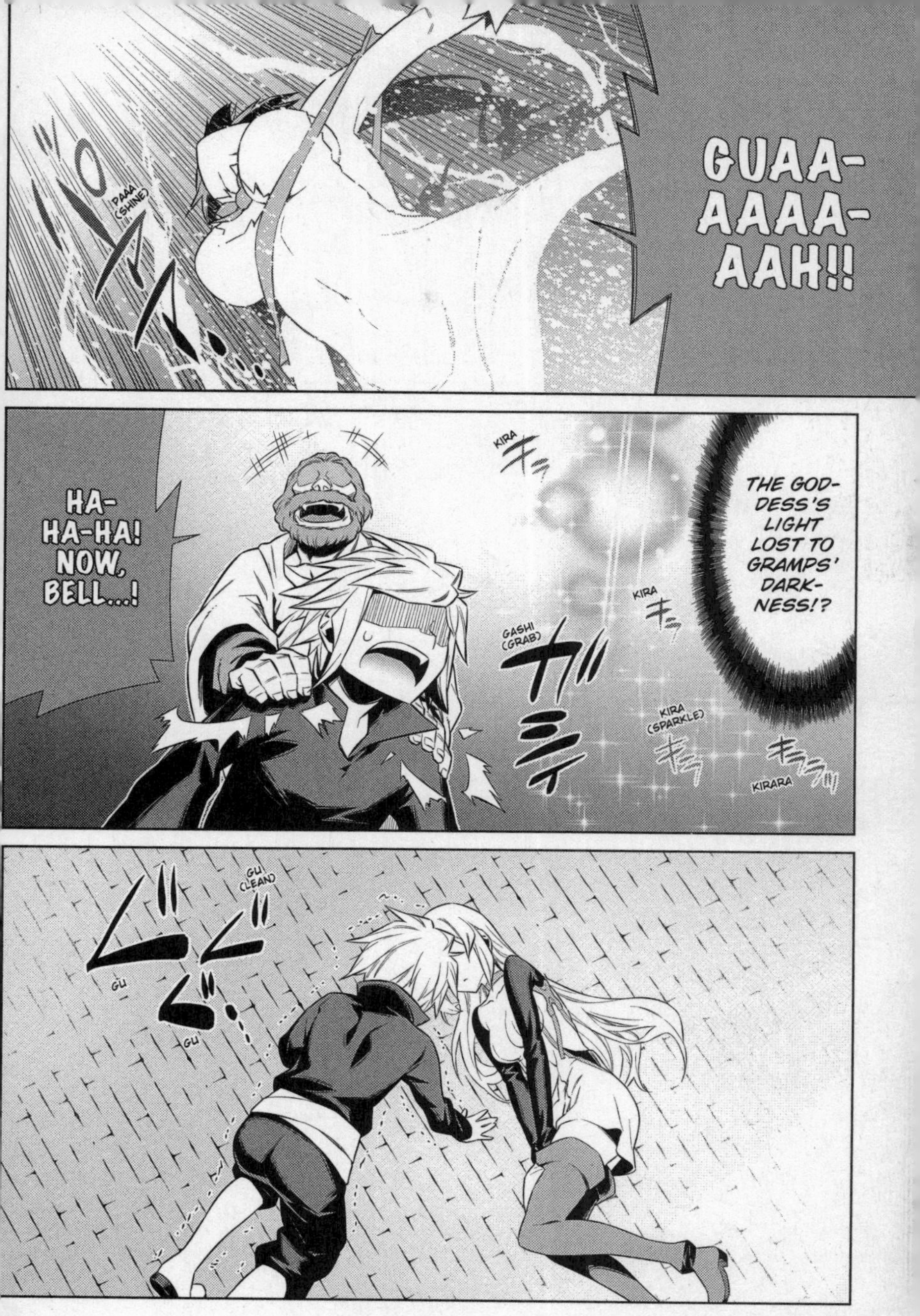
GUAA-AAAA-AAH!!
PAAA (SHINE)
THE GOD-DESS'S LIGHT LOST TO GRAMPS' DARK-NESS!?
KIRA
KIRA
GASHI (GRAB)
KIRA (SPARKLE)
KIRARA
HA-HA-HA! NOW, BELL...!
GU (LEAN)
GU
GU

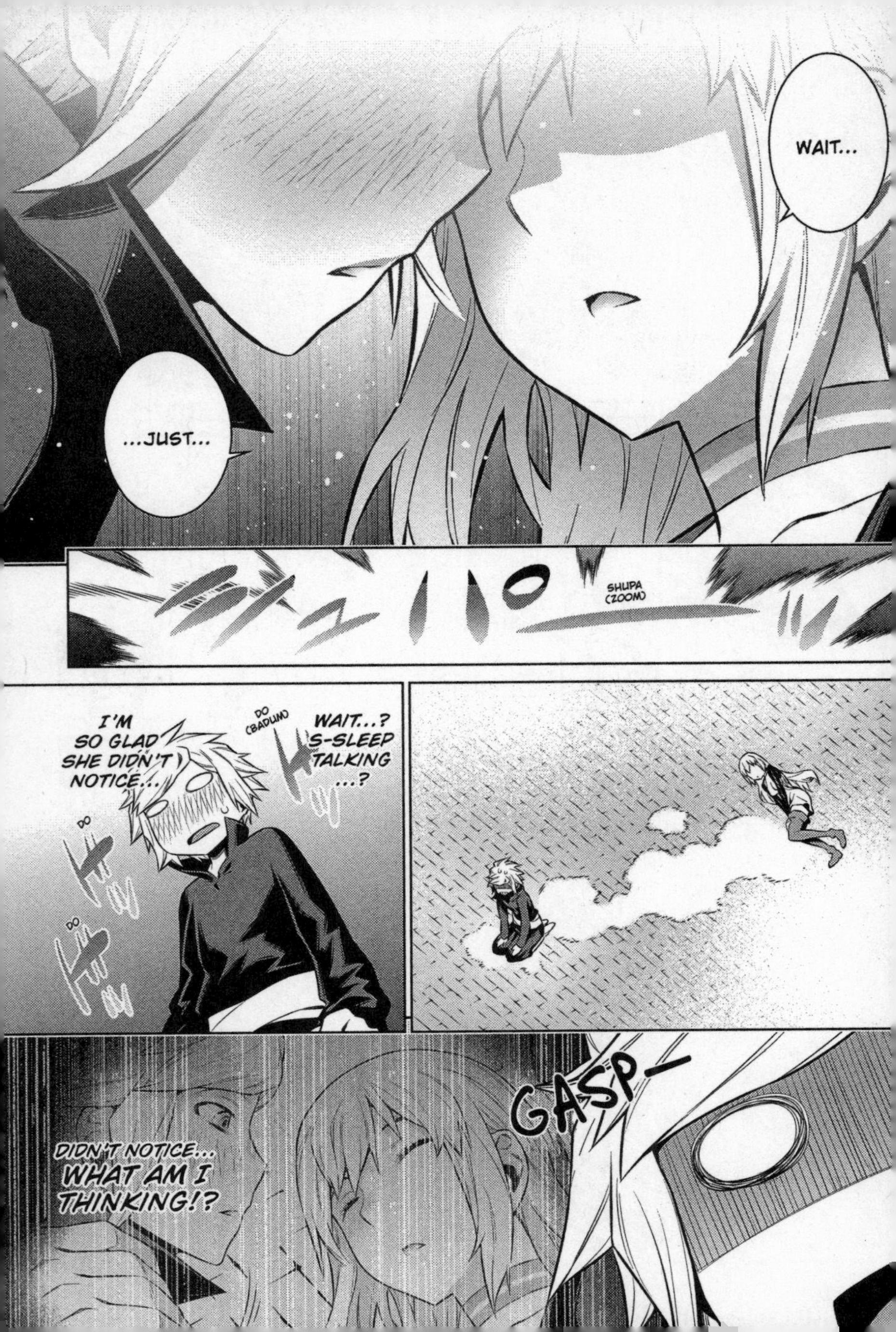
WAIT...
...JUST...
SHUPA (ZOOM)
WAIT...? S-SLEEP TALKING ...?
DO (BADUM)
I'M SO GLAD SHE DIDN'T NOTICE...
DO
DO
GASP—
DIDN'T NOTICE... WHAT AM I THINKING!?

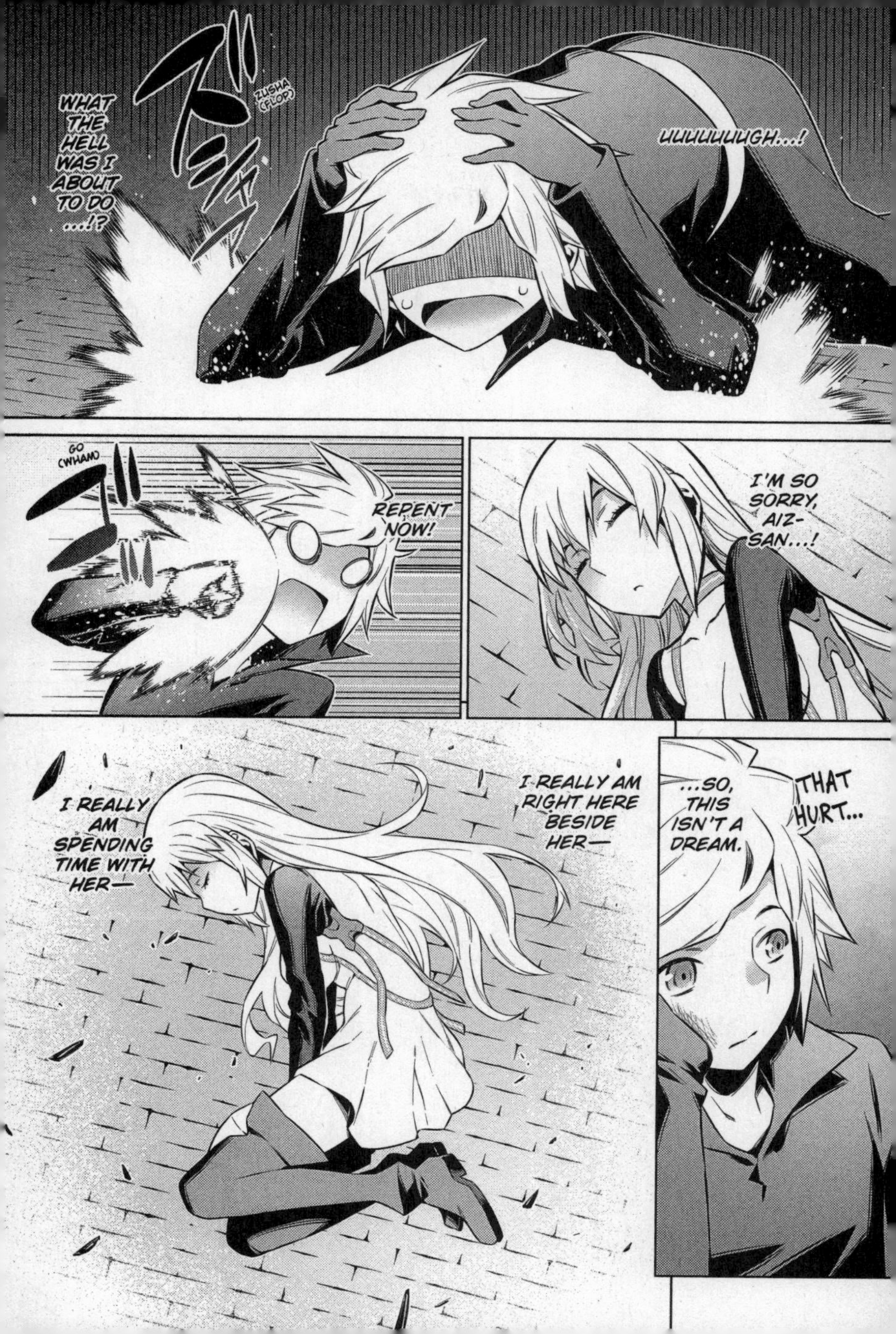
UUUUUUUGH...!
ZUSHA (FLOP)
WHAT THE HELL WAS I ABOUT TO DO...!?
I'M SO SORRY, AIZ-SAN...!
GO (WHAM)
REPENT NOW!
THAT HURT...
...SO, THIS ISN'T A DREAM.
I REALLY AM RIGHT HERE BESIDE HER—
I REALLY AM SPENDING TIME WITH HER—

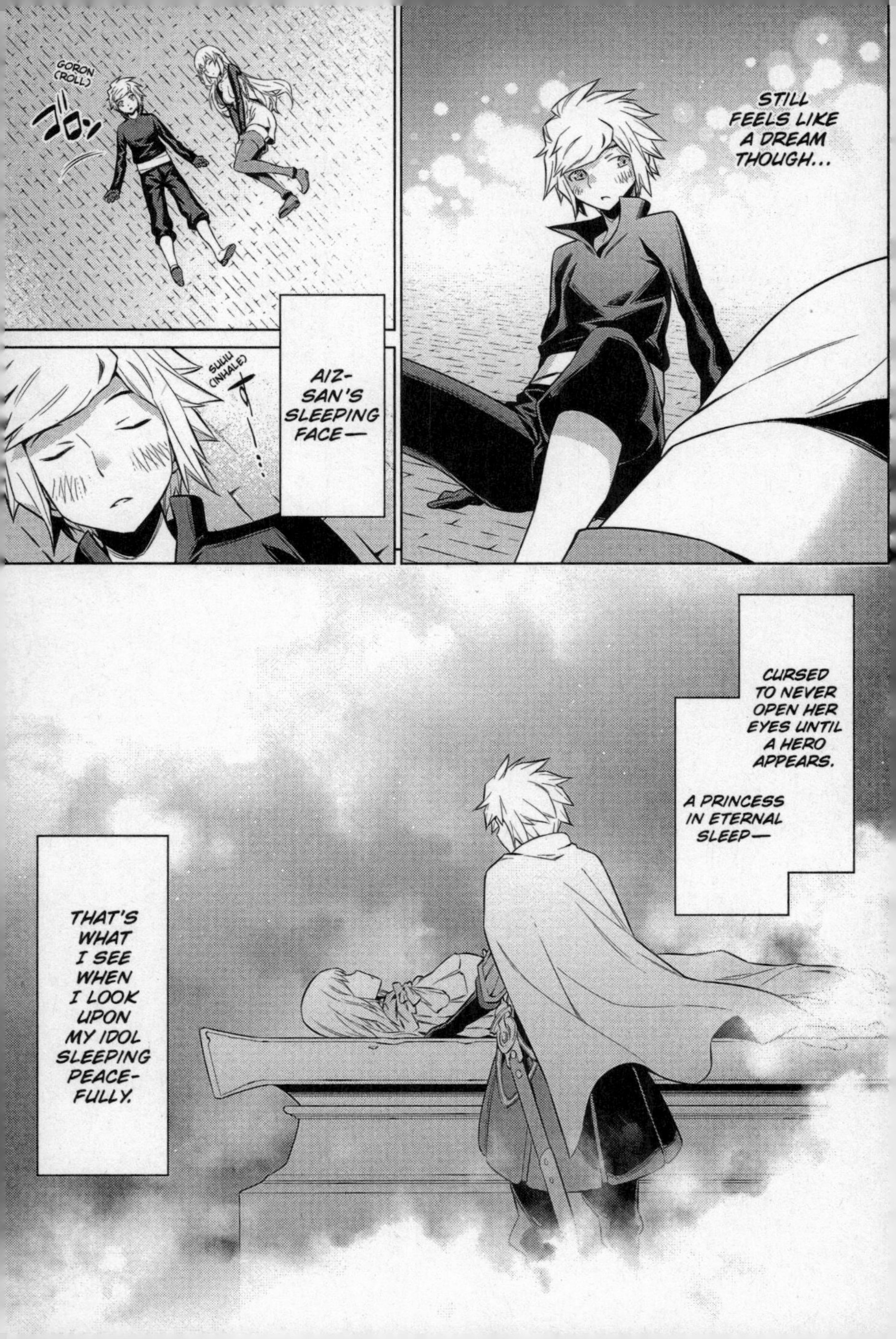

STILL FEELS LIKE A DREAM THOUGH...
GORON (ROLL)
AIZ-SAN'S SLEEPING FACE—
SUUU (INHALE)
CURSED TO NEVER OPEN HER EYES UNTIL A HERO APPEARS.
A PRINCESS IN ETERNAL SLEEP—
THAT'S WHAT I SEE WHEN I LOOK UPON MY IDOL SLEEPING PEACE-FULLY.

Is it WRONG to TRY to PICK UP GIRLS IN A DUNGEON?

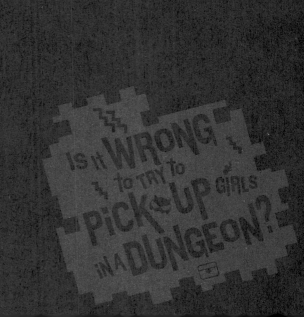

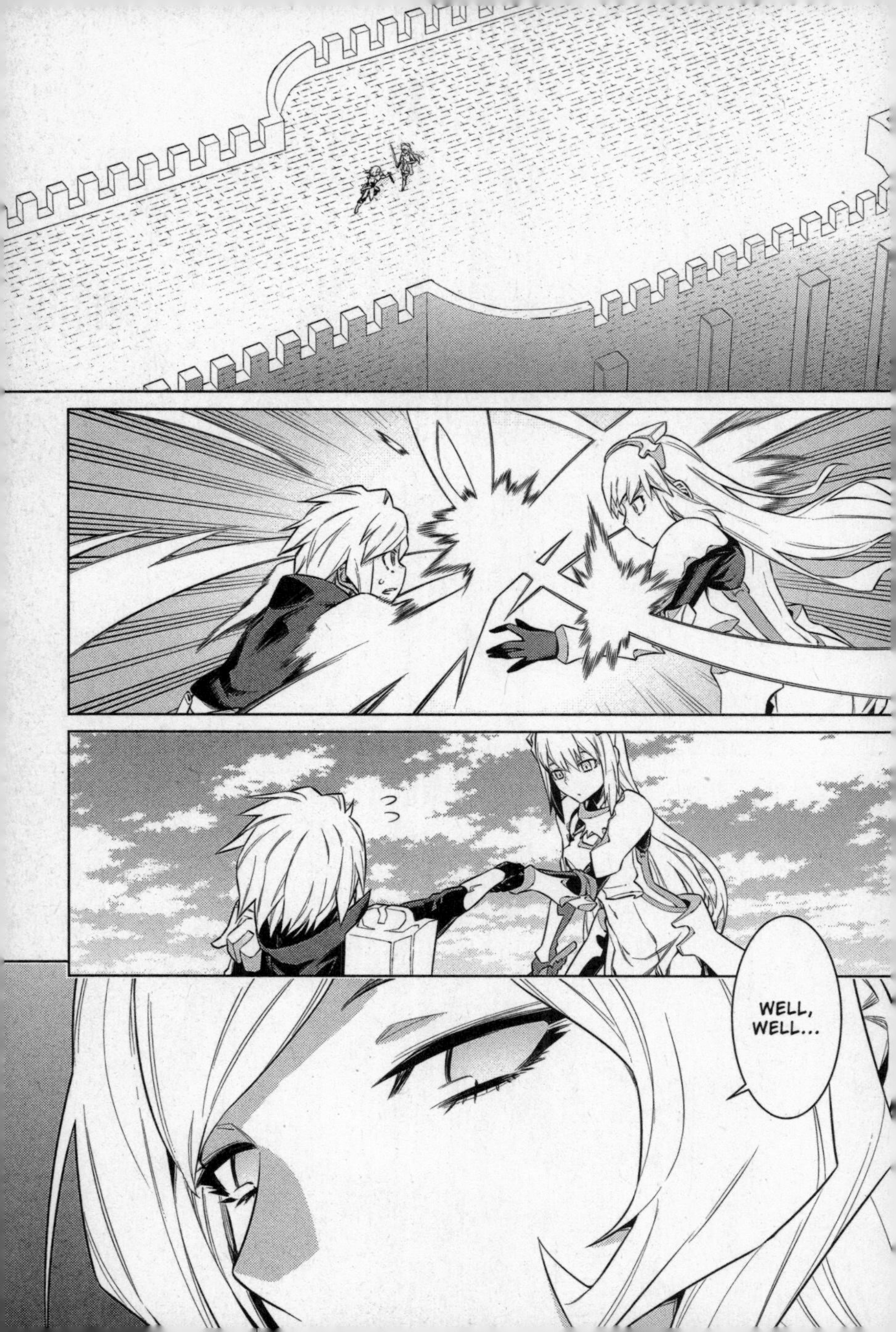
WELL, WELL...

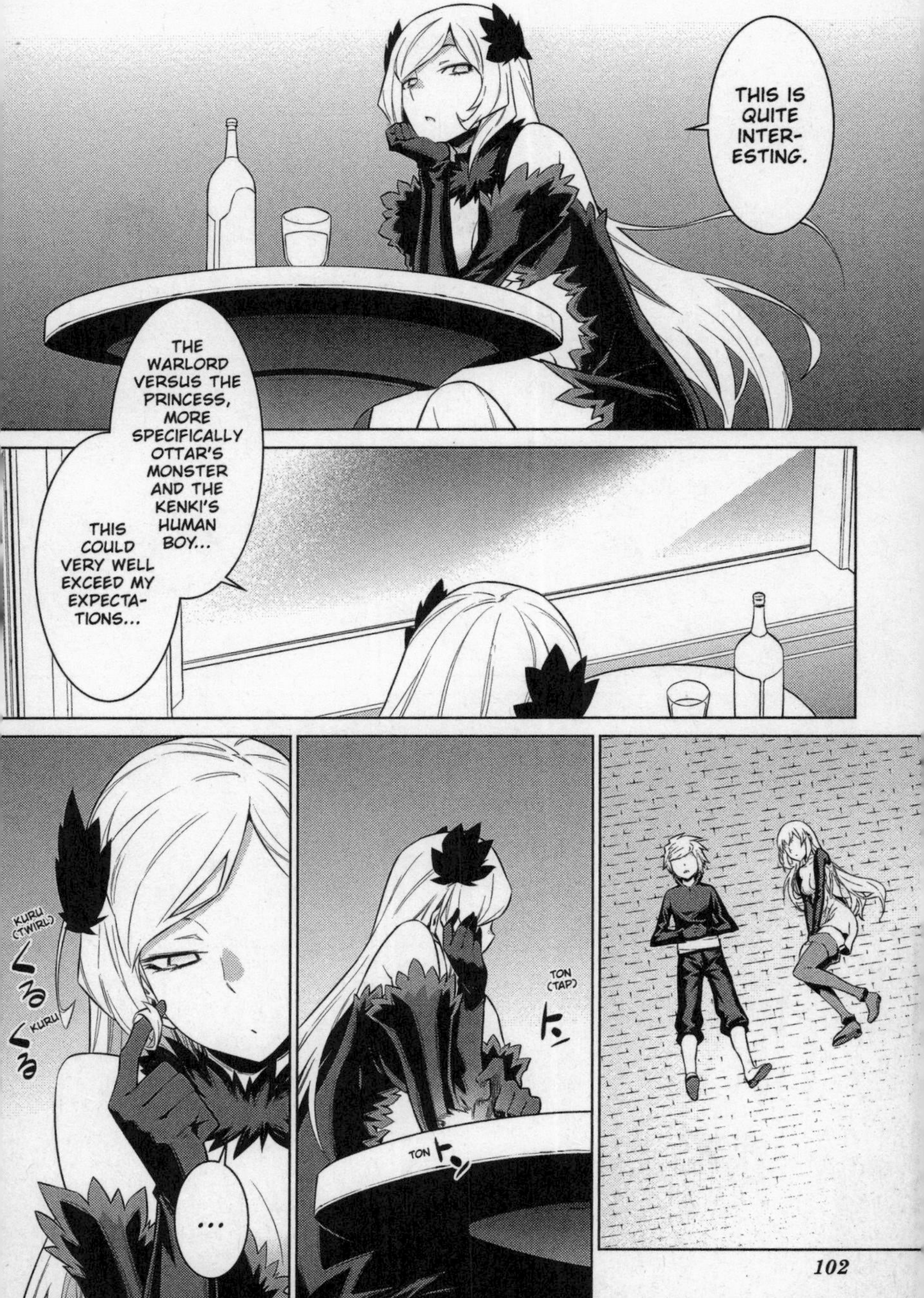
THIS IS QUITE INTER-ESTING.
THE WARLORD VERSUS THE PRINCESS, MORE SPECIFICALLY OTTAR'S MONSTER AND THE KENKI'S HUMAN BOY...
THIS COULD VERY WELL EXCEED MY EXPECTA-TIONS...
TON (TAP)
トン
TON
トン
KURU (TWIRL)
くる
KURU
くる
...

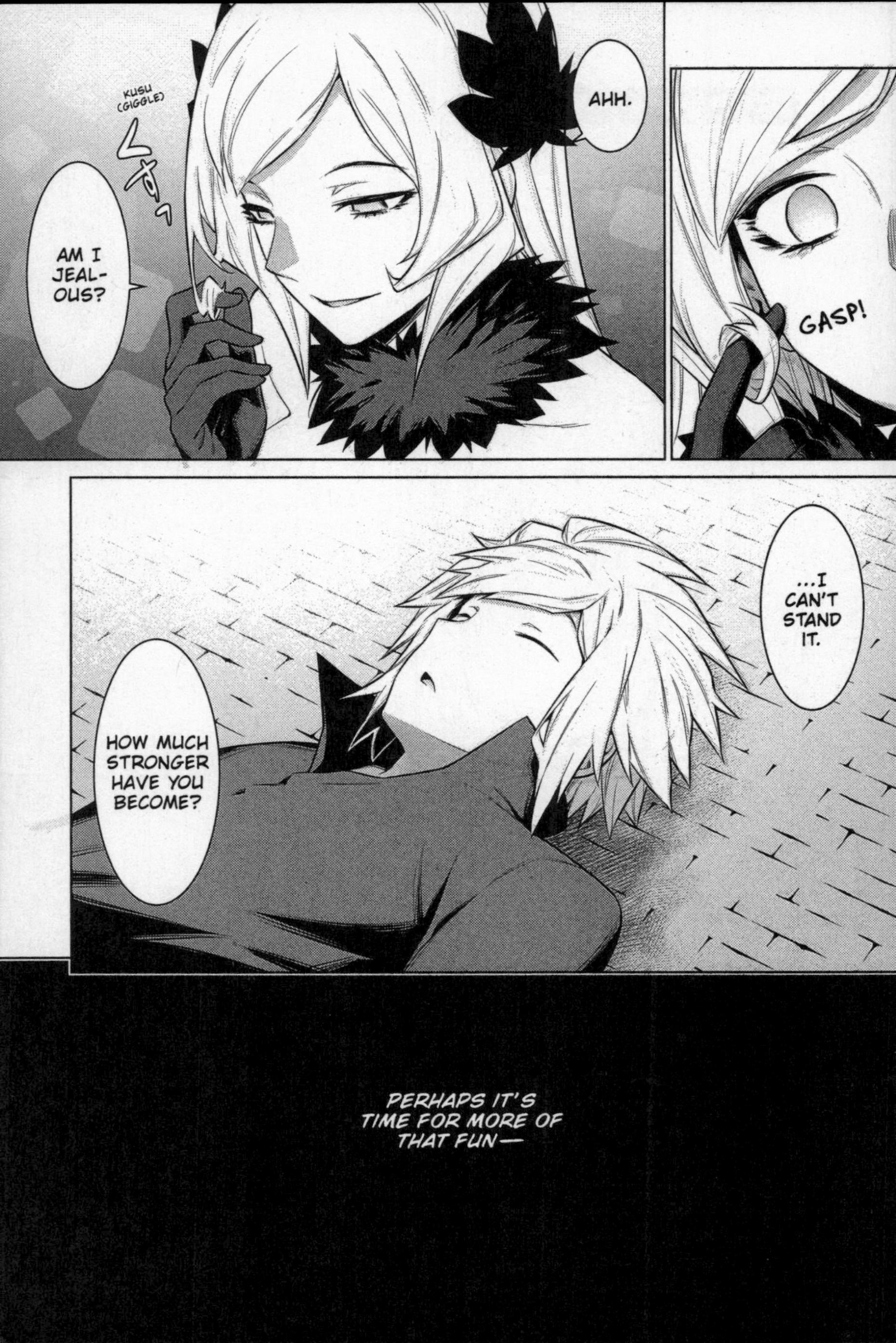
GASP!
AHH.
KUSU (GIGGLE)
AM I JEAL-OUS?
...I CAN'T STAND IT.
HOW MUCH STRONGER HAVE YOU BECOME?
PERHAPS IT'S TIME FOR MORE OF THAT FUN—

STEP 36 ▸▸ ASSAULT

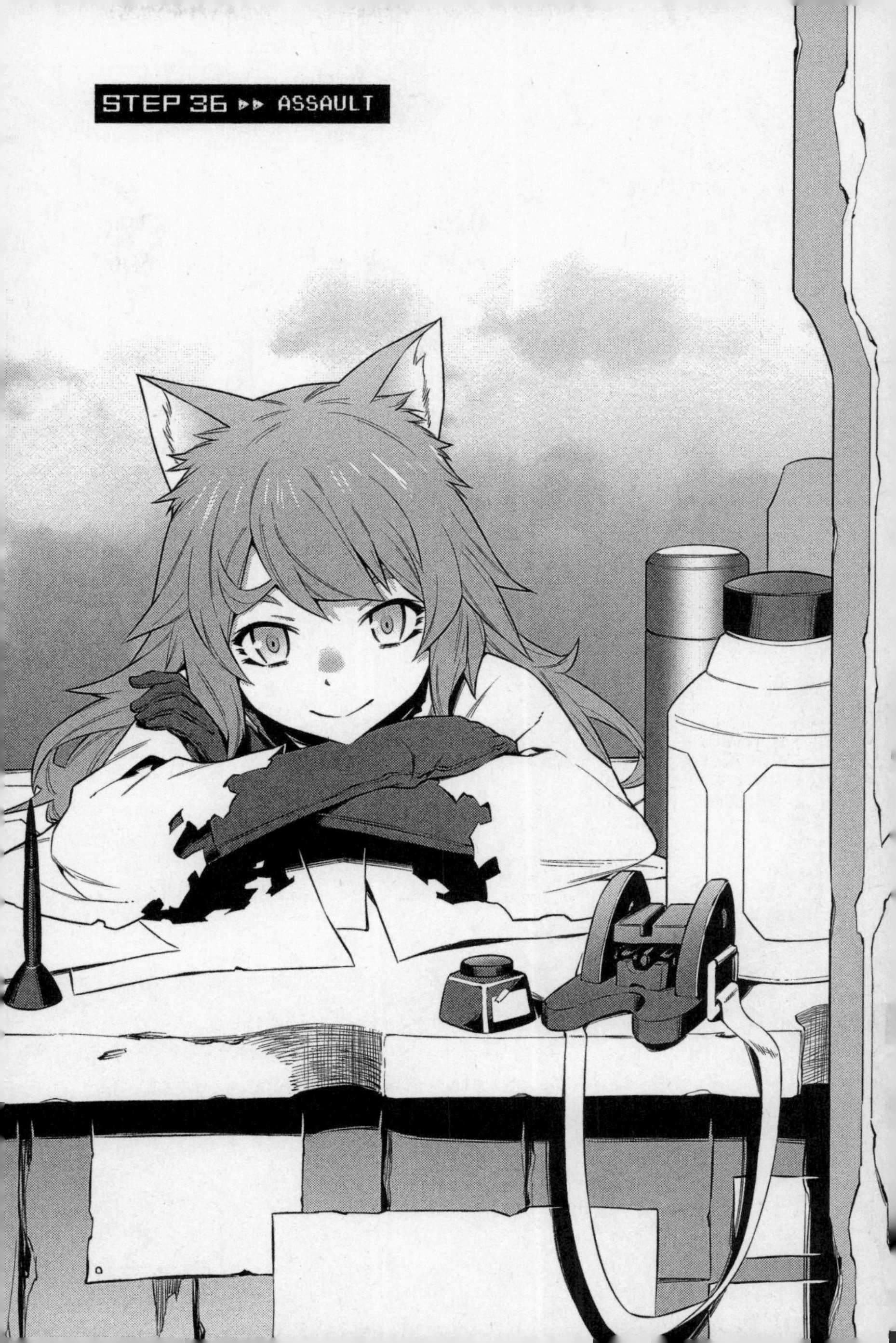

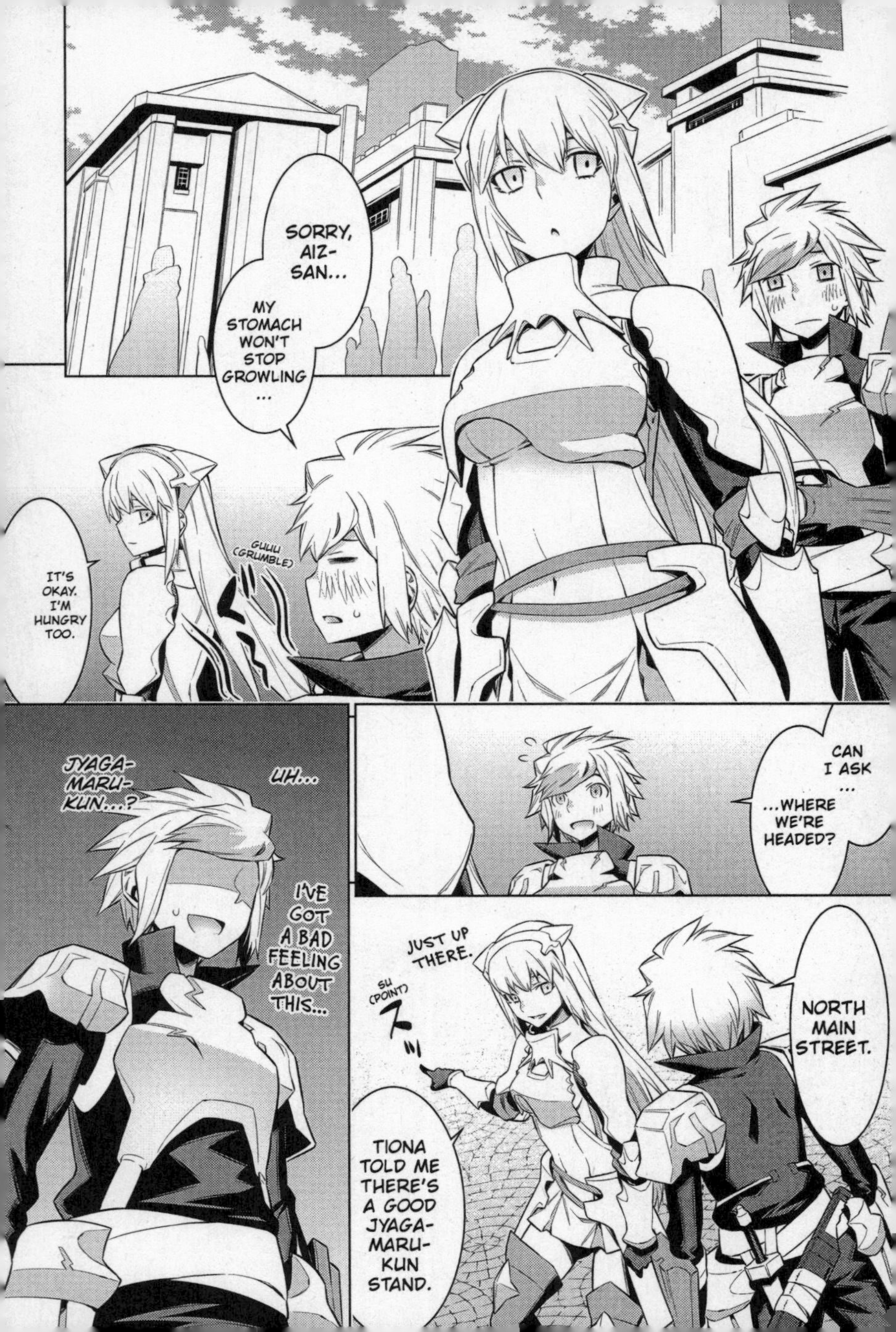

SORRY, AIZ-SAN... MY STOMACH WON'T STOP GROWLING...
GUUU (GRUMBLE)
IT'S OKAY. I'M HUNGRY TOO.
CAN I ASK ... ...WHERE WE'RE HEADED?
NORTH MAIN STREET.
JUST UP THERE.
SU (POINT)
TIONA TOLD ME THERE'S A GOOD JYAGA-MARU-KUN STAND.
JYAGA-MARU-KUN...?
UH...
I'VE GOT A BAD FEELING ABOUT THIS...

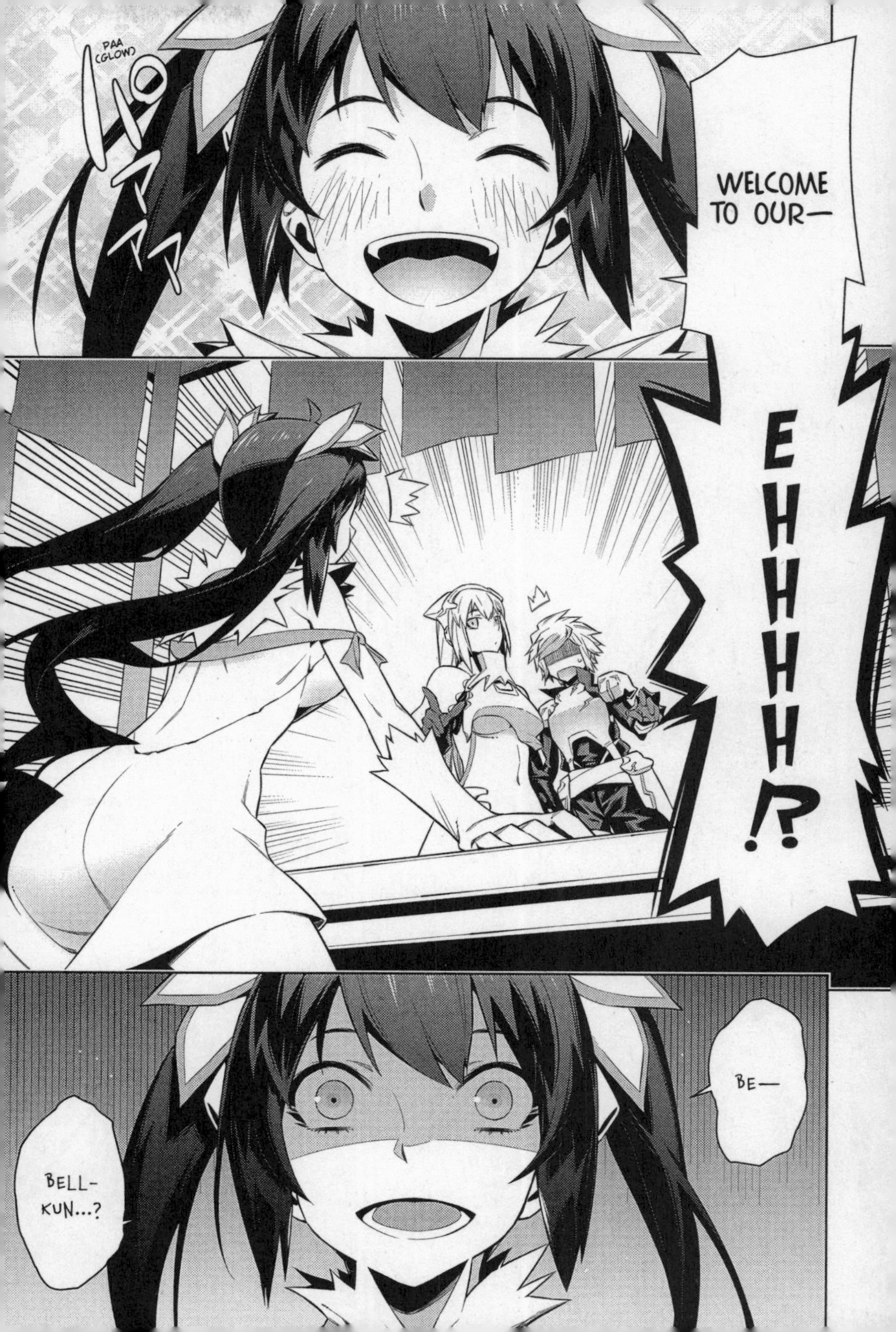
WELCOME TO OUR—
PAA (GLOW)
EHHHH!?
BE—
BELL-KUN...?

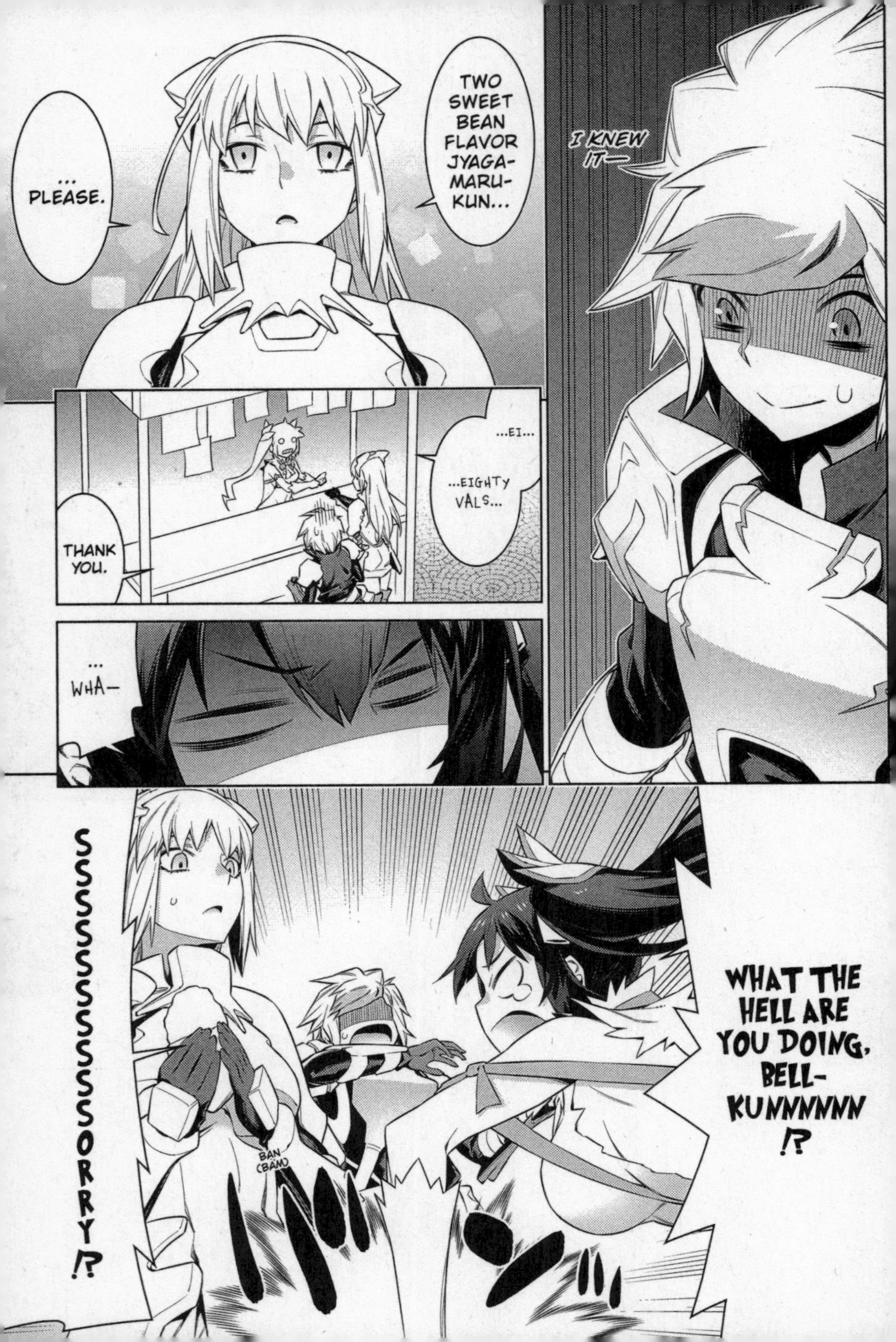
I KNEW IT—
TWO SWEET BEAN FLAVOR JYAGA-MARU-KUN...
...PLEASE.
...EI...
...EIGHTY VALS...
THANK YOU.
... WHA—
WHAT THE HELL ARE YOU DOING, BELL-KUNNNNNN!?
BAN (BAM)
SSSSSSSSSSSSSORRY!?

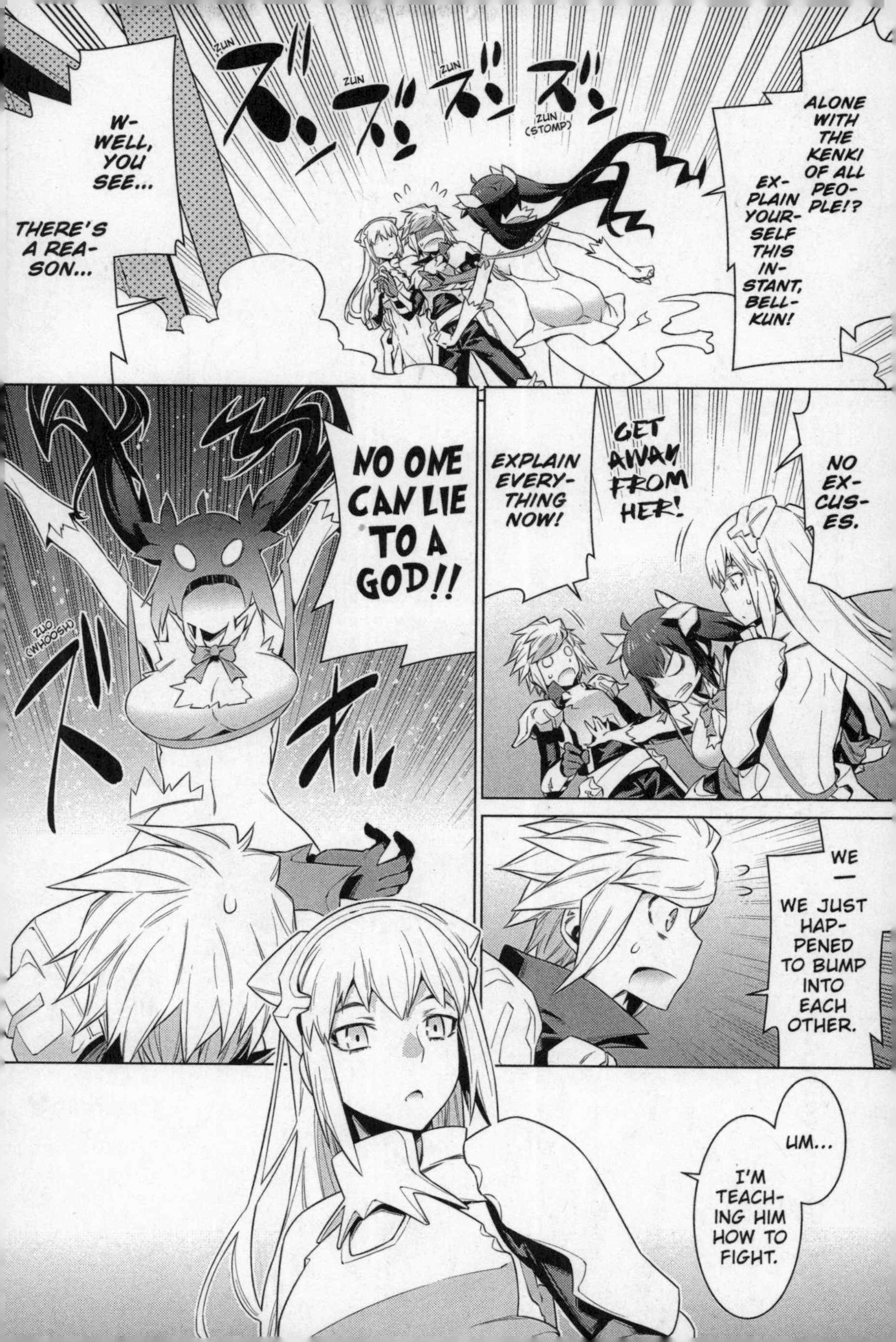
ALONE WITH THE KENKI OF ALL PEOPLE!?
EXPLAIN YOURSELF THIS INSTANT, BELL-KUN!
ZUN ZUN ZUN ZUN (STOMP)
W-WELL, YOU SEE...
THERE'S A REASON...
NO EXCUSES.
GET AWAY FROM HER!
EXPLAIN EVERYTHING NOW!
NO ONE CAN LIE TO A GOD!!
ZUO (WHOOSH)
WE—
WE JUST HAPPENED TO BUMP INTO EACH OTHER.
UM...
I'M TEACHING HIM HOW TO FIGHT.

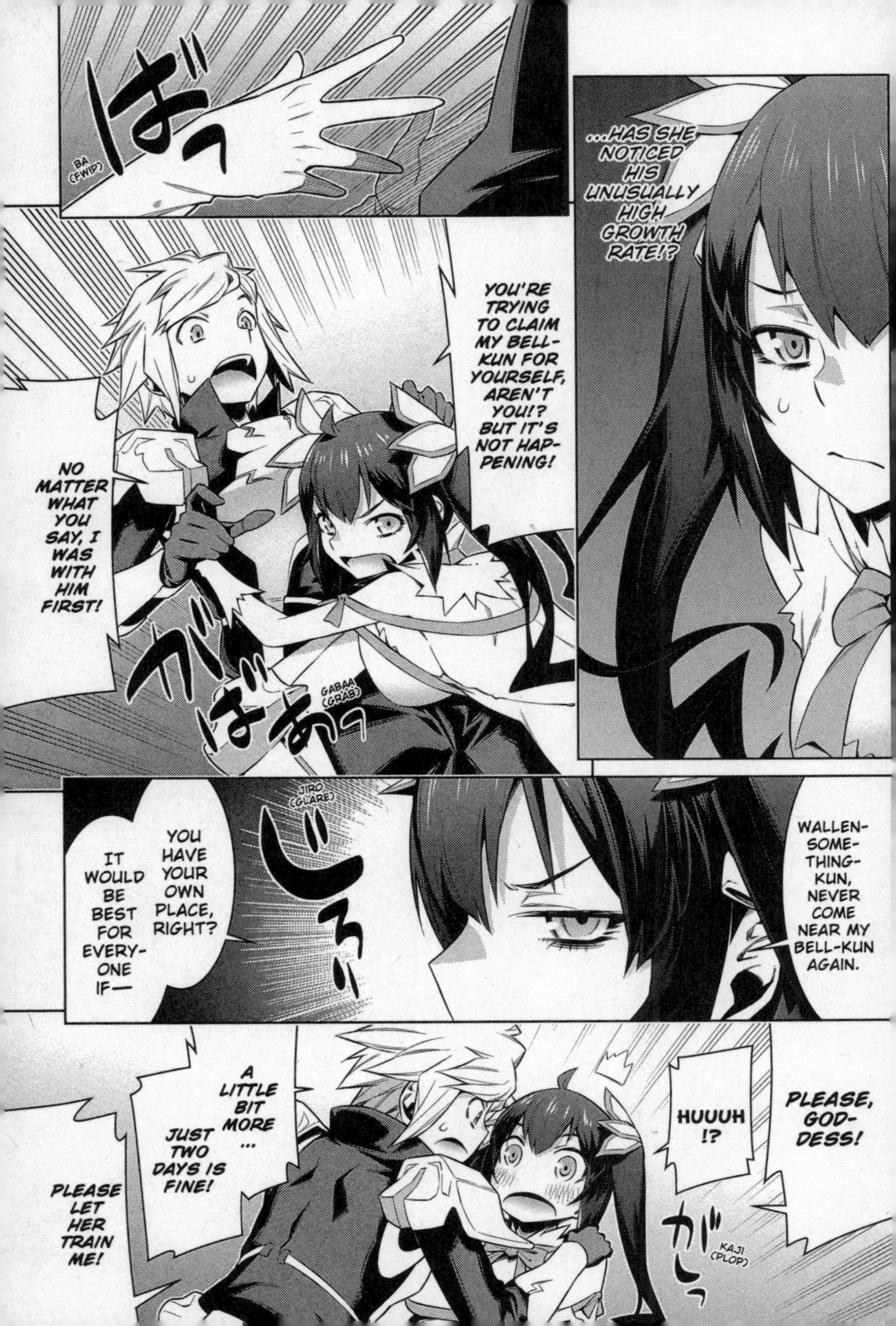
BA (FWIP)
...HAS SHE NOTICED HIS UNUSUALLY HIGH GROWTH RATE!?
YOU'RE TRYING TO CLAIM MY BELL-KUN FOR YOURSELF, AREN'T YOU!? BUT IT'S NOT HAPPENING!
NO MATTER WHAT YOU SAY, I WAS WITH HIM FIRST!
GABAA (GRAB)
WALLEN-SOMETHING-KUN, NEVER COME NEAR MY BELL-KUN AGAIN.
JIRO (GLARE)
YOU HAVE YOUR OWN PLACE, RIGHT?
IT WOULD BE BEST FOR EVERYONE IF—
PLEASE, GODDESS!
HUUUH!?
KAJI (PLOP)
A LITTLE BIT MORE...
JUST TWO DAYS IS FINE!
PLEASE LET HER TRAIN ME!

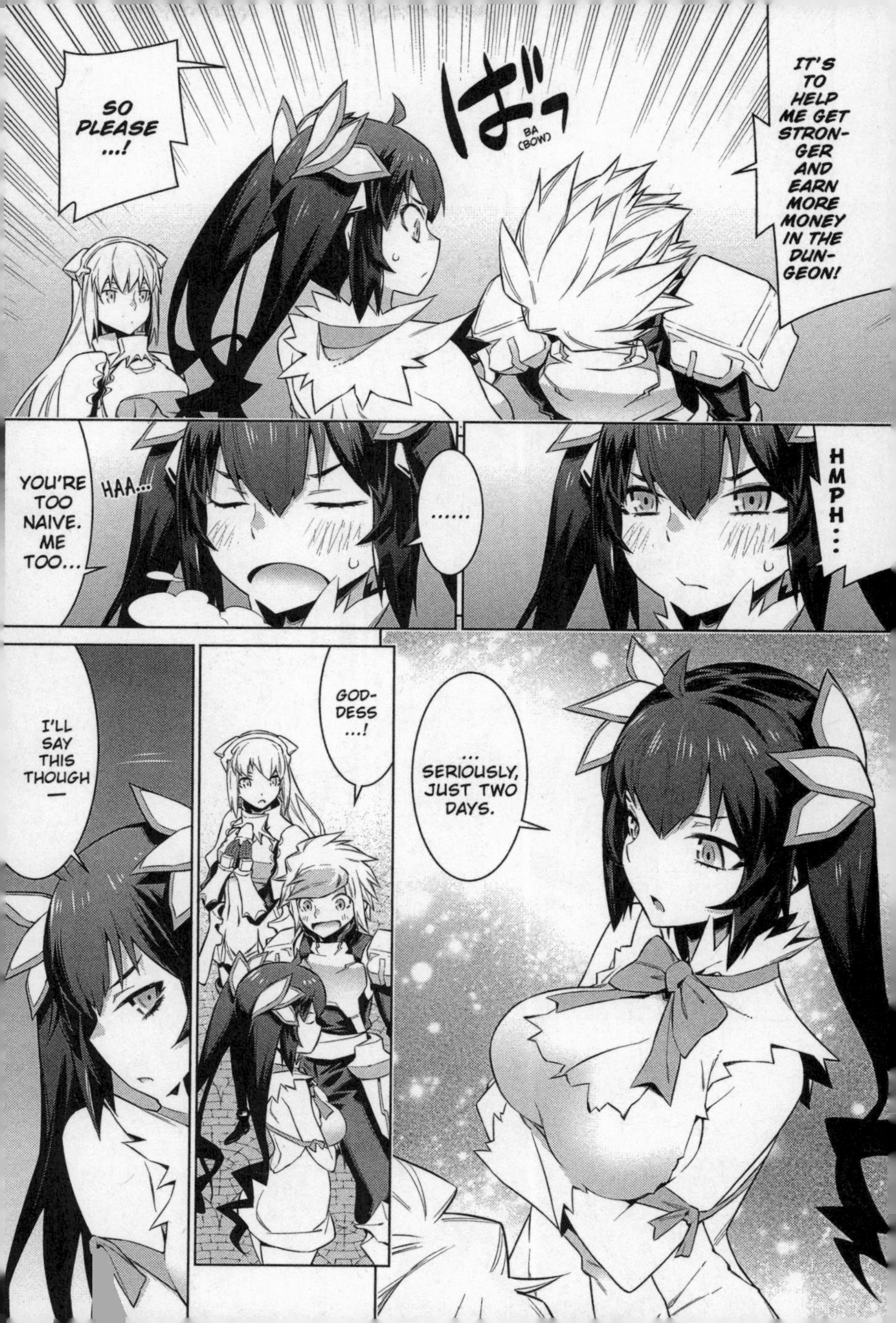
IT'S TO HELP ME GET STRONGER AND EARN MORE MONEY IN THE DUNGEON!
ばっ
BA (BOW)
SO PLEASE ...!
HMPH...
......
HAA...
YOU'RE TOO NAIVE. ME TOO...
... SERIOUSLY, JUST TWO DAYS.
GOD-DESS ...!
I'LL SAY THIS THOUGH—

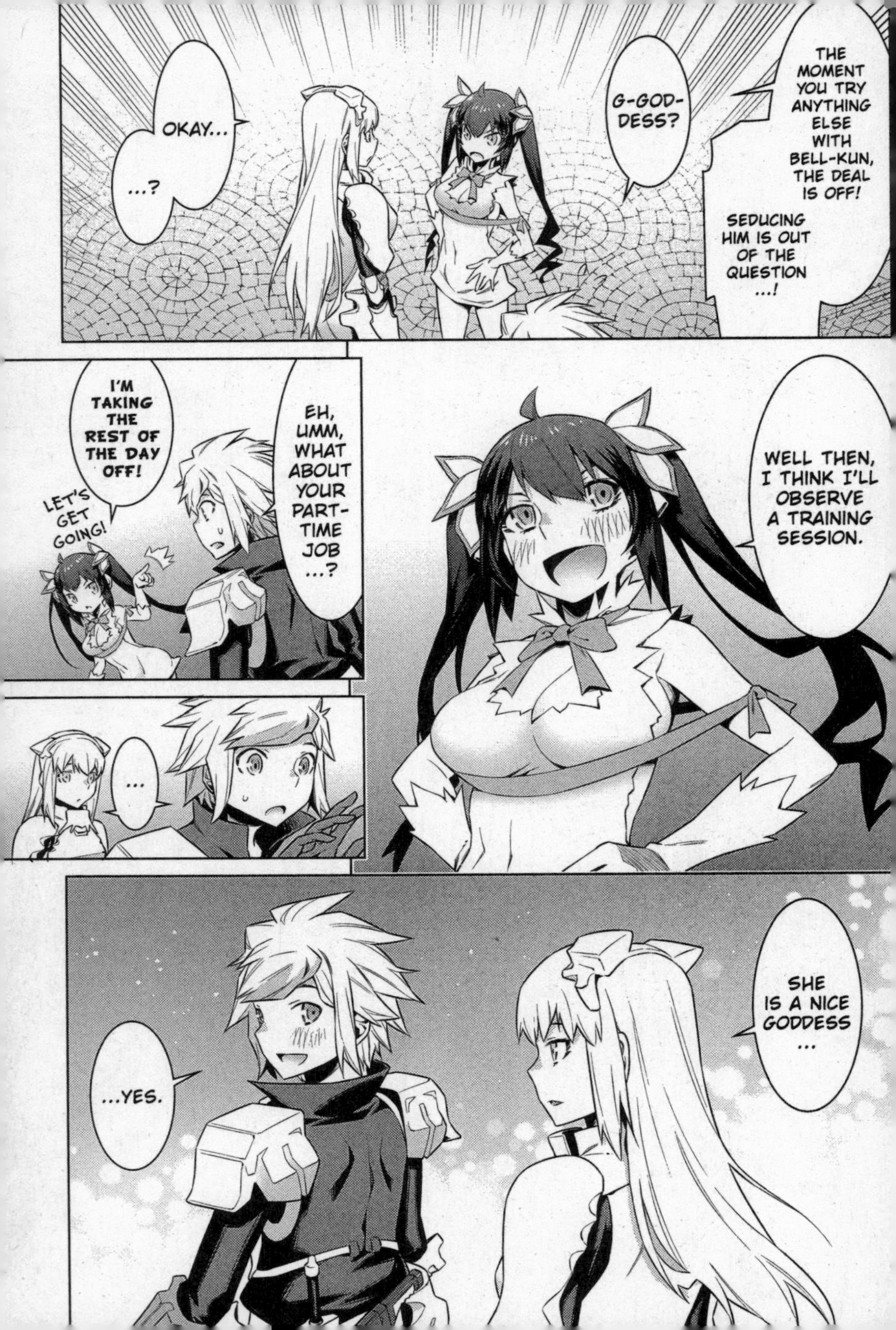
THE MOMENT YOU TRY ANYTHING ELSE WITH BELL-KUN, THE DEAL IS OFF!
SEDUCING HIM IS OUT OF THE QUESTION ...!
G-GOD-DESS?
OKAY...
...?
WELL THEN, I THINK I'LL OBSERVE A TRAINING SESSION.
EH, UMM, WHAT ABOUT YOUR PART-TIME JOB ...?
I'M TAKING THE REST OF THE DAY OFF!
LET'S GET GOING!
...
SHE IS A NICE GODDESS ...
...YES.

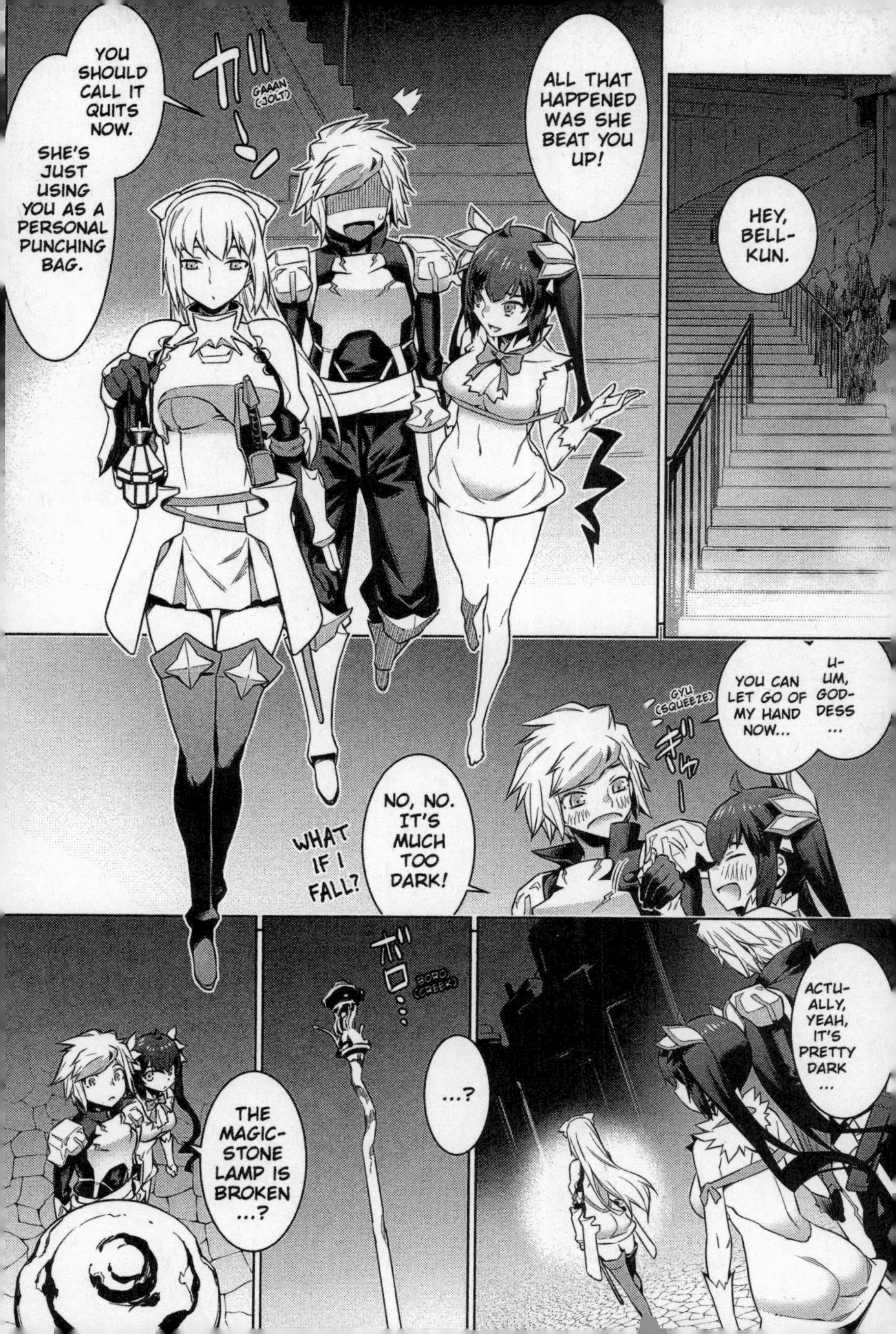
HEY, BELL-KUN.
U-UM, GODDESS...
YOU CAN LET GO OF MY HAND NOW...
GYU (SQUEEZE)
NO, NO. IT'S MUCH TOO DARK!
WHAT IF I FALL?
ALL THAT HAPPENED WAS SHE BEAT YOU UP!
GAAAN (JOLT)
YOU SHOULD CALL IT QUITS NOW.
SHE'S JUST USING YOU AS A PERSONAL PUNCHING BAG.
ACTUALLY, YEAH, IT'S PRETTY DARK...
BORO (CREEK)
...?
THE MAGIC-STONE LAMP IS BROKEN...?

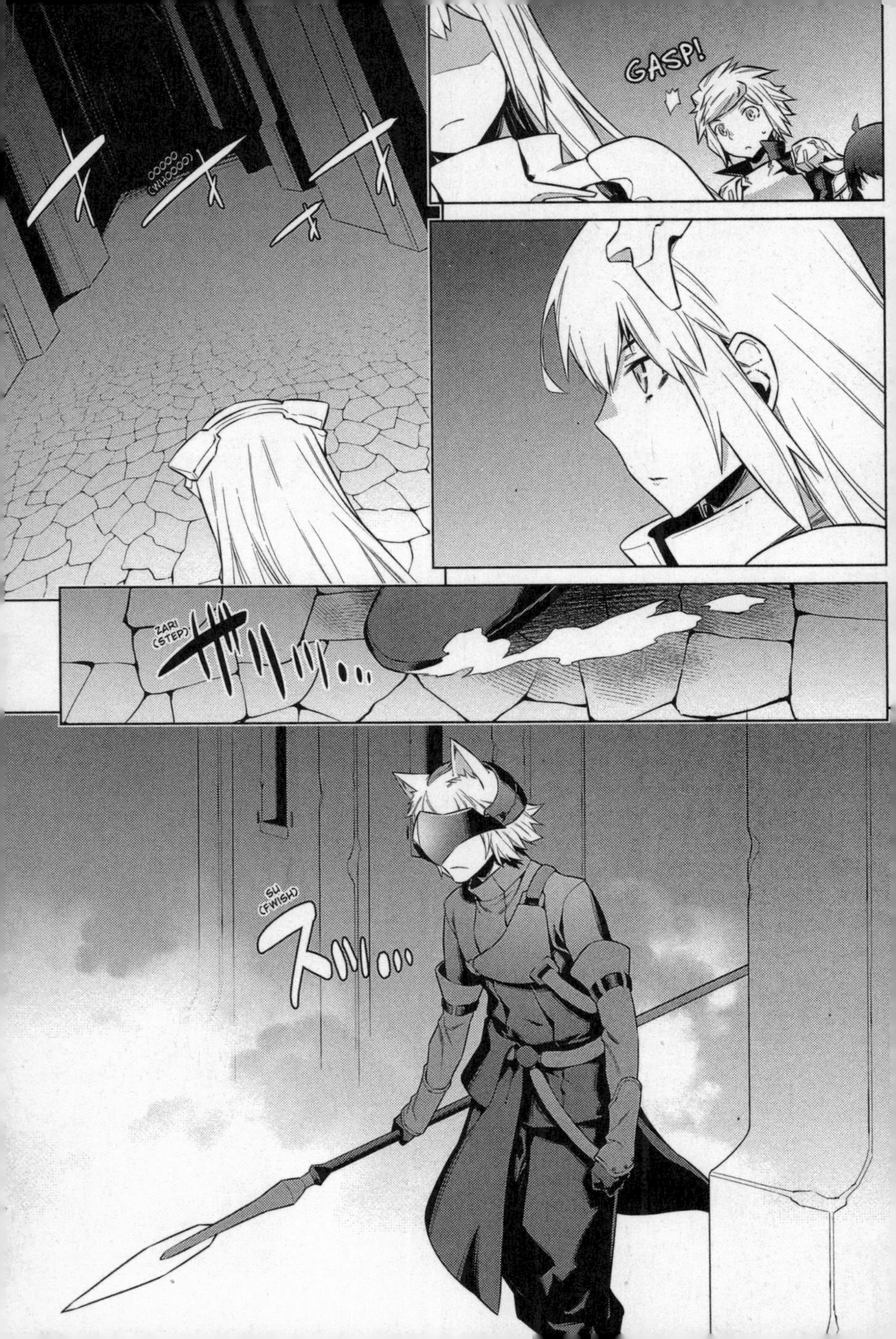
GASP!
OOOOO (WHOOOOO)
ZARI (STEP)
SU (FWISH)

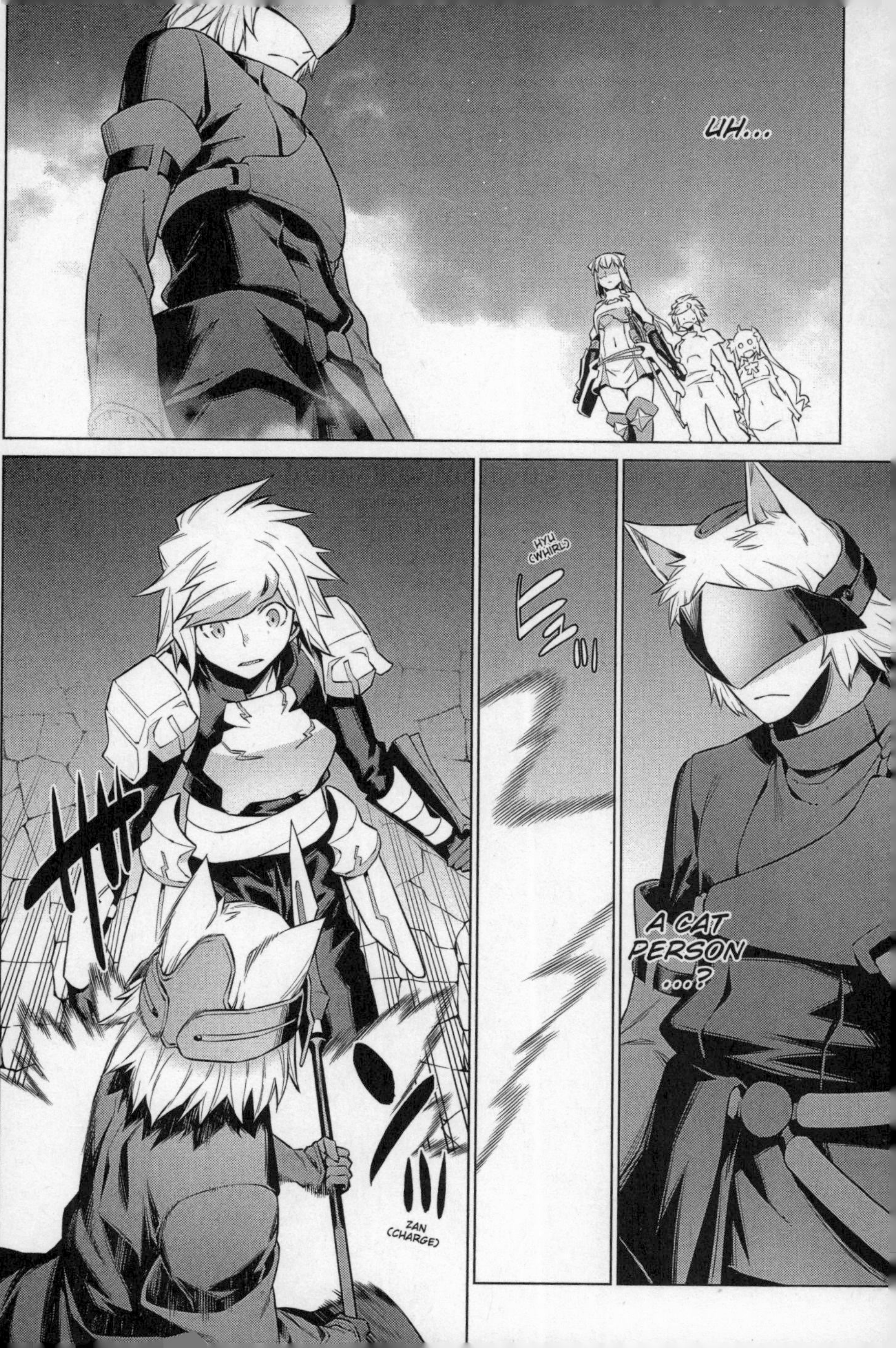
UH...
A CAT PERSON ...?
HYU (WHIRL)
ZAN (CHARGE)

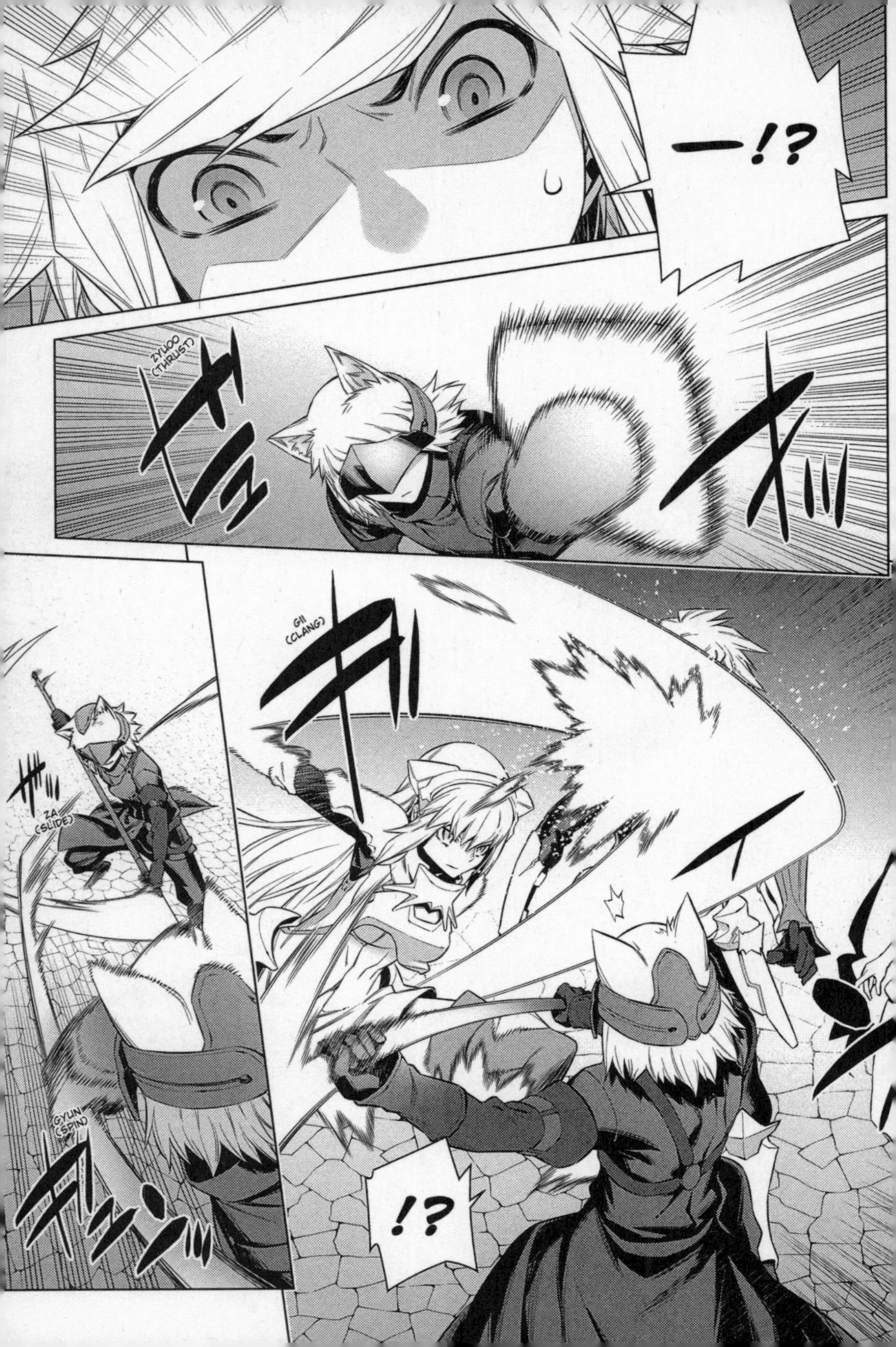
—!?
ZYUOO (THRUST)
GII (CLANG)
!?
ZA (SLIDE)
GYUN (SPIN)

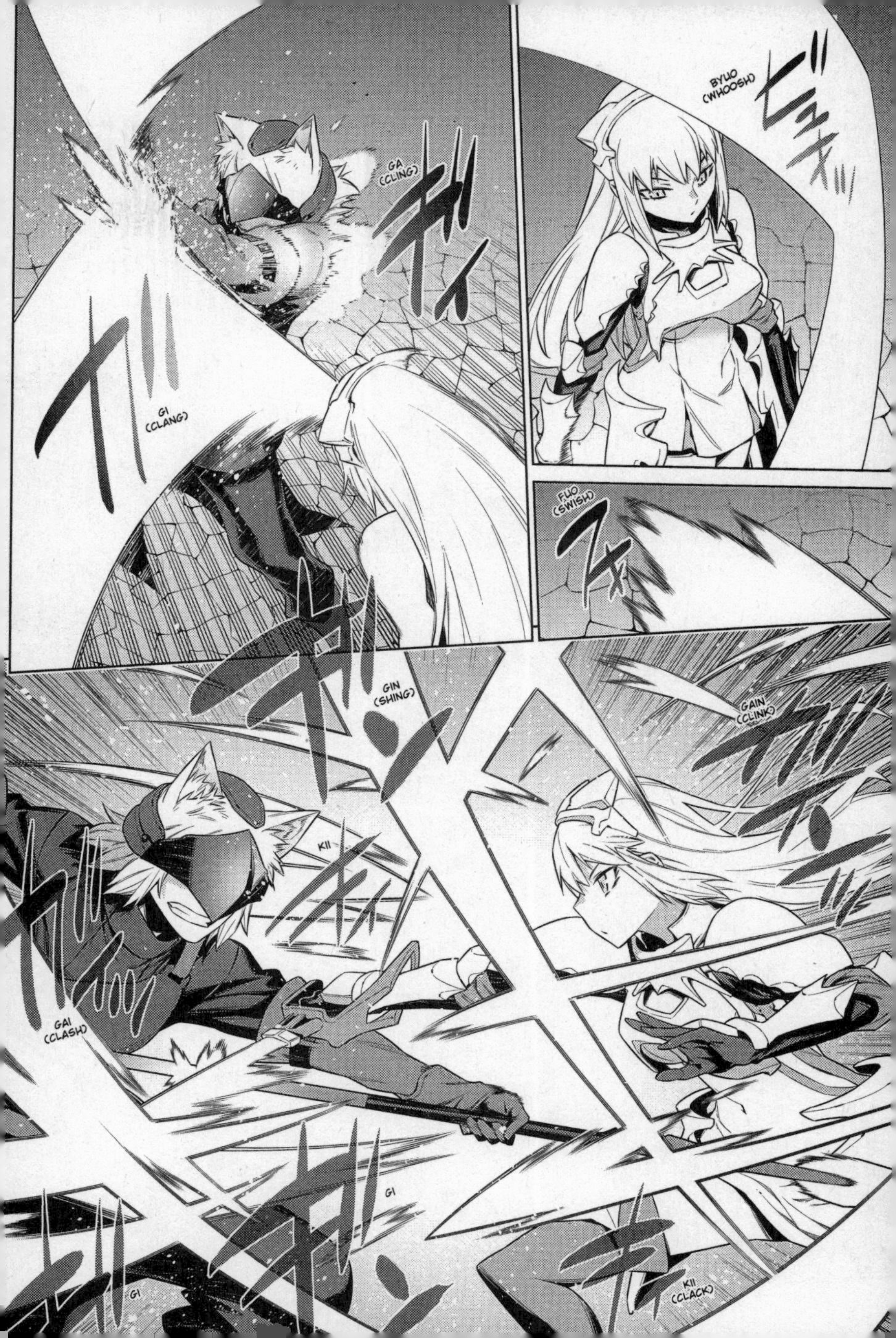
BYUO (WHOOSH)
FUO (SWISH)
GA (CLING)
GI (CLANG)
GAIN (CLINK)
GIN (SHING)
KII
GAI (CLASH)
KII (CLACK)
GI
GI

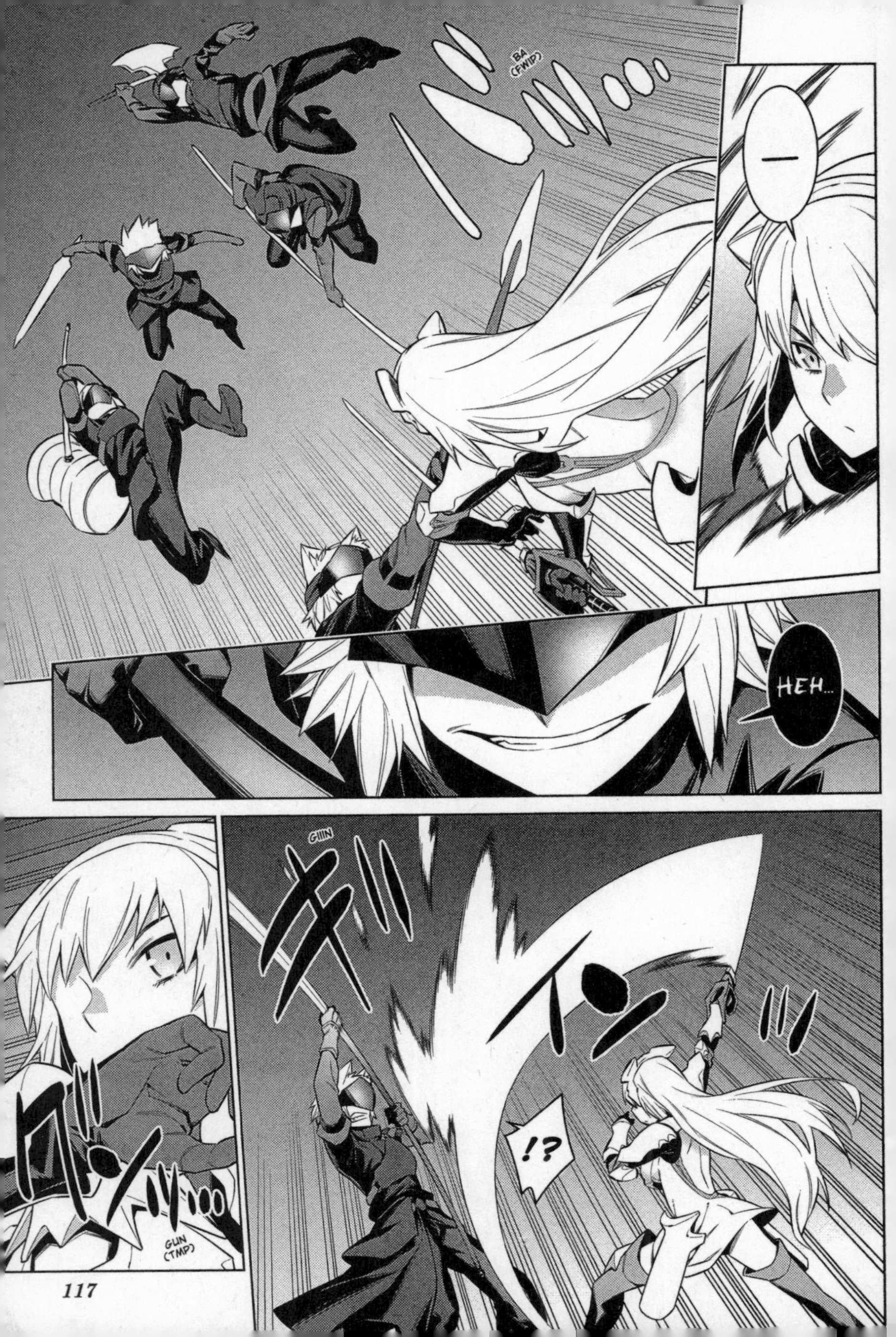
—
BA (FWIP)
HEH...
GIIN
!?
GUN (TMP)

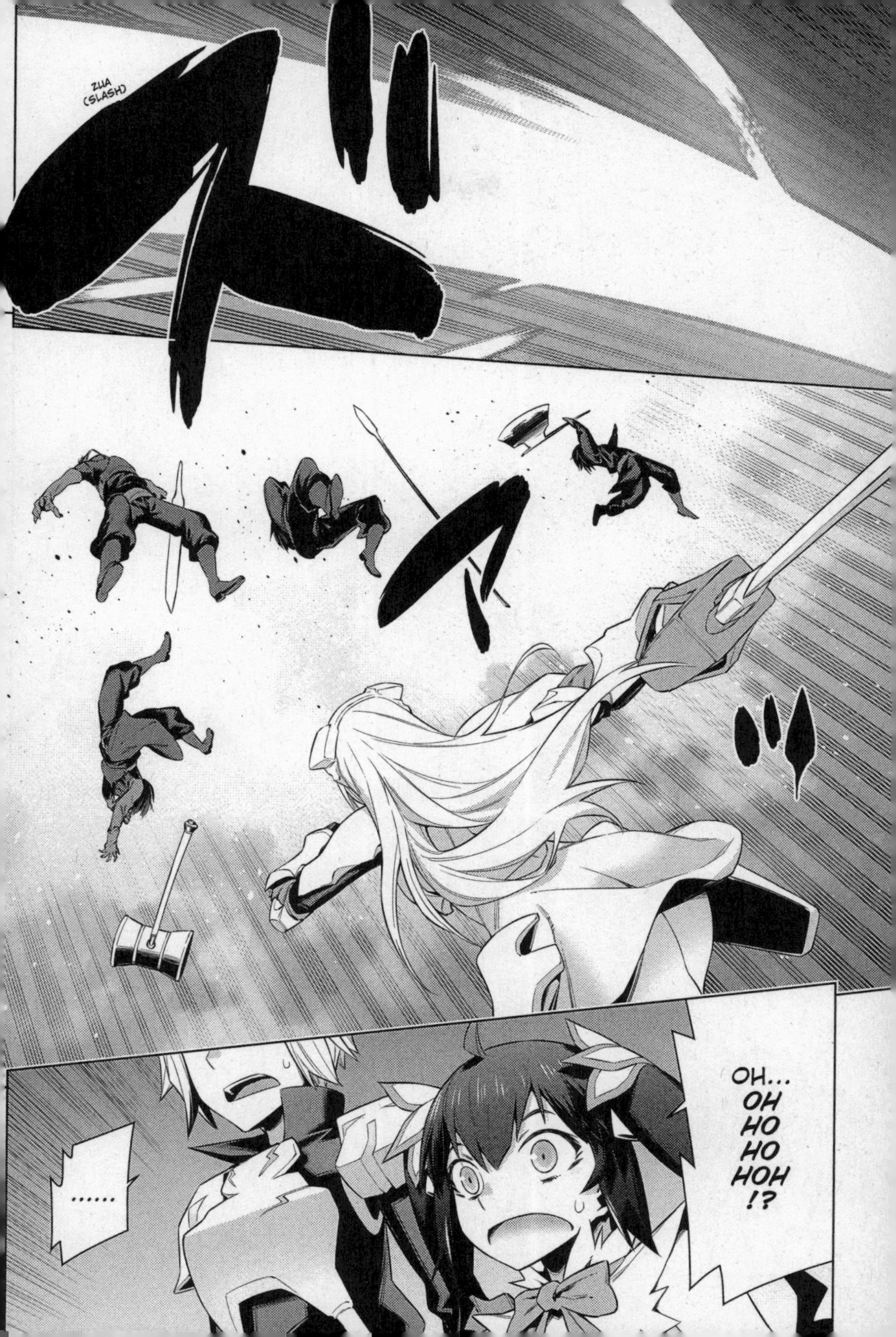
ZUA (SLASH)
OH... OH HO HO HOH!?
......

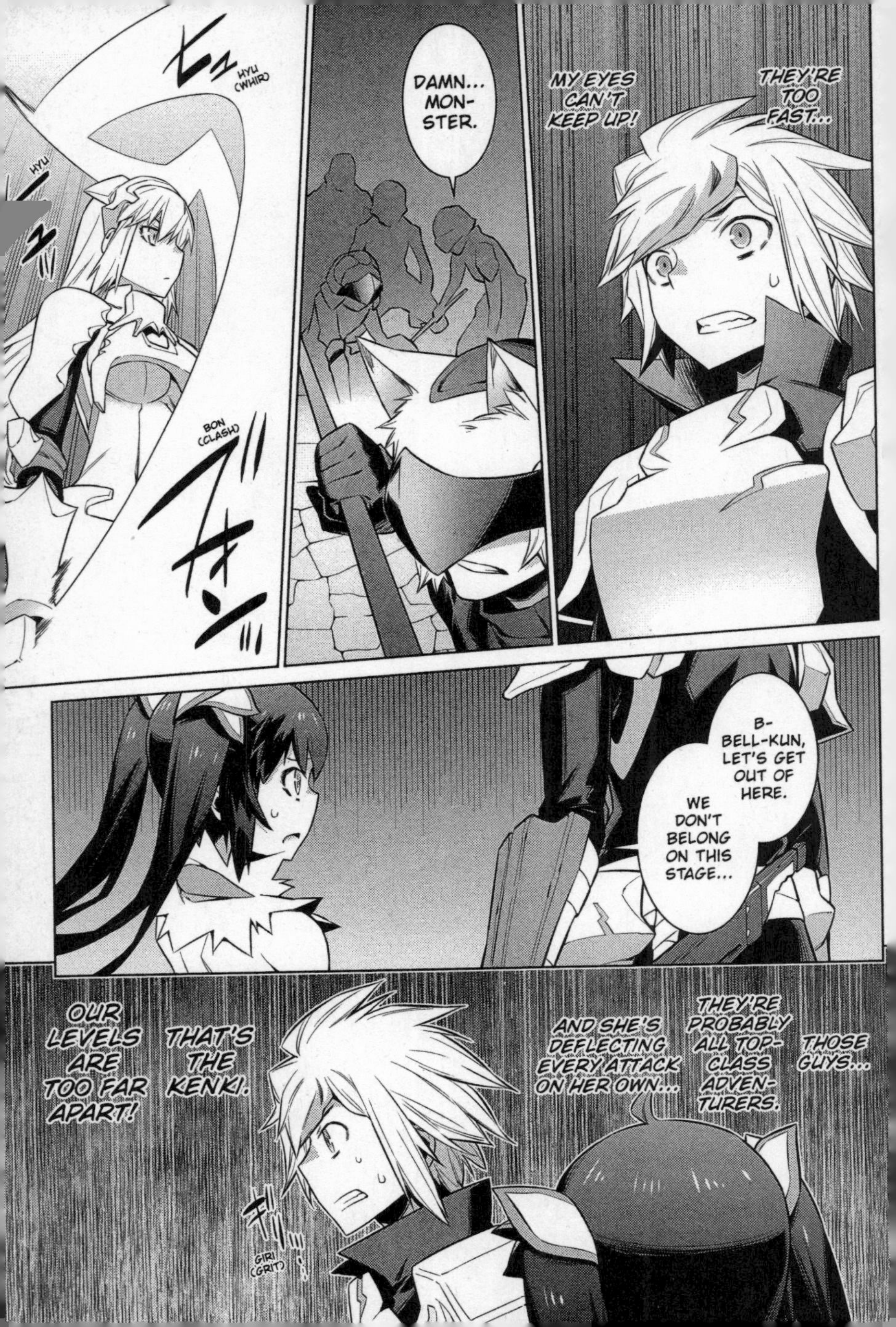
THEY'RE TOO FAST...
MY EYES CAN'T KEEP UP!
DAMN... MON-STER.
HYU (WHIR)
HYU
BON (CLASH)
B-BELL-KUN, LET'S GET OUT OF HERE.
WE DON'T BELONG ON THIS STAGE...
THOSE GUYS...
THEY'RE PROBABLY ALL TOP-CLASS ADVEN-TURERS.
AND SHE'S DEFLECTING EVERY ATTACK ON HER OWN...
THAT'S THE KENKI.
OUR LEVELS ARE TOO FAR APART!
GIRI (GRIT)

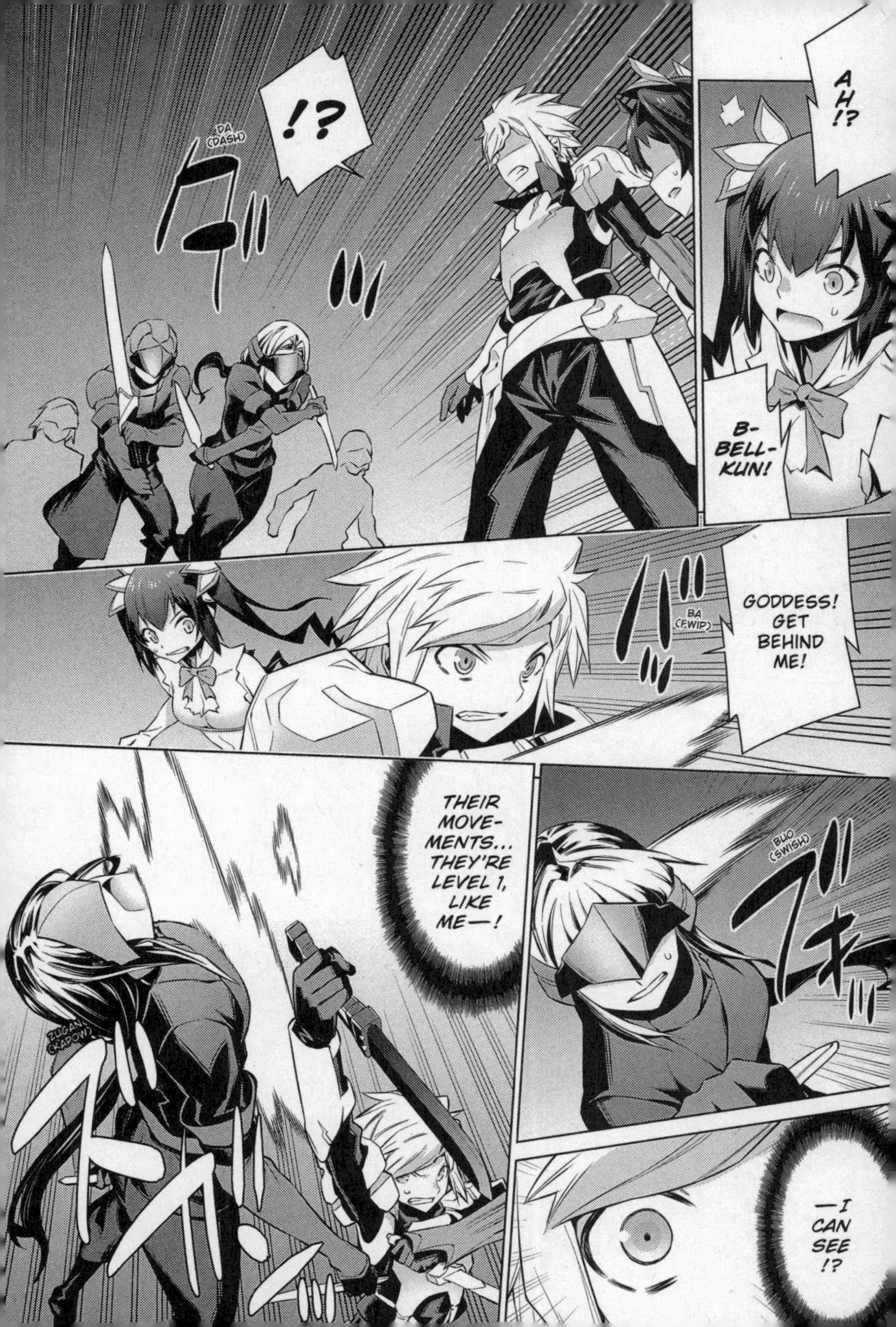
AH!?
B-BELL-KUN!
!?
DA (DASH)
GODDESS! GET BEHIND ME!
BA (FWIP)
BUO (SWISH)
—I CAN SEE!?
THEIR MOVE-MENTS... THEY'RE LEVEL 1, LIKE ME—!
ZUGAN (KAPOW)

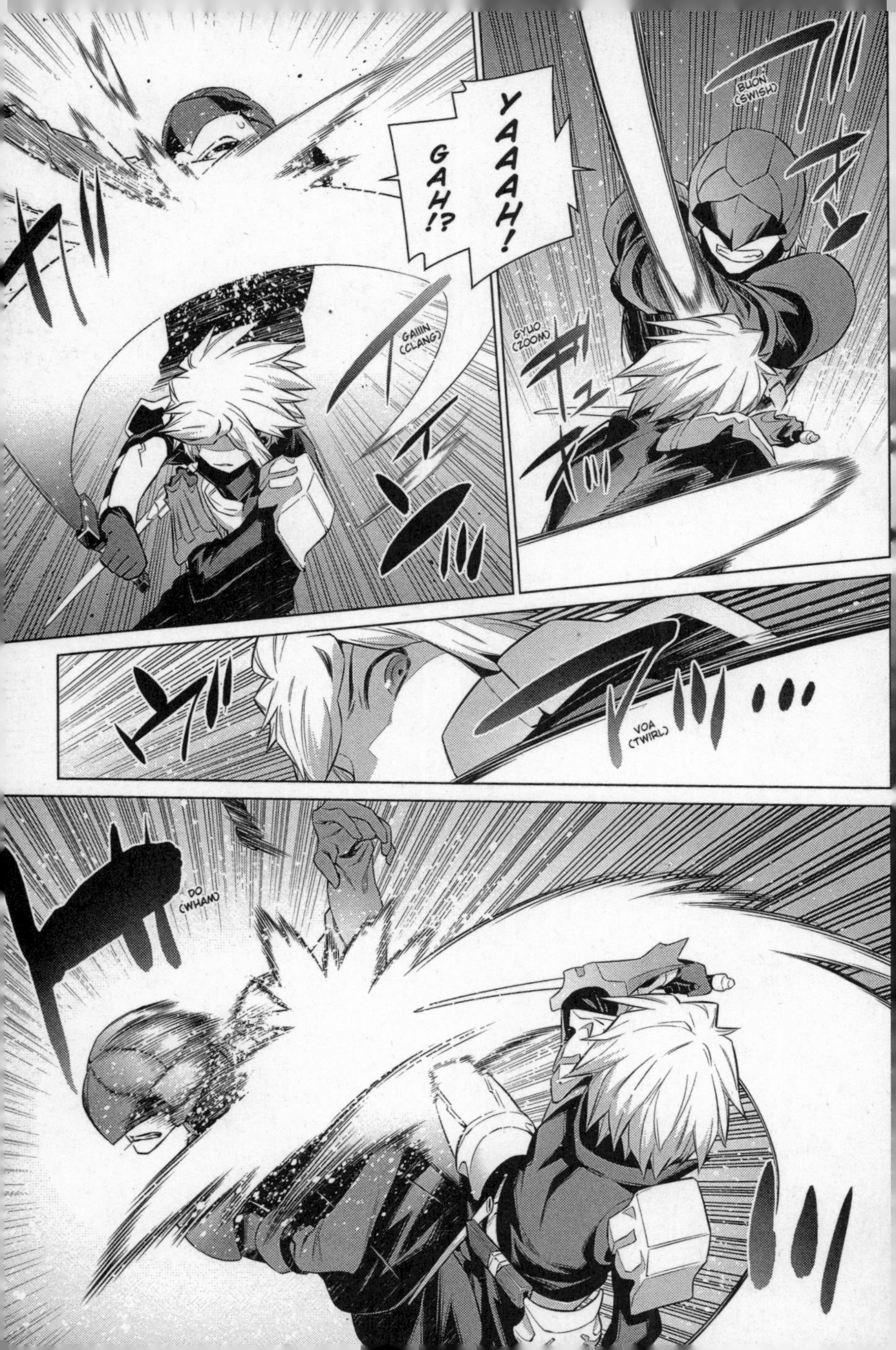
BUON (SWISH)
GYUO (ZOOM)
YAAAAH!
GAH!?
GAIIIN (CLANG)
VOA (TWIRL)
DO (WHAM)

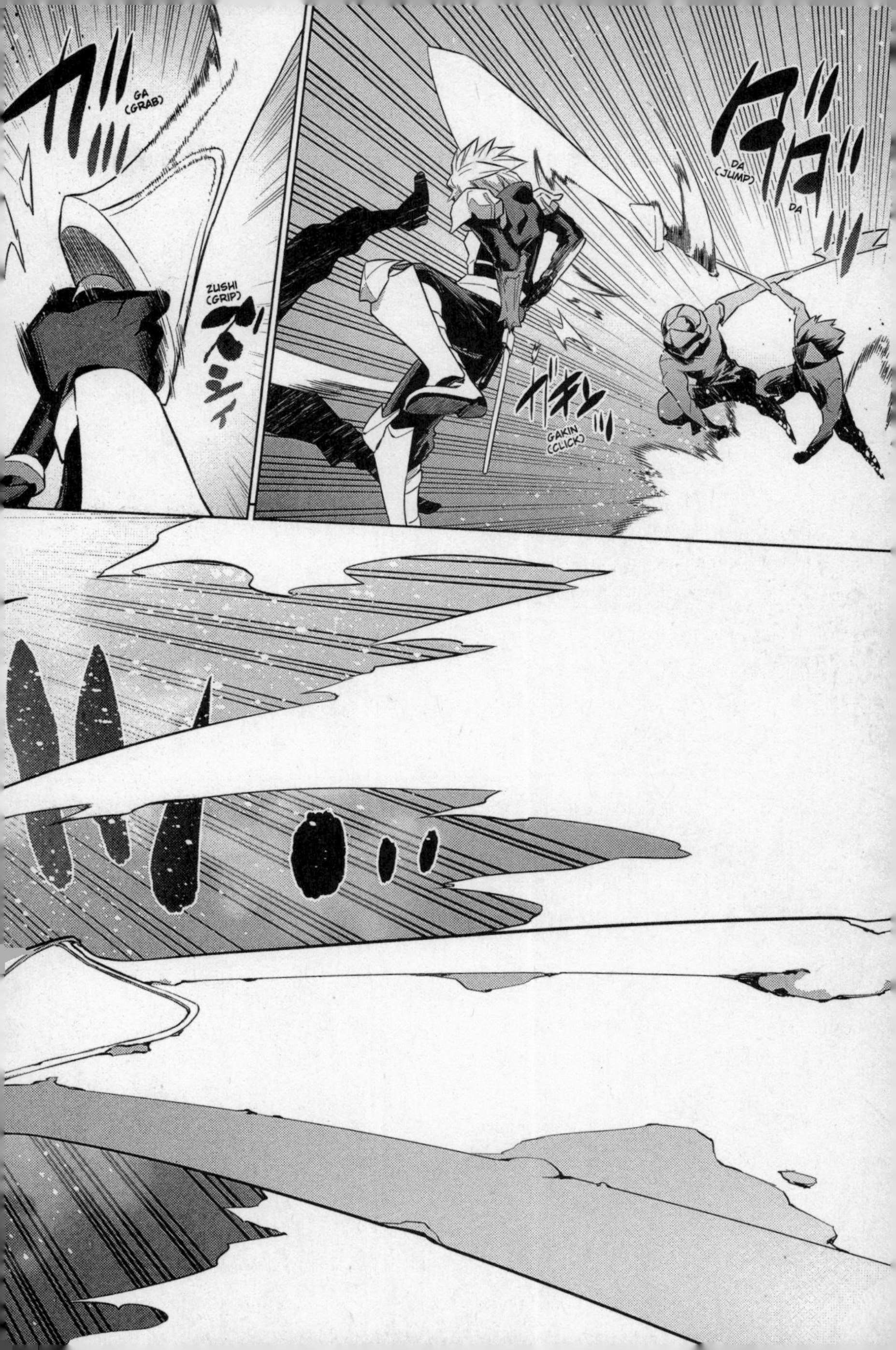
タダッ
DA (JUMP)
DA
ガキン
GAKIN (CLICK)
ズシィ
ZUSHI (GRIP)
ガッ
GA (GRAB)

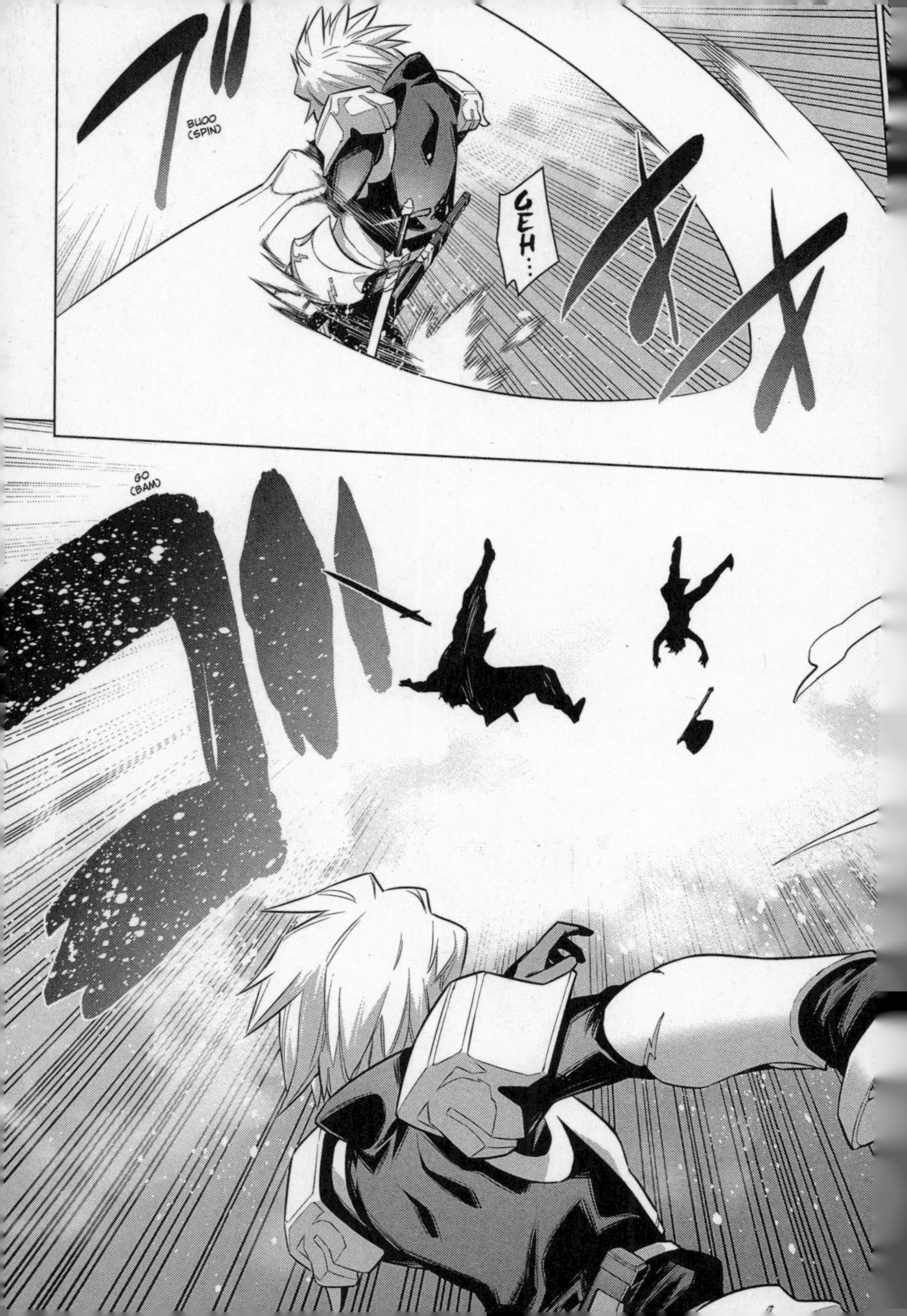
GEH...
BUOO (SPIN)
GO (BAM)

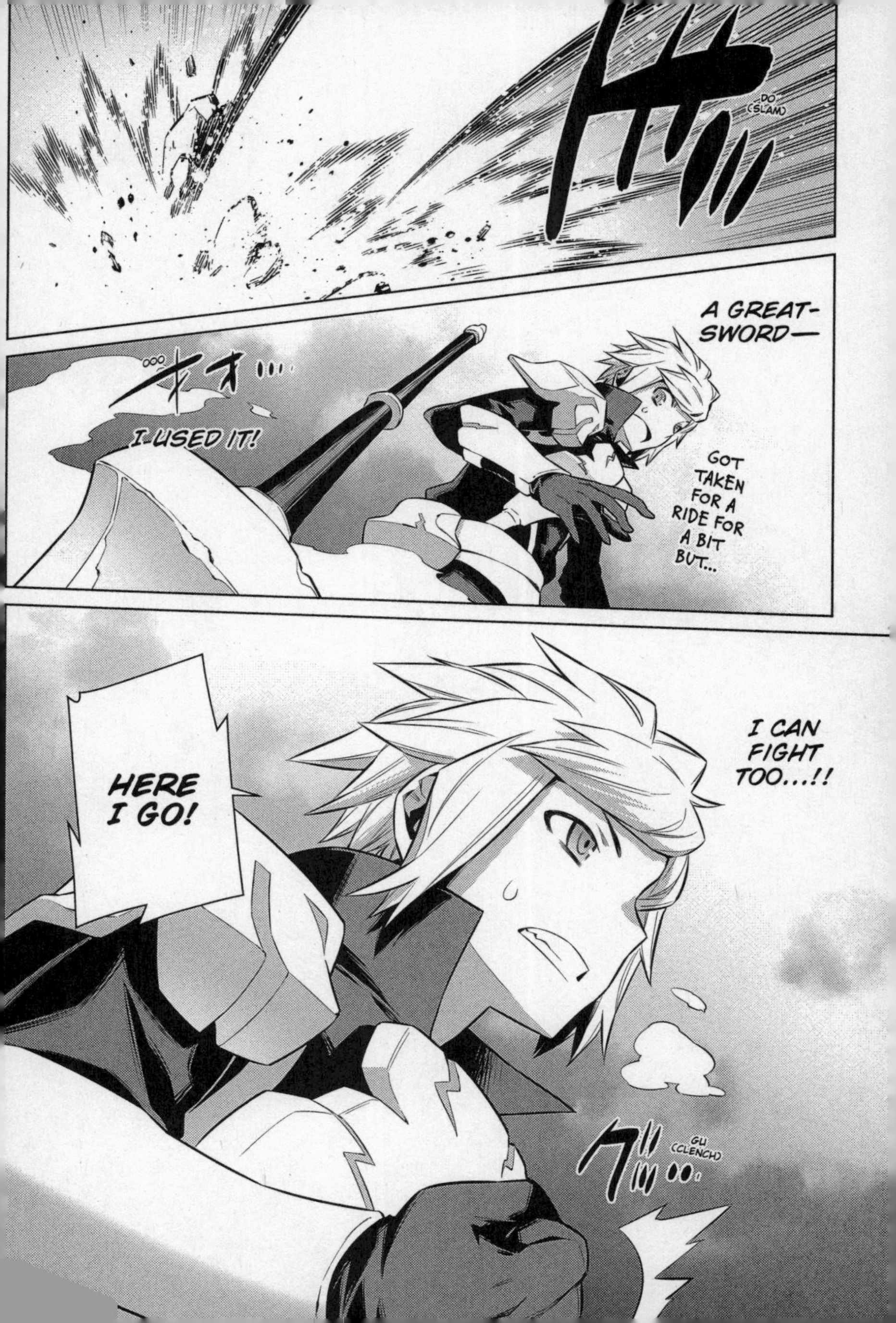
DO
(SLAM)
A GREAT-SWORD—
GOT TAKEN FOR A RIDE FOR A BIT BUT...
I USED IT!
I CAN FIGHT TOO...!!
HERE I GO!
GU
(CLENCH)

IS IT WRONG TO TRY TO PICK UP GIRLS IN A DUNGEON?

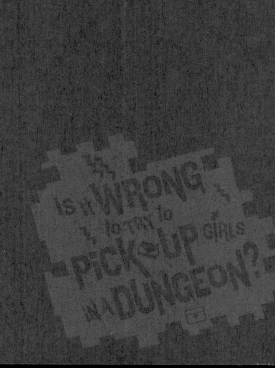

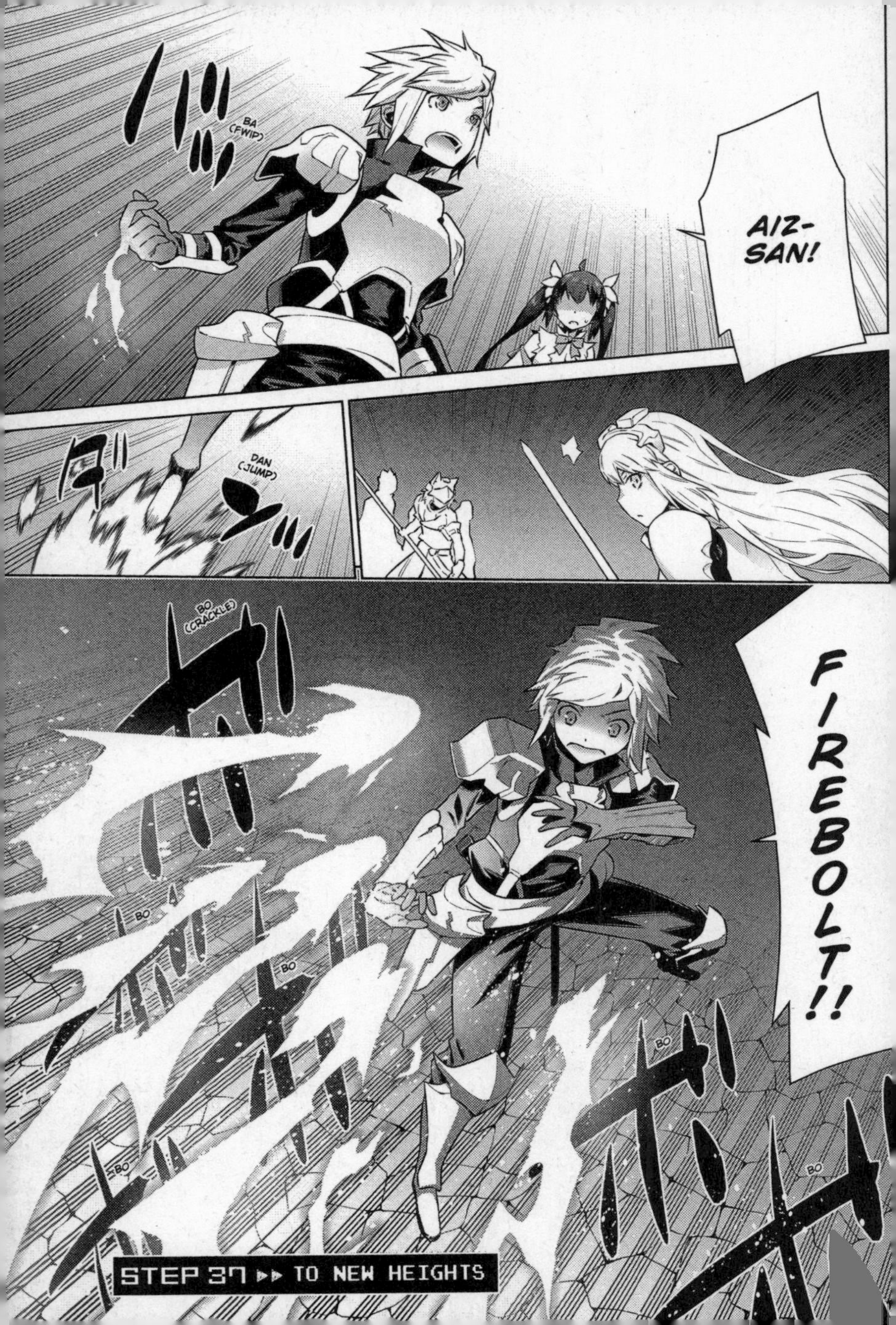
AIZ-SAN!
BA (FWIP)
DAN (JUMP)
FIREBOLT!!
BO (CRACKLE)
BO
BO
BO
BO
BO
STEP 37 ▸▸ TO NEW HEIGHTS

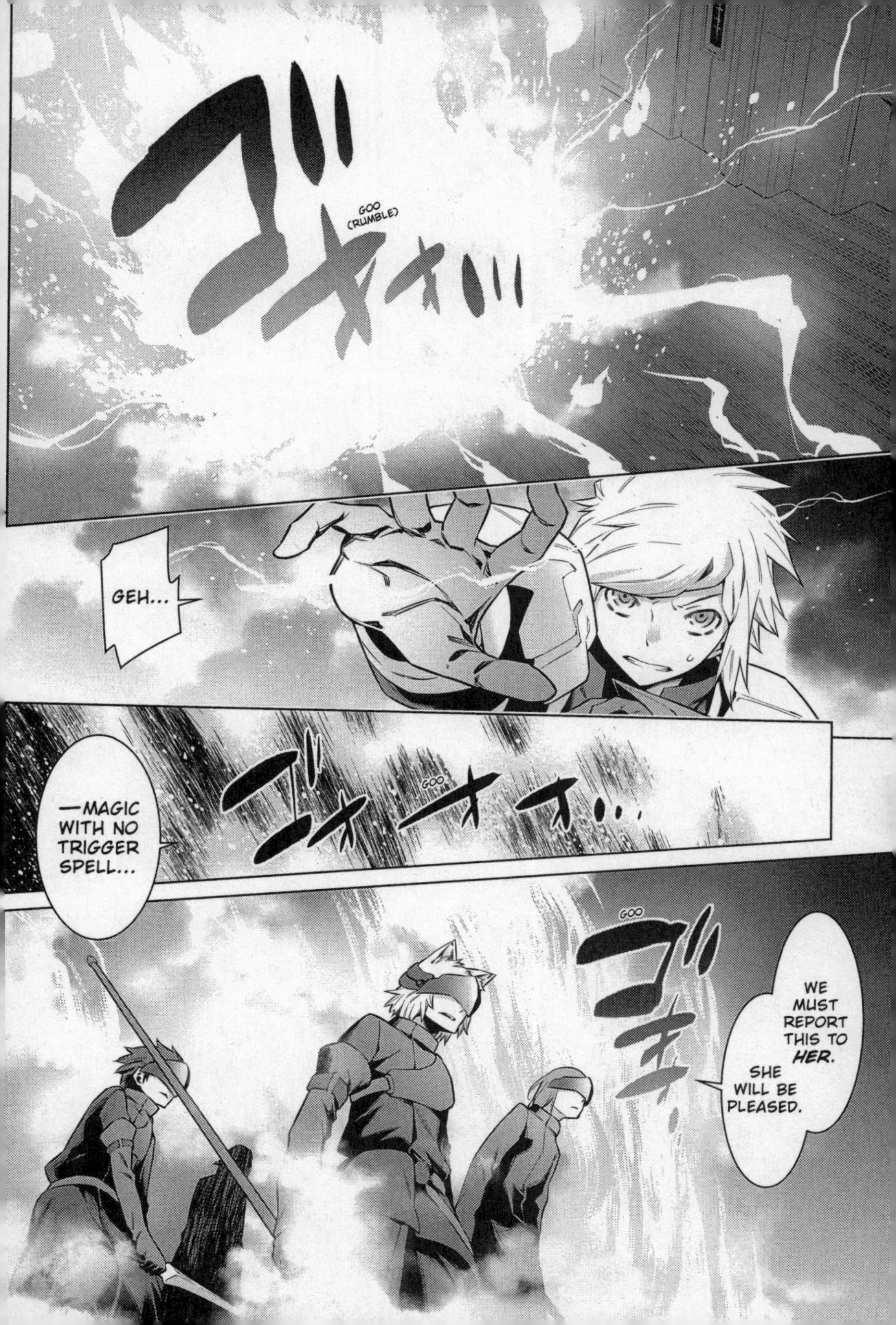
GOO (RUMBLE)
GEH...
—MAGIC WITH NO TRIGGER SPELL...
GOO
GOO
WE MUST REPORT THIS TO ***HER***. SHE WILL BE PLEASED.

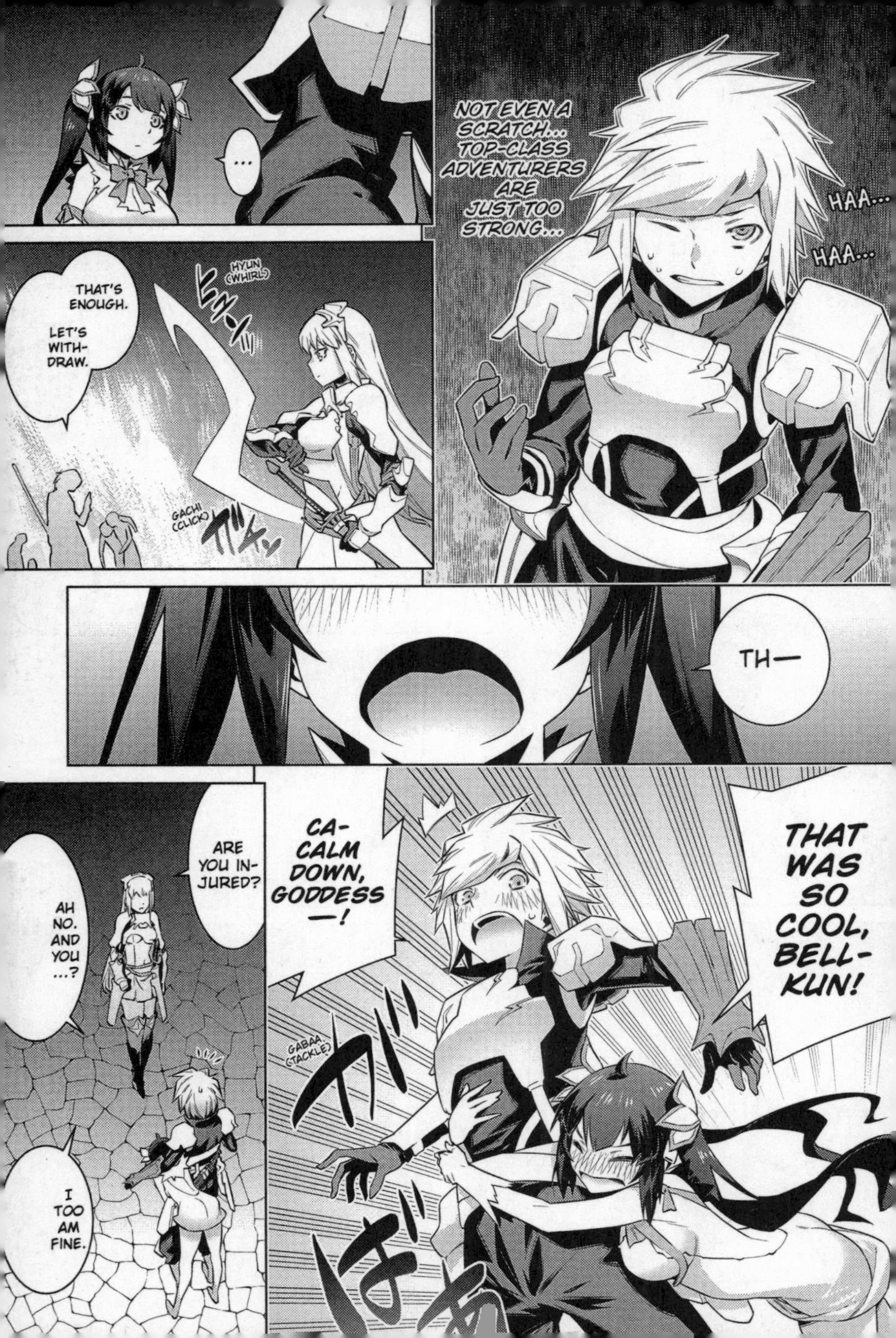
NOT EVEN A SCRATCH... TOP-CLASS ADVENTURERS ARE JUST TOO STRONG...
HAA...
HAA...
...
HYUN (WHIRL)
THAT'S ENOUGH.
LET'S WITH-DRAW.
GACHI (CLICK)
TH—
THAT WAS SO COOL, BELL-KUN!
CA-CALM DOWN, GODDESS—!
GABAA (TACKLE)
ARE YOU IN-JURED?
AH NO. AND YOU...?
I TOO AM FINE.

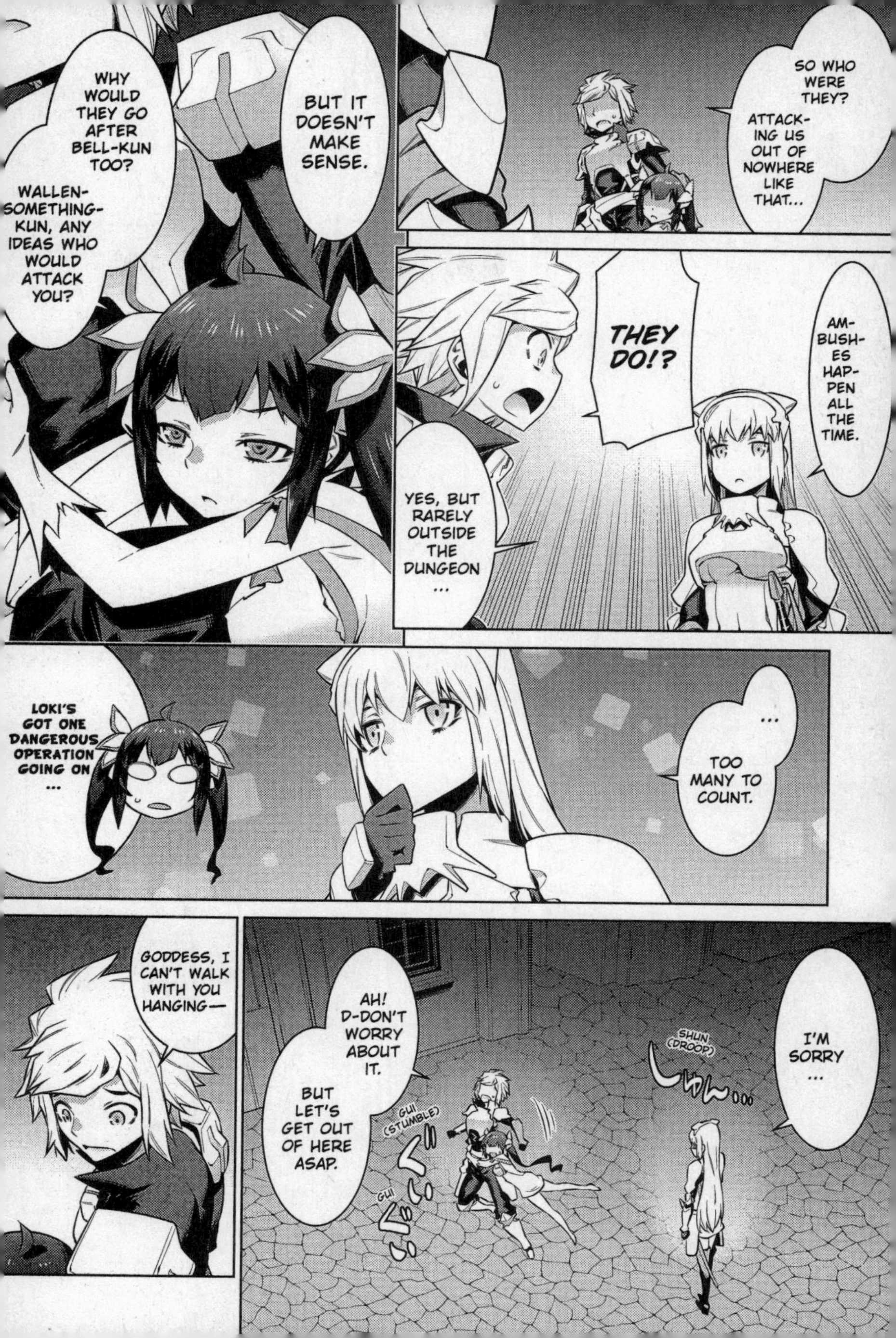
SO WHO WERE THEY?
ATTACKING US OUT OF NOWHERE LIKE THAT...
AMBUSHES HAPPEN ALL THE TIME.
THEY DO!?
YES, BUT RARELY OUTSIDE THE DUNGEON...
BUT IT DOESN'T MAKE SENSE.
WHY WOULD THEY GO AFTER BELL-KUN TOO?
WALLEN-SOMETHING-KUN, ANY IDEAS WHO WOULD ATTACK YOU?
... TOO MANY TO COUNT.
LOKI'S GOT ONE DANGEROUS OPERATION GOING ON...
I'M SORRY...
SHUN (DROOP)
AH! D-DON'T WORRY ABOUT IT.
BUT LET'S GET OUT OF HERE ASAP.
GUI (STUMBLE)
GUI
GODDESS, I CAN'T WALK WITH YOU HANGING—

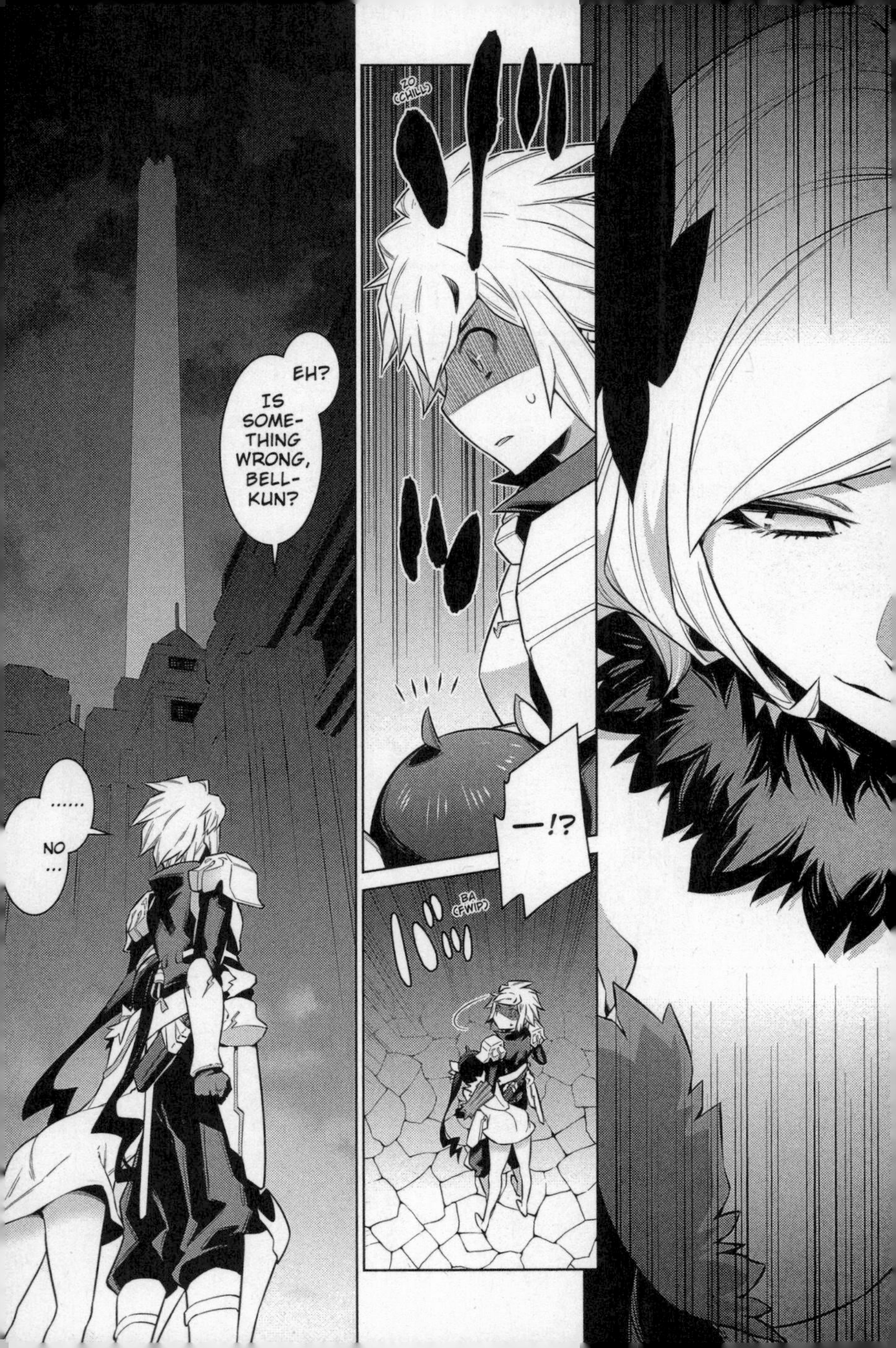
ZO (CHILL)
—!?
BA (FWIP)
EH? IS SOMETHING WRONG, BELL-KUN?
...... NO ...

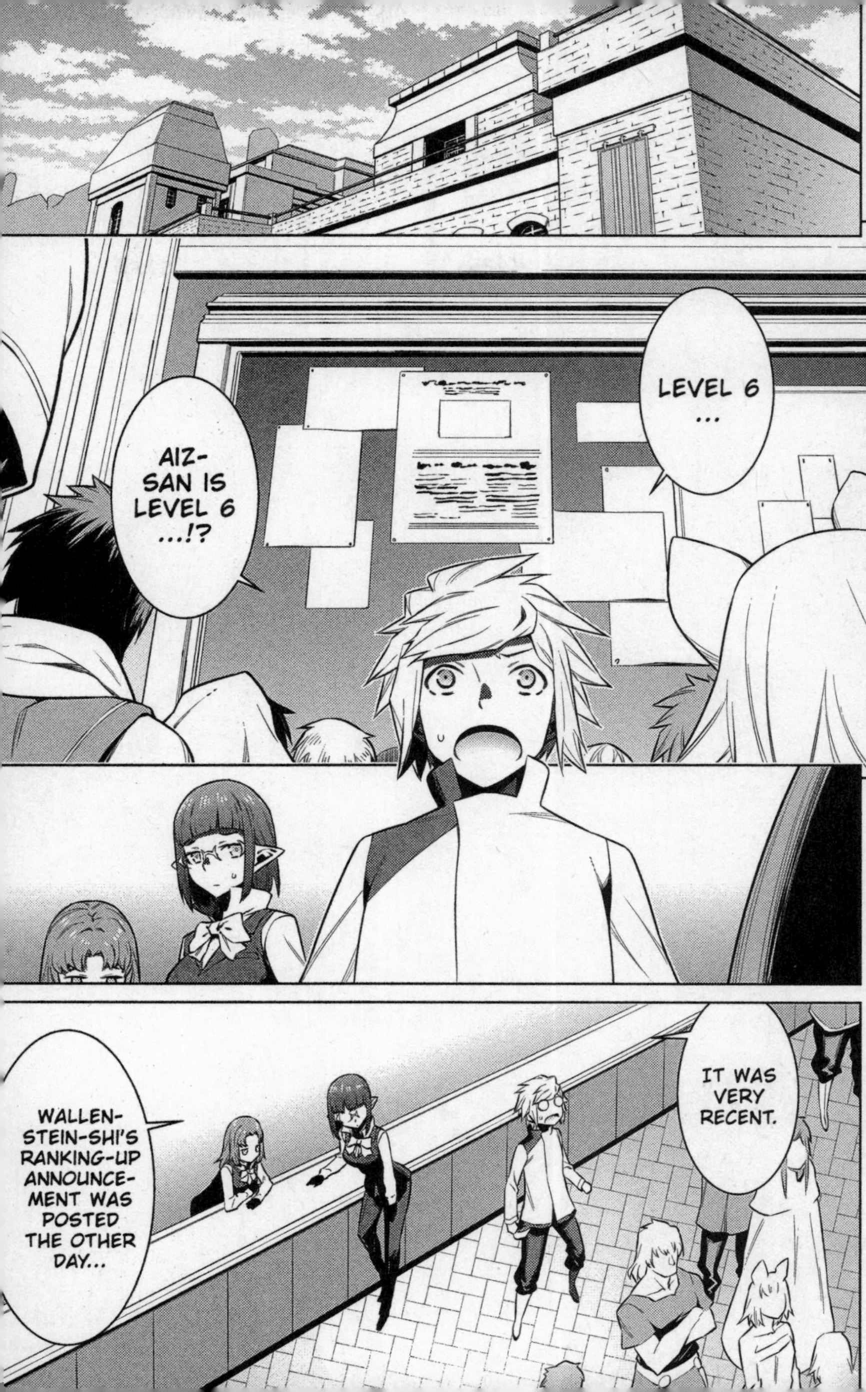
LEVEL 6 ...
AIZ-SAN IS LEVEL 6 ...!?
IT WAS VERY RECENT.
WALLEN-STEIN-SHI'S RANKING-UP ANNOUNCE-MENT WAS POSTED THE OTHER DAY...

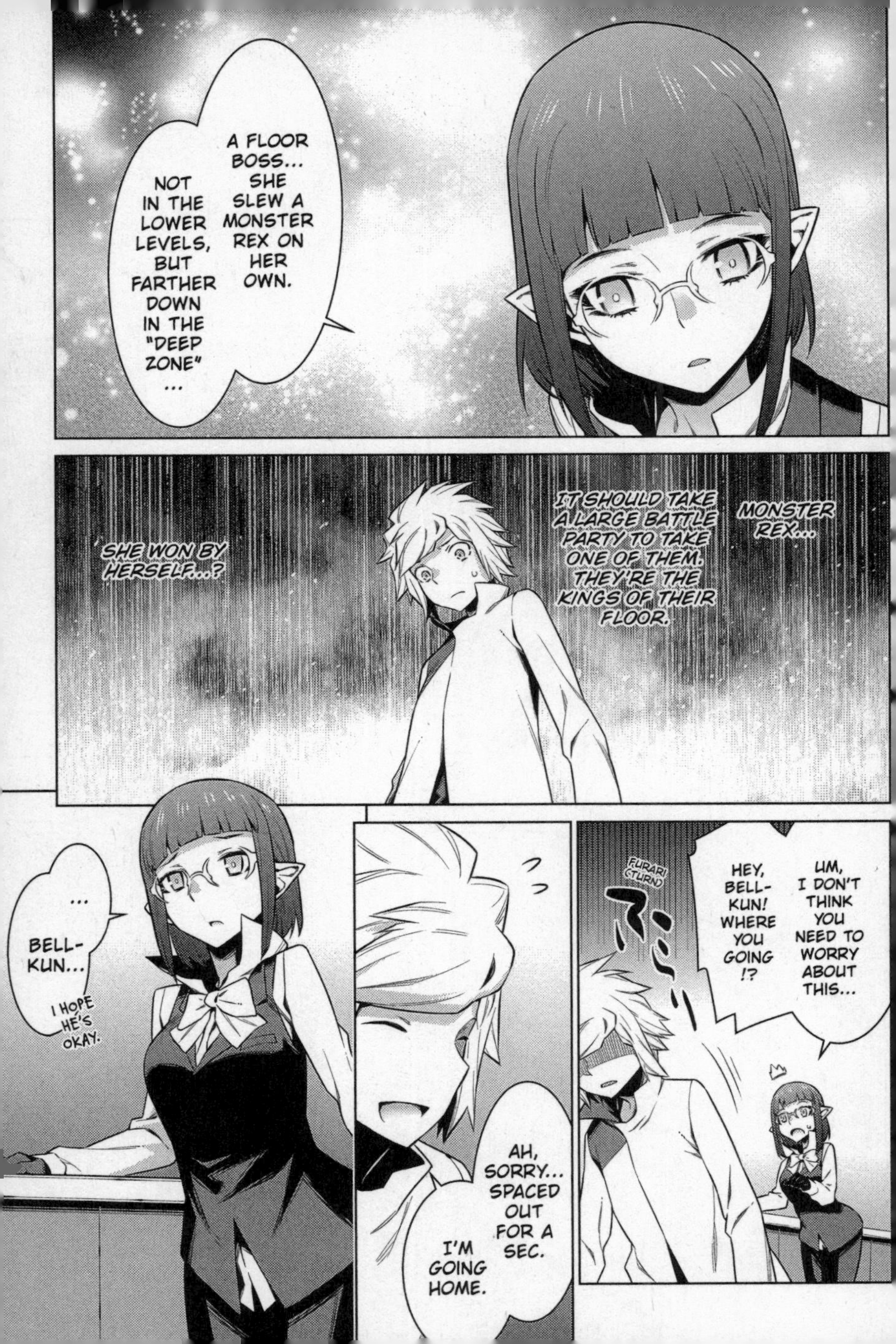
A FLOOR BOSS... SHE SLEW A MONSTER REX ON HER OWN.
NOT IN THE LOWER LEVELS, BUT FARTHER DOWN IN THE "DEEP ZONE" ...
MONSTER REX...
IT SHOULD TAKE A LARGE BATTLE PARTY TO TAKE ONE OF THEM. THEY'RE THE KINGS OF THEIR FLOOR.
SHE WON BY HERSELF...?
UM, I DON'T THINK YOU NEED TO WORRY ABOUT THIS...
HEY, BELL-KUN! WHERE YOU GOING!?
FURARI (TURN)
AH, SORRY... SPACED OUT FOR A SEC.
I'M GOING HOME.
...
BELL-KUN...
I HOPE HE'S OKAY.

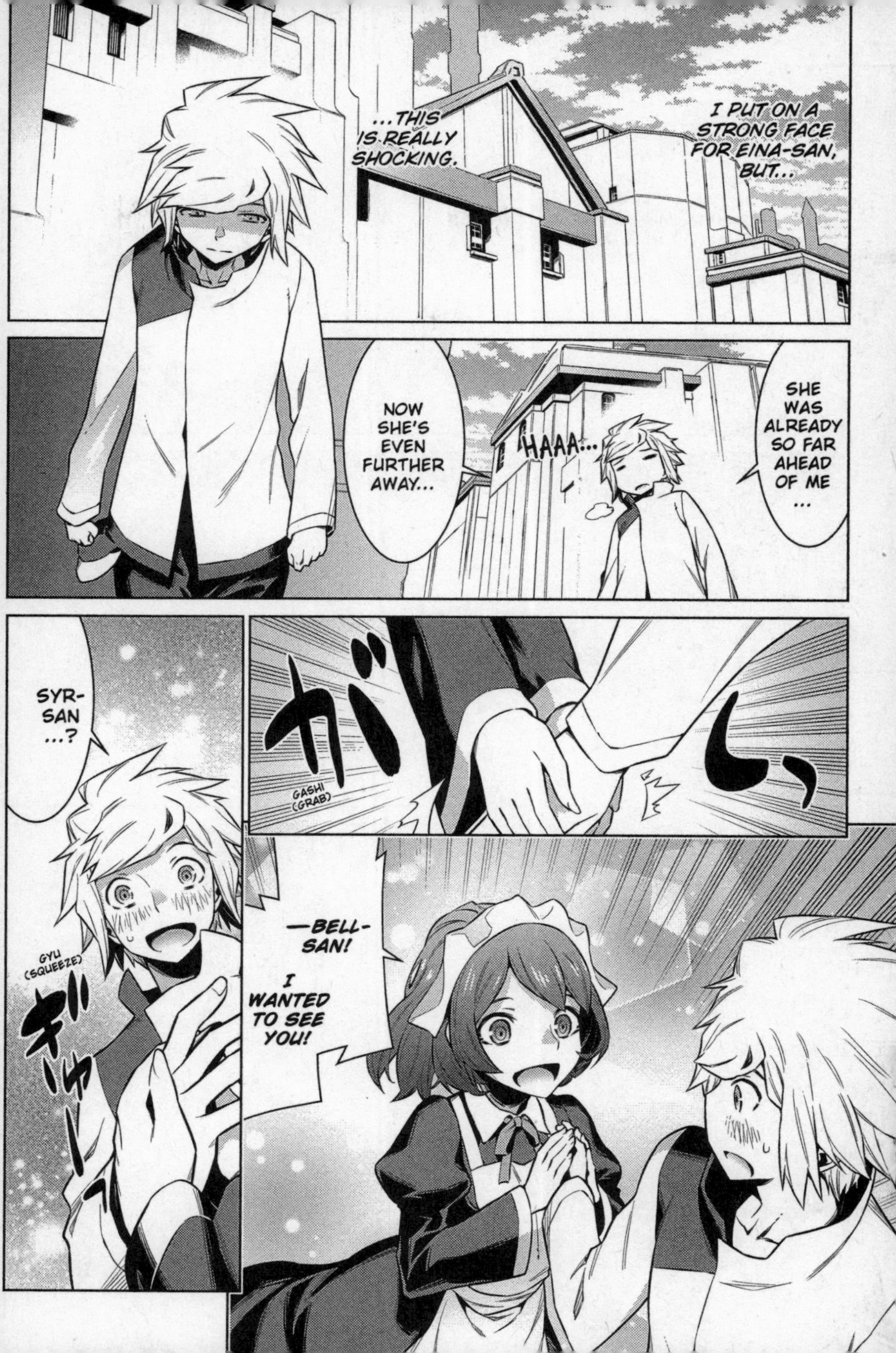
I PUT ON A STRONG FACE FOR EINA-SAN, BUT...
...THIS IS REALLY SHOCKING.
SHE WAS ALREADY SO FAR AHEAD OF ME ...
HAAA...
NOW SHE'S EVEN FURTHER AWAY...
GASHI (GRAB)
—BELL-SAN!
I WANTED TO SEE YOU!
SYR-SAN ...?
GYU (SQUEEZE)

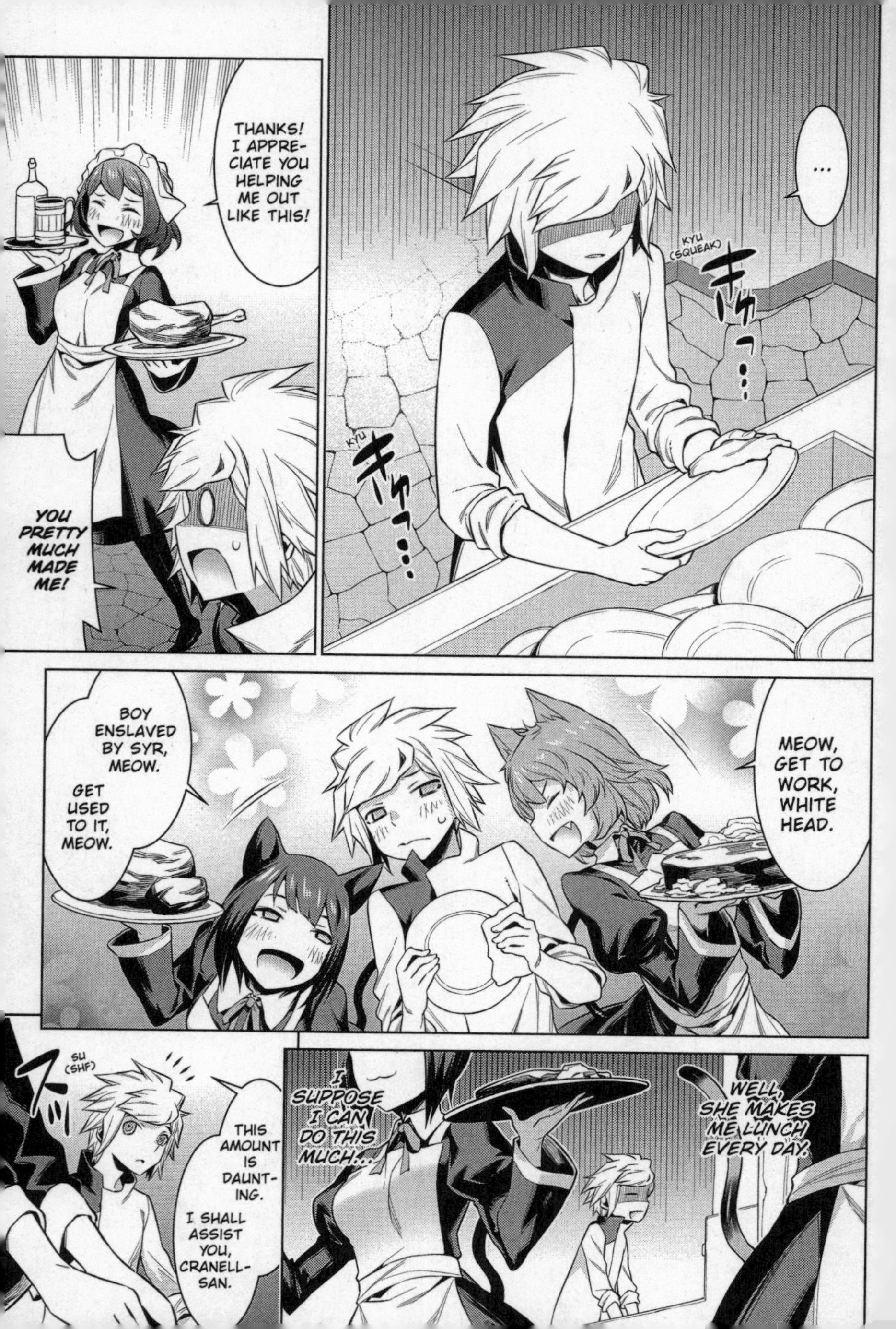
...
KYU (SQUEAK)
KYU
THANKS! I APPRECIATE YOU HELPING ME OUT LIKE THIS!
YOU PRETTY MUCH MADE ME!
MEOW, GET TO WORK, WHITE HEAD.
BOY ENSLAVED BY SYR, MEOW.
GET USED TO IT, MEOW.
WELL, SHE MAKES ME LUNCH EVERY DAY.
I SUPPOSE I CAN DO THIS MUCH...
SU (SHF)
THIS AMOUNT IS DAUNTING.
I SHALL ASSIST YOU, CRANELL-SAN.

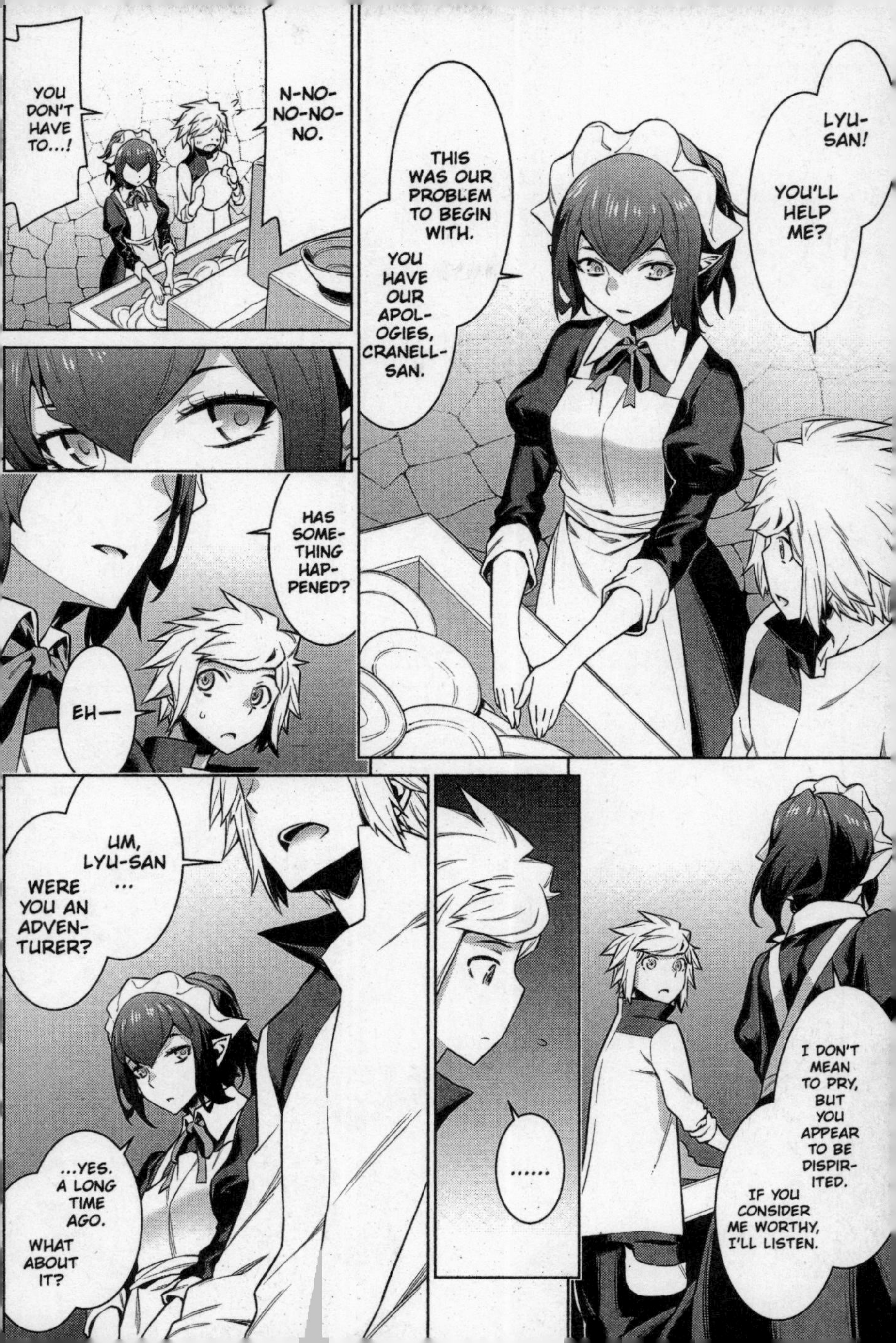
LYU-SAN!
YOU'LL HELP ME?
THIS WAS OUR PROBLEM TO BEGIN WITH.
YOU HAVE OUR APOLOGIES, CRANELL-SAN.
N-NO-NO-NO-NO.
YOU DON'T HAVE TO...!
HAS SOMETHING HAPPENED?
EH—
I DON'T MEAN TO PRY, BUT YOU APPEAR TO BE DISPIRITED.
IF YOU CONSIDER ME WORTHY, I'LL LISTEN.
......
UM, LYU-SAN ...
WERE YOU AN ADVENTURER?
...YES. A LONG TIME AGO.
WHAT ABOUT IT?

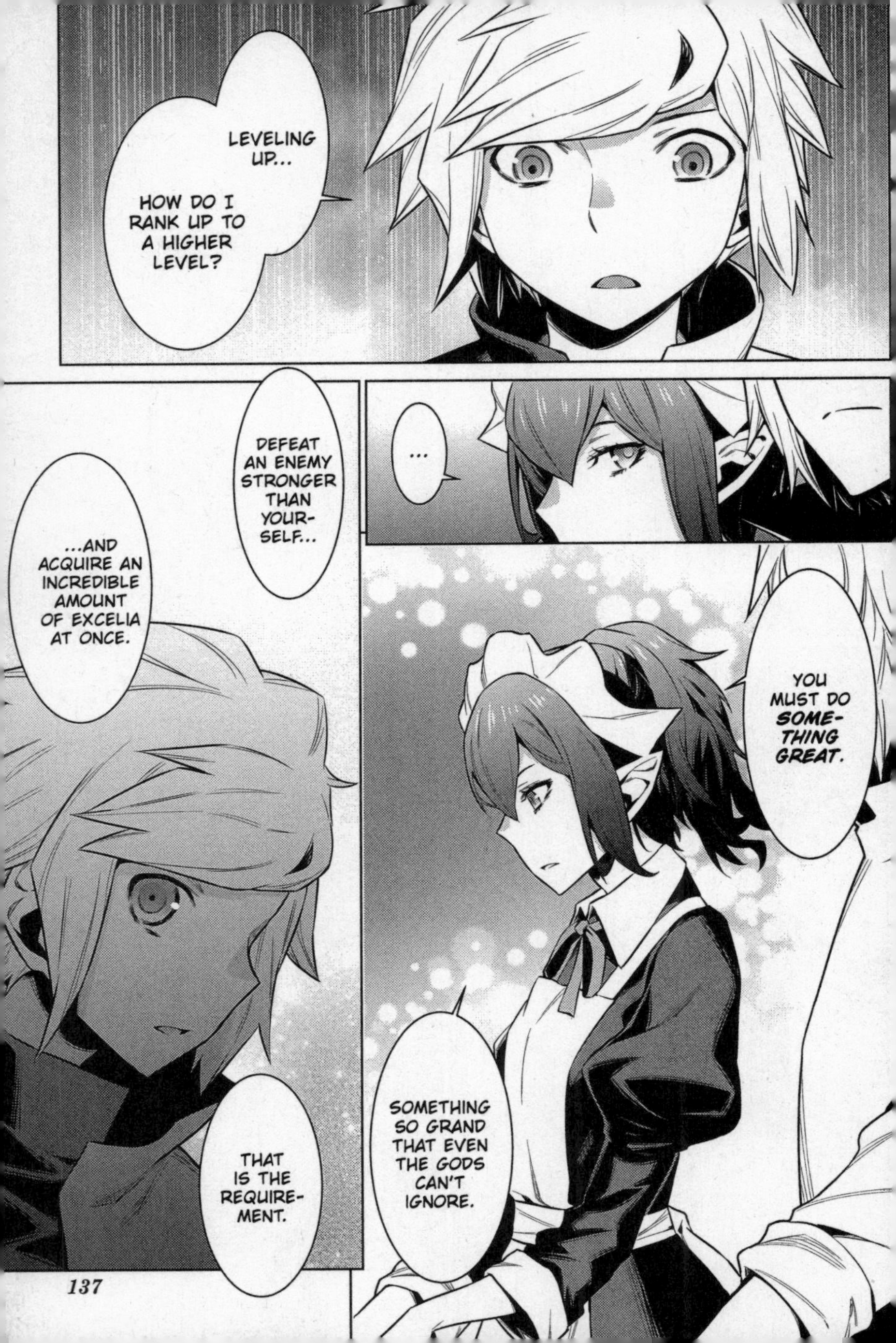

LEVELING UP...
HOW DO I RANK UP TO A HIGHER LEVEL?
...
YOU MUST DO *SOMETHING GREAT*.
SOMETHING SO GRAND THAT EVEN THE GODS CAN'T IGNORE.
DEFEAT AN ENEMY STRONGER THAN YOURSELF...
...AND ACQUIRE AN INCREDIBLE AMOUNT OF EXCELIA AT ONCE.
THAT IS THE REQUIREMENT.

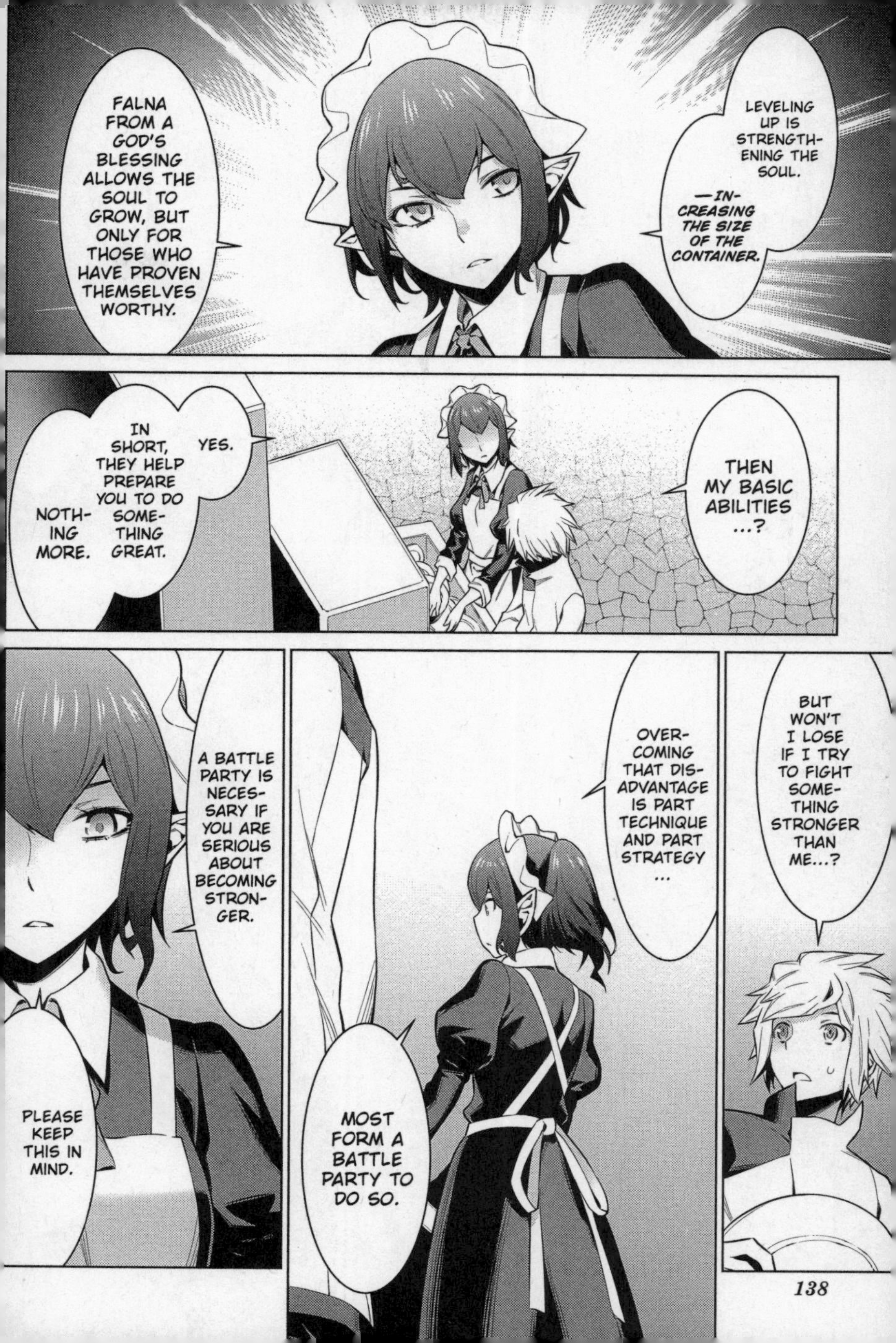
LEVELING UP IS STRENGTHENING THE SOUL.
—INCREASING THE SIZE OF THE CONTAINER.
FALNA FROM A GOD'S BLESSING ALLOWS THE SOUL TO GROW, BUT ONLY FOR THOSE WHO HAVE PROVEN THEMSELVES WORTHY.
THEN MY BASIC ABILITIES...?
YES.
IN SHORT, THEY HELP PREPARE YOU TO DO SOMETHING GREAT.
NOTHING MORE.
BUT WON'T I LOSE IF I TRY TO FIGHT SOMETHING STRONGER THAN ME...?
OVERCOMING THAT DISADVANTAGE IS PART TECHNIQUE AND PART STRATEGY...
MOST FORM A BATTLE PARTY TO DO SO.
A BATTLE PARTY IS NECESSARY IF YOU ARE SERIOUS ABOUT BECOMING STRONGER.
PLEASE KEEP THIS IN MIND.

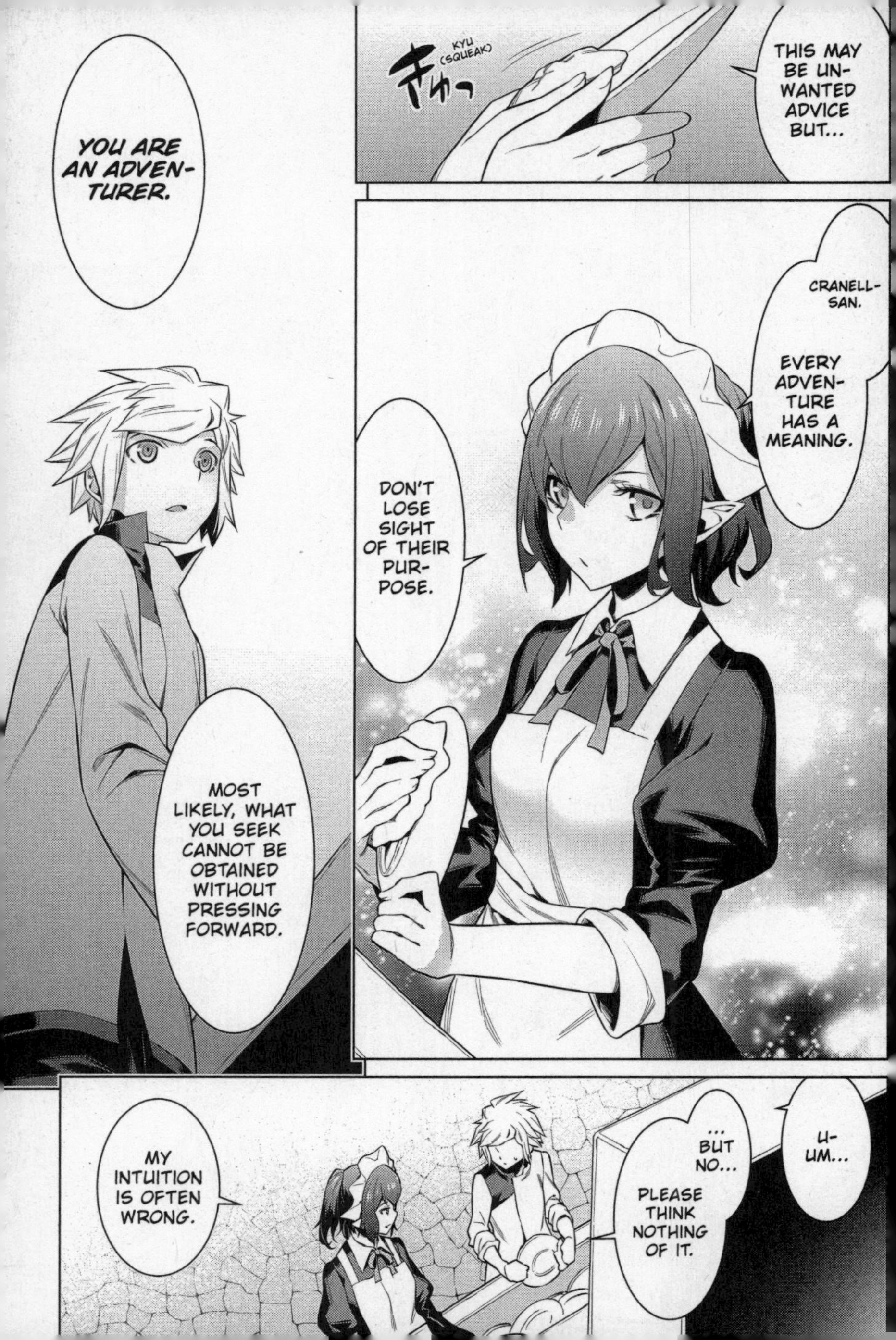
KYU (SQUEAK)
THIS MAY BE UN-WANTED ADVICE BUT...
CRANELL-SAN.
EVERY ADVEN-TURE HAS A MEANING.
DON'T LOSE SIGHT OF THEIR PUR-POSE.
YOU ARE AN ADVEN-TURER.
MOST LIKELY, WHAT YOU SEEK CANNOT BE OBTAINED WITHOUT PRESSING FORWARD.
U-UM...
...BUT NO...
PLEASE THINK NOTHING OF IT.
MY INTUITION IS OFTEN WRONG.

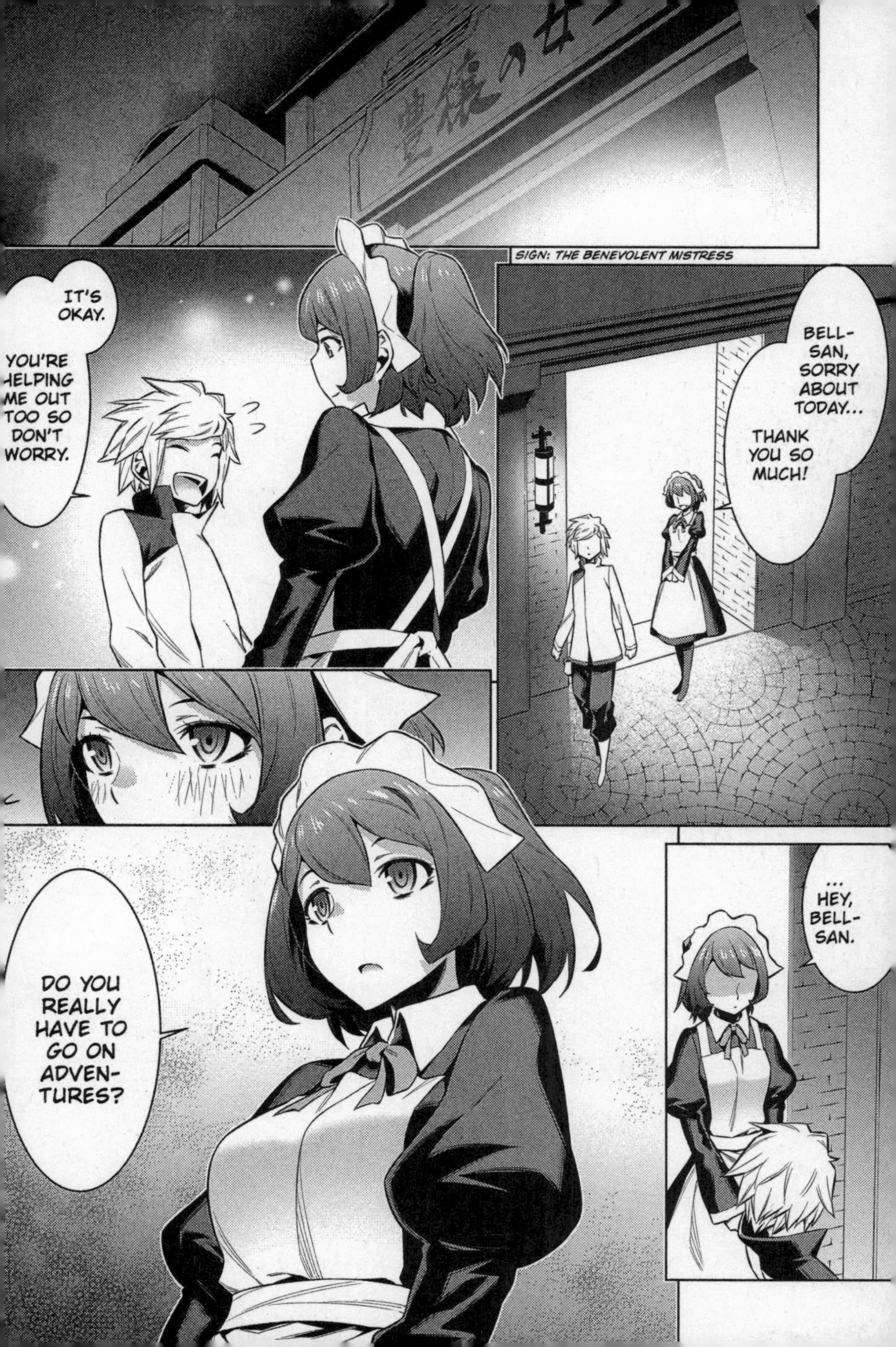
SIGN: THE BENEVOLENT MISTRESS
BELL-SAN, SORRY ABOUT TODAY...
THANK YOU SO MUCH!
IT'S OKAY.
YOU'RE HELPING ME OUT TOO SO DON'T WORRY.
... HEY, BELL-SAN.
DO YOU REALLY HAVE TO GO ON ADVENTURES?

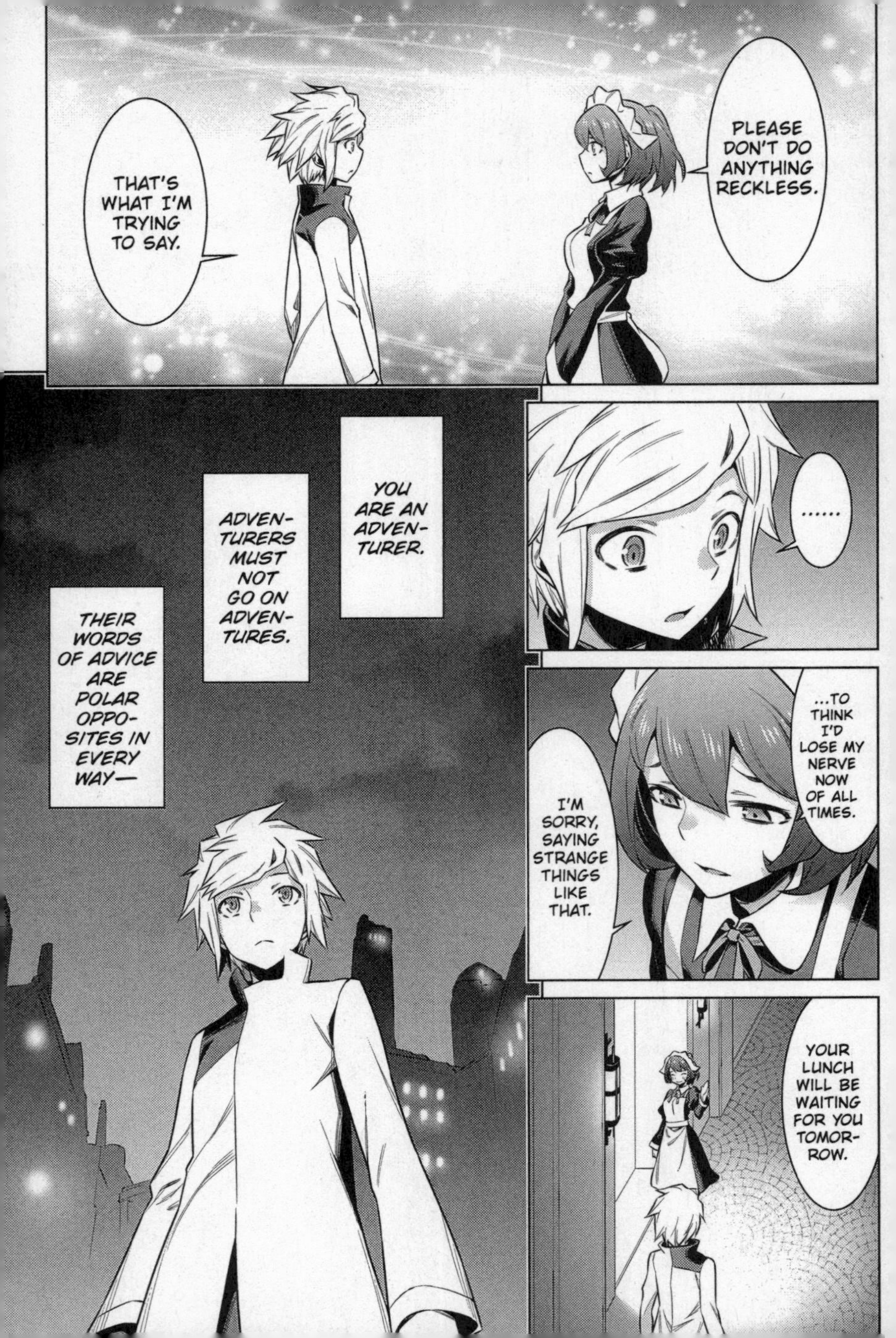
PLEASE DON'T DO ANYTHING RECKLESS.
THAT'S WHAT I'M TRYING TO SAY.
......
...TO THINK I'D LOSE MY NERVE NOW OF ALL TIMES.
I'M SORRY, SAYING STRANGE THINGS LIKE THAT.
YOUR LUNCH WILL BE WAITING FOR YOU TOMORROW.
YOU ARE AN ADVENTURER.
ADVENTURERS MUST NOT GO ON ADVENTURES.
THEIR WORDS OF ADVICE ARE POLAR OPPOSITES IN EVERY WAY—

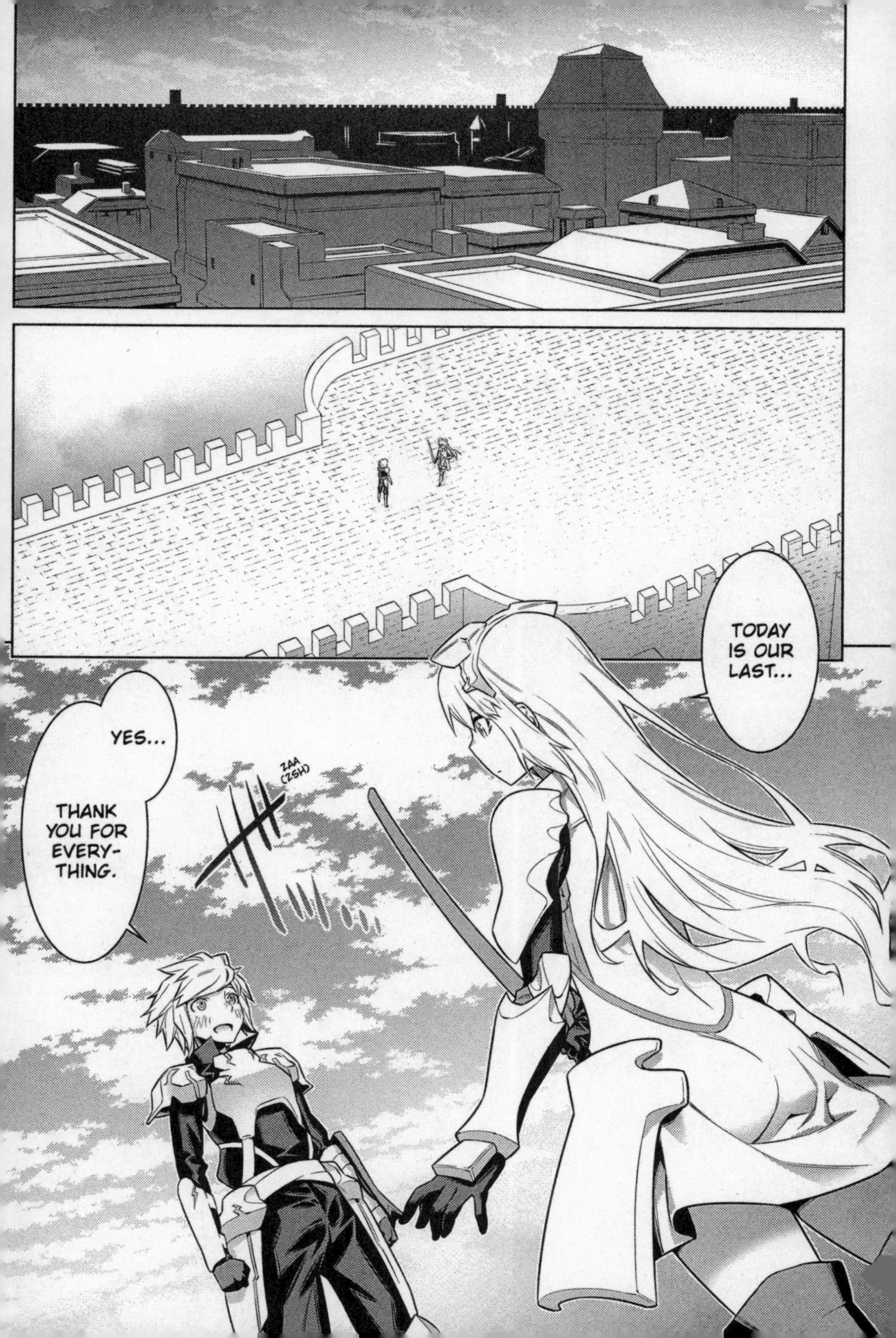
TODAY IS OUR LAST...
YES...
THANK YOU FOR EVERY-THING.
ZAA (ZSH)

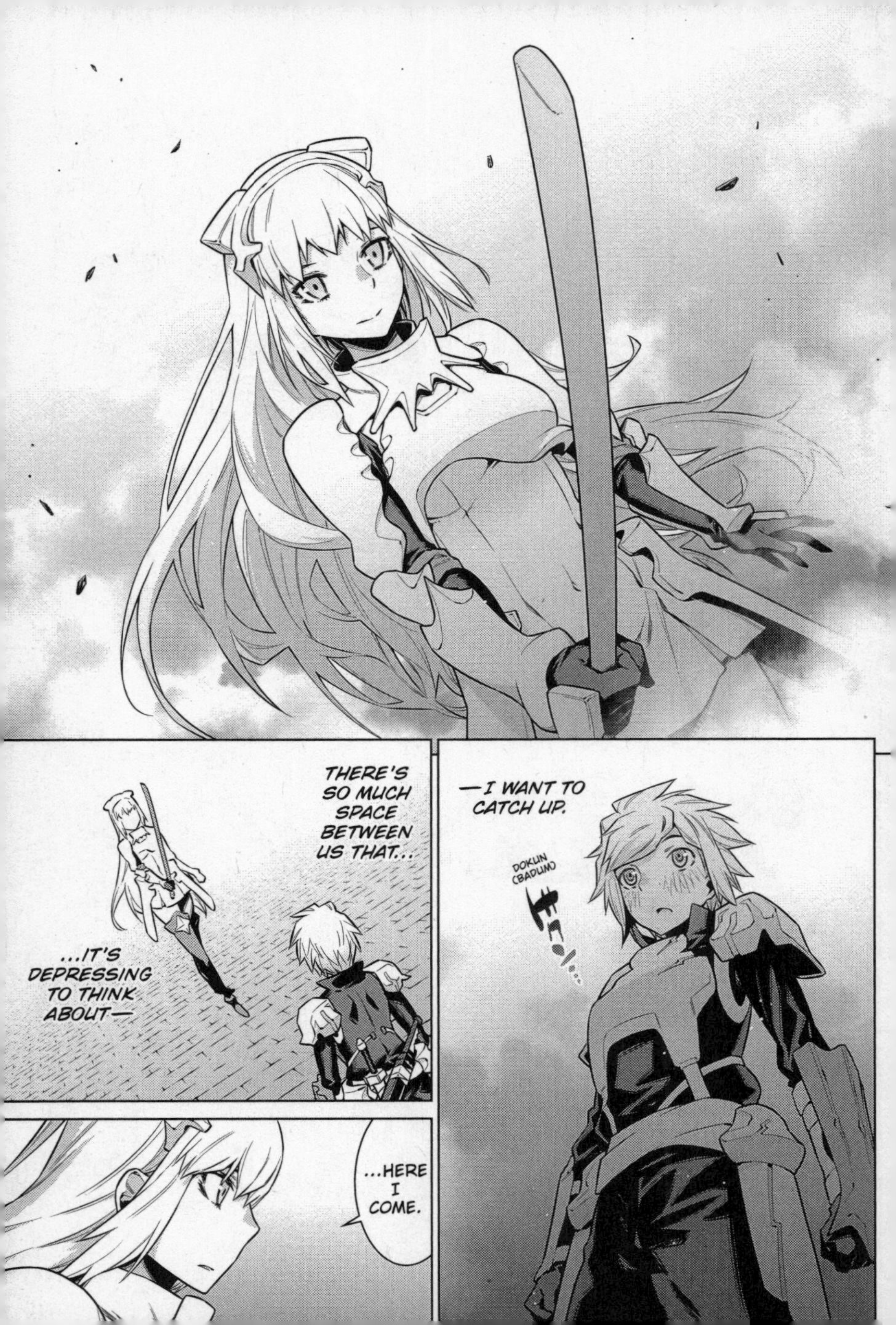
—I WANT TO CATCH UP.
DOKUN (BADUM)
THERE'S SO MUCH SPACE BETWEEN US THAT...
...IT'S DEPRESSING TO THINK ABOUT—
...HERE I COME.

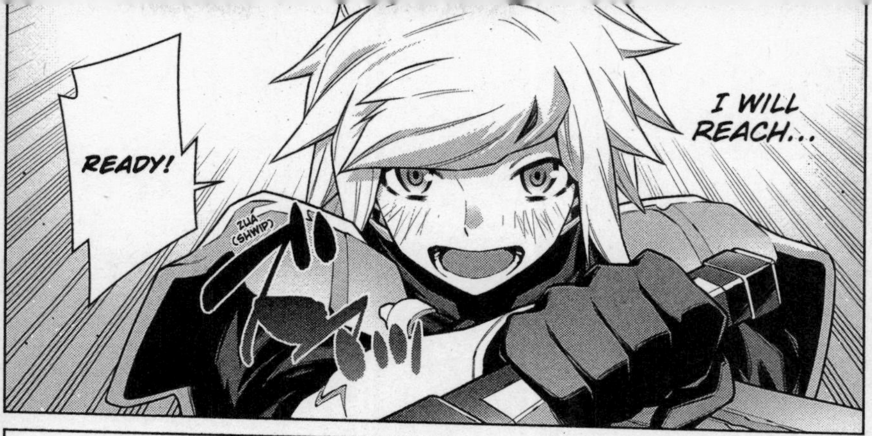
I WILL REACH...
READY!
ZUA (SHWIP)

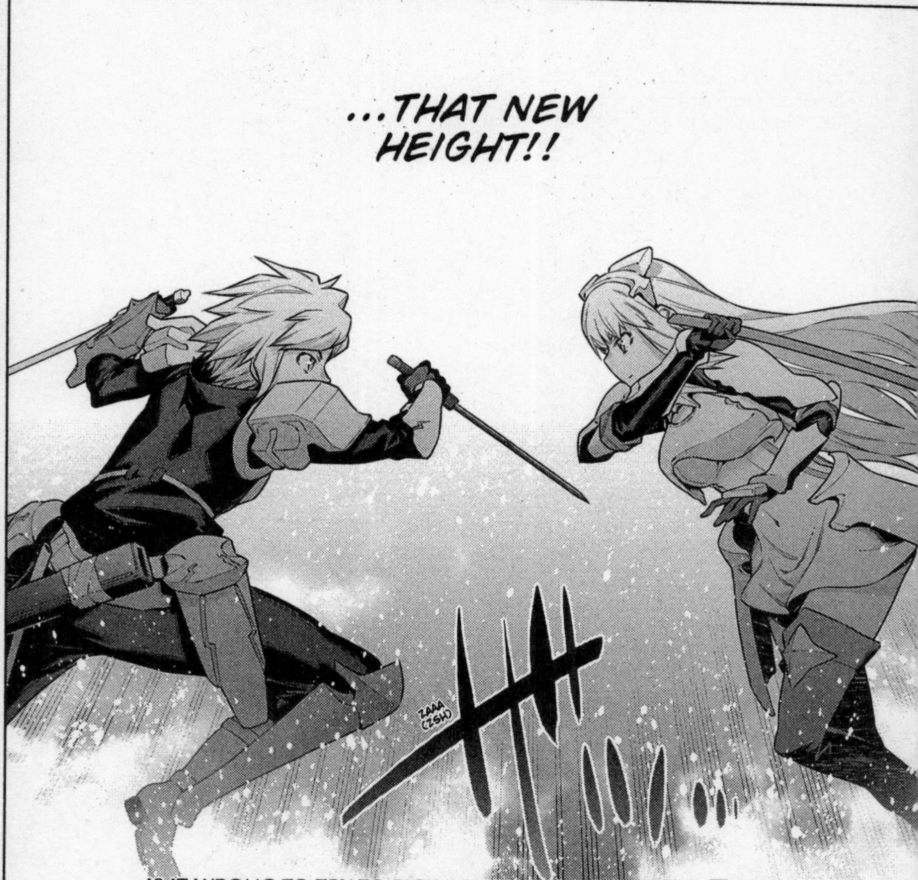
...THAT NEW HEIGHT!!
ZAAA (ZSH)

IS IT WRONG TO TRY TO PICK UP GIRLS IN A DUNGEON? 5 END

TRANSLATION NOTES

Common Honorifics
no honorific: Indicates familiarity or closeness; if used without permission or reason, addressing someone in this manner would constitute an insult.
-san: The Japanese equivalent of Mr./Mrs./Miss. If a situation calls for politeness, this is the failsafe honorific.
-shi: Not unlike -san; the equivalent of Mr./Mrs./Miss but conveying a more official or bureaucratic mood.
-sama: Conveys great respect; may also indicate that the social status of the speaker is lower than that of the addressee.
-kun: Used most often when referring to boys, this indicates affection or familiarity. Occasionally used by older men among their peers, but it may also be used by anyone referring to a person of lower standing.
-chan: An affectionate honorific indicating familiarity used mostly in reference to girls; also used in reference to cute persons or animals of either gender.

PAGE 73
Falna: A god's blessing on the adventurers in their *Familia*, a Falna is tattooed on the back of every member and, like a character sheet in an RPG, is a record of experience and abilities accrued by the adventurer while in the Dungeon.

PAGE 105
Jyaga-maru-kun: Fried potato puffs

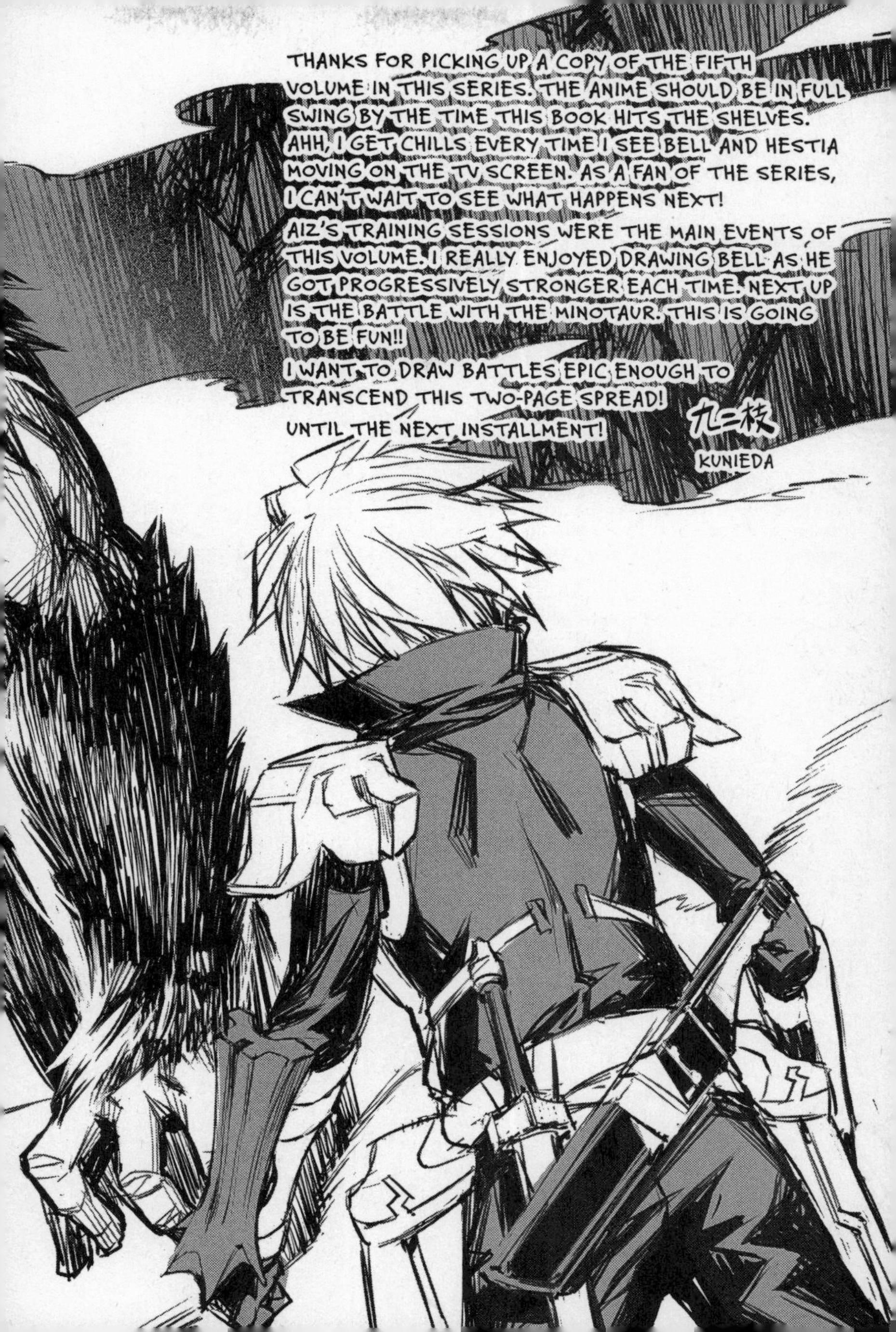
THANKS FOR PICKING UP A COPY OF THE FIFTH VOLUME IN THIS SERIES. THE ANIME SHOULD BE IN FULL SWING BY THE TIME THIS BOOK HITS THE SHELVES. AHH, I GET CHILLS EVERY TIME I SEE BELL AND HESTIA MOVING ON THE TV SCREEN. AS A FAN OF THE SERIES, I CAN'T WAIT TO SEE WHAT HAPPENS NEXT!
AIZ'S TRAINING SESSIONS WERE THE MAIN EVENTS OF THIS VOLUME. I REALLY ENJOYED DRAWING BELL AS HE GOT PROGRESSIVELY STRONGER EACH TIME. NEXT UP IS THE BATTLE WITH THE MINOTAUR. THIS IS GOING TO BE FUN!!
I WANT TO DRAW BATTLES EPIC ENOUGH TO TRANSCEND THIS TWO-PAGE SPREAD!
UNTIL THE NEXT INSTALLMENT!
九二枝
KUNIEDA

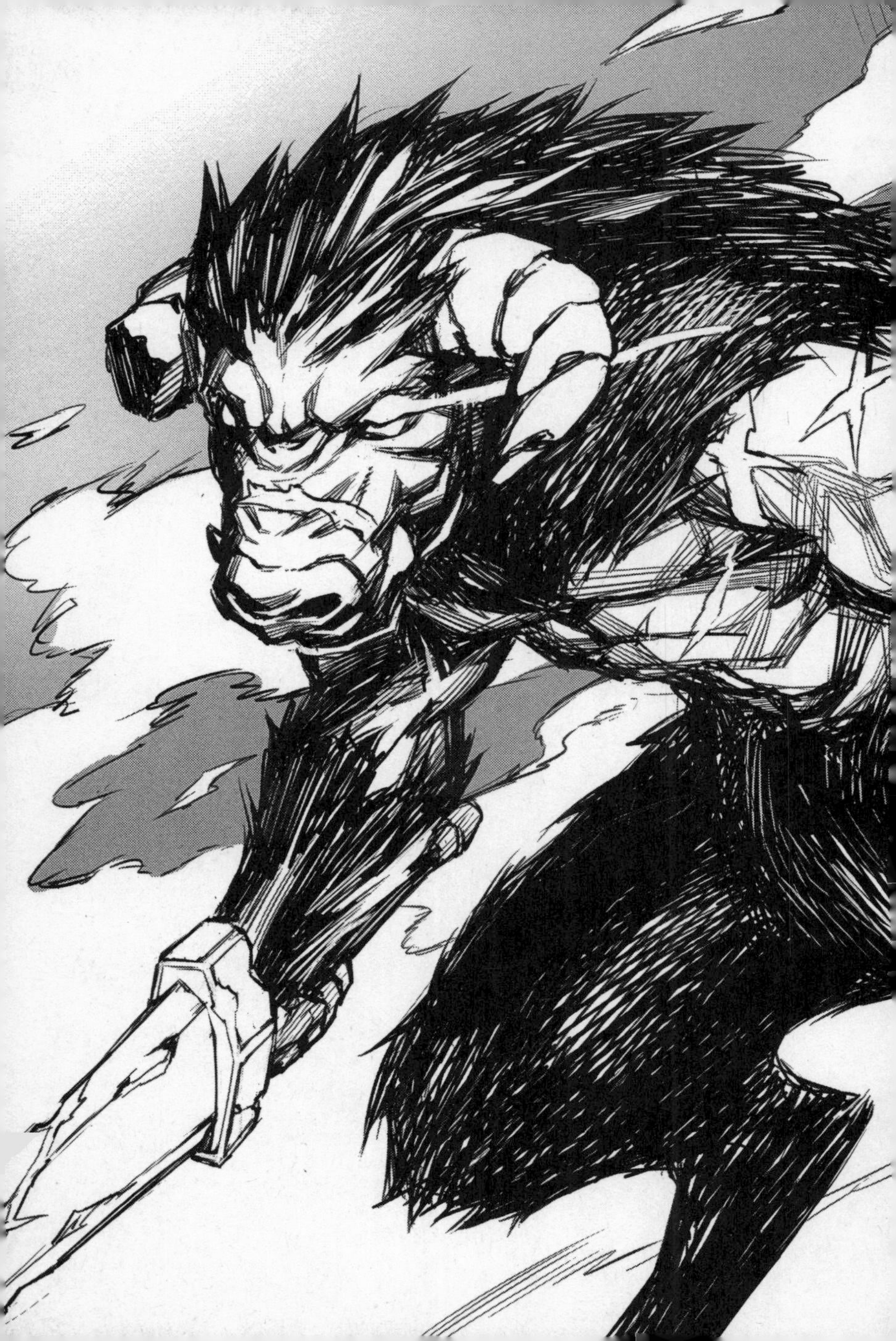